A VISUAL GUIDE
TO BIBLE EVENTS

A VISUAL GUIDE
TO BIBLE EVENTS

*Fascinating Insights into
Where They Happened and Why*

JAMES C. MARTIN,
JOHN A. BECK, AND
DAVID G. HANSEN

BakerBooks

a division of Baker Publishing Group
Grand Rapids, Michigan

© 2009 by James C. Martin, John A. Beck, and David G. Hansen

Published by Baker Books
a division of Baker Publishing Group
P.O. Box 6287, Grand Rapids, MI 49516-6287
www.bakerbooks.com

Paperback edition published 2015
ISBN 978-0-8010-1727-8

Printed in the United States of America

The Library of Congress has cataloged the previous edition as follows:
Martin, James C., 1952–
    A visual guide to Bible events : fascinating insights into where they happened and why / James C. Martin, John A. Beck, and David G. Hansen.
        p.   cm.
    Includes bibliographical references and index.
    ISBN 978-0-8010-1285-3 (cloth)
    1. Bible—Geography. 2. Bible stories, English. 3. Bible—Criticism, interpretation, etc. I. Beck, John A., 1956– II. Hansen, David G., 1938– III. Title.

BS630.B38 2008
220.9′1—dc22   2008017079

Maps by International Mapping

Routes, roads, and regions indicated on the maps are approximate. Buildings, and placement of them in city maps, are representative and approximations of actual locations.

Maps focusing on the Israel/Palestine/Lebanon area were created on an Albers Conic Equal-Area Projection with a central meridian of 35°E and standard parallel at 33°N. The lines of latitude are curved and bend northward at the edges of the subject area.

Maps showing areas outside of Israel were created on an Albers Conic Equal-Area Projection with a central meridian of 40°E and standard parallels at 25°N and 45°N. The lines of latitude are curved and bend northward at the edges of the subject area.

Because of these more correct spatial representations and projections, relative locations on maps in this volume may appear slightly different than on maps in other sources.

Photographs from the photo archives of Dr. James C. Martin, Bible World Seminars (bibleworld seminars@gmail.com), P.O. Box 2687, Amarillo, TX 79105.

Photo copyrights include: © Dr. James C. Martin; © Direct Design; © Garo Nalbandian; © The Israel Museum; and © The British Museum.

Credits to all those providing special photographic permissions:

Egypt
    The Egyptian Ministry of Antiquities.
    The Isma-iliya Museum. Isma-iliya, Egypt.
    The Cairo Museum. Cairo, Egypt.

France
    Mus'ee du Louvre; Autorisation de photographer et de filmer—LOUVRE. Paris, France.

Greece
    The Greek Ministry of Antiquities (Athens, Corinth, Delphi, Thessalonica).

Israel
    Collection of the Israel Museum, Jerusalem, and courtesy of the Israel Antiquities Authority, exhibited at the Israel Museum, Jerusalem.
    Collection of the Israel Museum, Jerusalem, and courtesy of the Israel Antiquities Authority, exhibited at the Shrine of the Book, the Israel Museum, Jerusalem.
    Collection of the Israel Museum, Jerusalem, and courtesy of the Israel Antiquities Authority, exhibited at the Rockefeller Museum, Jerusalem.
    The Church of Annunciation Museum. Nazareth, Israel.
    The House of Anchors. Kibbutz Ein Gev. Sea of Galilee, Israel.
    "Reproduction of the City of Jerusalem at the time of the Second Temple—located on the grounds of the Holyland Hotel, Jerusalem." Photographed by permission.
    The Eretz Israel Museum. Tel Aviv, Israel.
    The Skirball Museum, Hebrew Union College—Jewish Institute of Religion. 13 King David St., Jerusalem 94101.
    The Yigal Allon Center. Kibbutz Ginosar, on the western shore of the Sea of Galilee, Israel.

Italy
    On licence Ministero per I Beni e le Attivita Culturali—Soprintendenza Archaeologica di Roma. Rome, Italy.

Jordan
    The Jordanian Ministry of Antiquities. Amman, Jordan.
    The Amman Archaeological Museum. Amman, Jordan.

Turkey
    The Turkish Ministry of Antiquities. Ankara, Turkey.
    The Ankara Archaeological Museum. Ankara, Turkey.
    The Ephesus Archaeological Museum. Selchuk, Turkey.
    The Istanbul Archaeological Museum. Istanbul, Turkey.

United Kingdom
    The British Museum. London, England.

United States
    Sola Scriptura. The Van Kampen Collection on display at the Holy Land Experience in Orlando, Florida.

15 16 17 18 19 20 21   7 6 5 4 3 2 1   Interior design by Brian Brunsting

CONTENTS

ACKNOWLEDGMENTS

We would like to extend special thanks to Dixie and Gray Keller (the Leader Foundation) and Bruce Bordine for their support and participation in the numerous photo shoots and acquisitions. Additional thanks to Carolyn Hansen, family, and friends for assistance in the development of this manuscript.

Personal Note

Over the past twenty-five years it has been our privilege to travel, study, and teach the Bible in the land of the Bible. The information provided in this book is a synthesis of information from our professors who walked the land before us, and our own personal experiences with Scripture in its geographical, historical, and cultural setting. This book is not intended to be a proof text for any theory, but rather a door through which to enter the world of the Bible and encounter the power and love of our Lord Jesus and the unity of Scripture. It is our hope that this resource will be a blessing in your journey through God's Word.

This book is dedicated to the memory of Robert E. Fraley, an honored friend.

PART 1

THE NEED FOR RESCUE AND THE PROMISED LAND

"By faith Abraham . . . made his home in the promised land like a stranger in a foreign country; he lived in tents" (Heb. 11.8-9).

GENESIS

Genesis is a book of beginnings. Throughout this book, we find ourselves reading about events that happened where they did for a reason. We read about gardens and towers, a Promised Land that has no water and unpromised lands that do, roadways and memorials, trips to Egypt, delays at Beersheba, and a longing to be buried in Hebron. Each of these events happened where it did for a reason.

In part 1 we will see that water concerns often affected the decisions people made. The Lord placed Adam and Eve in his water-rich Garden of Eden. But when the serpent tempted them to eat the forbidden fruit, he directly contradicted the Lord's warning that this act of mutiny would bring death. The new sin-ruined world became so steeped in mutiny that it threatened the hope of any rescue. The Lord then used water to remove wickedness from the world—a judgment on evil that opened the door for a new beginning that Noah's family could enjoy. Mutiny, however, was progressive. Noah's descendants, through his son Ham, moved east and into deep trouble. Thus the new beginning of Noah's descendants ended badly as they tried to set down roots in the well-watered region of Babel only to build structures that misrepresented the nature and power of the one true God and distorted the Lord's purpose for humanity.

Thus in the Lord's plan, Abraham was directed to the land of Canaan with its unpredictable supply of water. The Lord chose Abraham and his descendants to be messengers of the one true God whose plan to rescue all nations occurred on the podium of Canaan (the Promised Land). Throughout the life of Abraham, Isaac, Jacob, and other members of this family, we observe their struggles, falling, rising, and continuing their journey. Water-rich areas of the Fertile Crescent that espoused self-reliance proved alluring. So we find them weighing decisions to leave the Promised Land only to return to their divinely assigned mission, and a life marked by tombs, altars, and memorials, whose locations and messages go hand in hand. The book of Genesis ends with Abraham's family in Egypt, but their hope for return is forged in the minds of all through the burial requests of Jacob and Joseph, who constantly turn their eyes to the Promised Land and call for their descendants to remember they are messengers of the one true God through whom all nations will be blessed.

So although Adam and Eve succumbed to the serpent's temptation in the Garden of Eden—a temptation to mutiny against the King of the Universe—their loving Creator proclaimed a message of rescue and restoration from the consequences of that mutiny. In time, that promise would intimately involve the family of Abraham and would one day be fulfilled in the coming of the Rescuer.

"In the beginning God created the heavens and the earth" (Gen. 1:1).

Neo-Sumerian cylinder seal (2200–2100 BC) reveals similarities with Adam and Eve in the Garden of Eden.

Mount Ararat, eastern Turkey. Noah's ark rested on the mountains of Ararat.

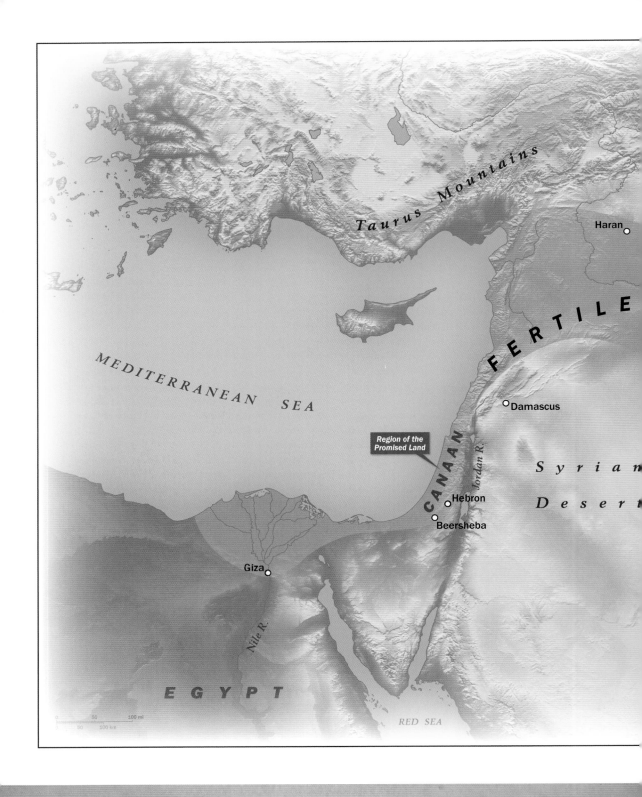

Taurus Mountains

Haran

MEDITERRANEAN SEA

FERTILE

Damascus

Region of the Promised Land

CANAAN

Jordan R.

Syrian

Desert

Hebron

Beersheba

Giza

Nile R.

EGYPT

RED SEA

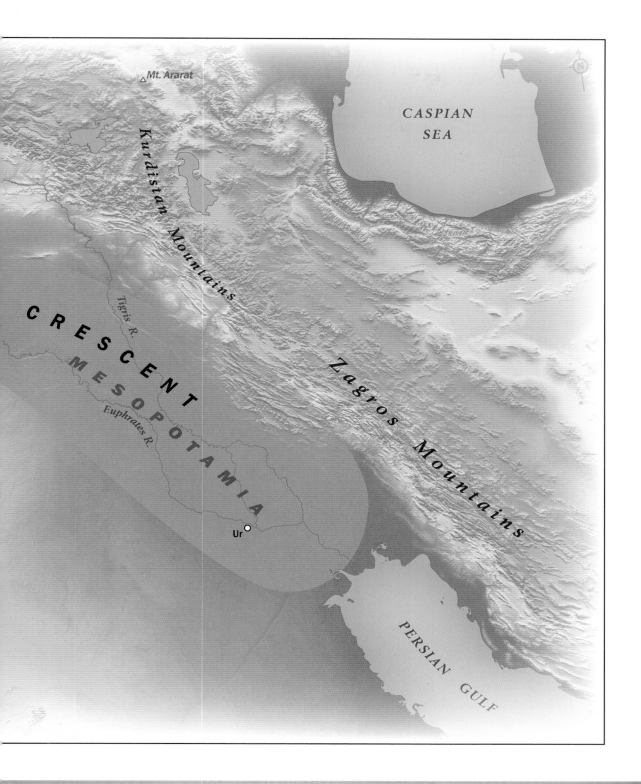

THE TEMPTATION IN THE GARDEN OF EDEN

GENESIS 2:4–3:24

*T*he beginning of our discussion takes us to the Garden of Eden. While the exact location of the Garden of Eden remains unknown,[1] one thing is certain: the description of this place as a water-rich region is key in establishing the geographical setting for this account and for those to come. The Lord placed Adam and Eve in this highly desirable living space, and the serpent used that place to shape his temptation of Adam and Eve.

Although the Garden of Eden no longer exists, following the Bible's lead, our search for its previous location takes us to one general region: Mesopotamia, the land between the Tigris and the Euphrates rivers (Gen. 2:14). Most place the Garden of Eden either in the Armenian Mountains of eastern Turkey, where we find the source of the Tigris and the Euphrates rivers, or in southeastern Iraq, near the effluence of those rivers into the Persian Gulf.[2] Nothing more conclusive than that can be said.

Even though its location remains a mystery, we do have a description of this place that became the home of Adam and Eve. The writer of Genesis called it a "garden" (*gan*), a living space akin to the royal parks and "King's Garden" (Neh. 3:15) of a later age.[3] Please note that this was not *paradise* in the popular sense of that term.[4] The Garden of Eden was not a luxury hotel filled with attendants whose job was to dote on vacationing visitors. It was an everyday living space of a royal garden by which the King offered his residents security from harm, plentiful food, and abundant water (Gen.

2:5–6, 10–14). The last item in that list is the one that would have especially caught the attention of those in antiquity living in the Middle East. To put the water issue in perspective, consider the following modern reality. The average United States citizen uses about 10,000 cubic meters (2.6 million gallons) of fresh water each

Sarcophagus lid (fourth century AD) depicting Adam and Eve in the Garden of Eden.

year. In Egypt the per capita total drops to 1,100 cubic meters and in Israel to 460 cubic meters per capita.[5]

Those of us who live with more fresh water than we need may not be solidly struck by this dimension of God's garden, but the people in this part of the ancient world were. Nothing meant contentment for the residents of this ancient world like a ready supply of fresh water. Because the Garden of Eden had it, Adam and Eve needed to change nothing so as to make their living circumstances better.

The serpent, a saboteur, used the blessings found in the King's royal Garden of Eden to sow the

Painted shrine offering with serpents (sixth century BC).

seeds of doubt and discontent. He proposed to Adam and Eve that the Lord was holding out on them, implying that the Lord had provided a royal living space and a living experience that was incomplete and less fulfilling than it could have been (Gen. 3:1–5). This first couple was persuaded to mutiny against the legitimate King in his royal garden. As a result, they became enemies of God and were required to leave the garden.

But the Lord would not have it be this way forever. So the Garden of Eden witnesses a third great event. Before they were driven into the clutches of a world corrupted and broken by mutiny, God promised that he would fix the problem by providing a Rescuer who would destroy the serpent (Gen. 3:15).

When the serpent tempted the first man and woman in the Garden of Eden, he did so for a reason. The Lord gave Adam and Eve dominion over his royal garden and provided them with water, food, and security. But the serpent wanted the allegiance of Adam and Eve, so he tempted them to mutiny against the Lord in God's royal garden. As the Lord warned, this

Euphrates River in northern Mesopotamia—a suggested location of the Garden of Eden.

brought death and destruction into creation and gave the serpent dominion over that which was intended for humanity. Even in the light of this mutiny and its consequences, the Lord promised to bring the Rescuer who would destroy the serpent and provide humanity with a means of rescue and restoration with the King of the Universe.

Possible locations of the Garden of Eden

Fertile Crescent

BUILDING THE TOWER AT BABEL

GENESIS 10:1–11:9

In the early chapters of Genesis, a good start went bad (Genesis 1–3), and mutiny proved itself to be progressive. By the end of Genesis 4 we have witnessed a murder, as Cain kills Abel. And by the time we get to Genesis 6, the mutiny is so pervasive that God elects to destroy his creation, save one family. We have hope that the new beginning Noah and his family enjoy will take the world to a better place. Yet even after the flood, some of Noah's descendants continued the mutiny as they attempted to replace the Lord's legitimate authority with their own by building a city with a tower in order to make a name for themselves (Gen. 11:4). They sought to build the city of Babel where they did for a reason.

The descendants of Ham (Noah's son) who initiated this building settled in a portion of the Fertile Crescent called the plain of Shinar (Gen. 10:8–10; 11:1–4). The Fertile Crescent is an arch of land that extends from the Nile River in Egypt northward through modern Israel, Lebanon, and coastal Syria before turning southeast as it follows the Tigris and the Euphrates rivers through Syria and Iraq toward the head of the Persian Gulf. A move north or south out of this arch moves into undesirable living circumstances. Moving north puts one into the Taurus,

Relief of Ashurbanipal's garden party (Assyria, 645–635 BC). The Creator's royal Garden of Eden is replaced by nations wishing to make a name for themselves.

Kurdistan, and Zagros mountains. Moving south puts one into the forbidding Syrian Desert. Choosing to avoid mountains and deserts, Ham's descendants wanted to live in the Fertile Crescent because it provided the necessary water and agricultural resources for those who wished to abandon a life of seasonal migration for a more settled, city life.[6]

In order to get to the region of Shinar, Ham's family traveled "eastward" (Gen. 11:2). This detail can easily escape our attention. But within the early chapters of Genesis, mention of travel direction has very important implications.[7] When Adam and Eve were driven from the Garden of Eden, they moved eastward (Gen. 3:24). When Cain went out from the Lord's

Model of a ziggurat at the Baghdad Archaeological Museum.

presence after murdering Abel, he too moved farther east (4:16). Each of these eastward moves is associated with negative circumstances. So when we read that Ham's descendants moved "eastward," we can expect things to get worse rather than better.

When humanity could no longer have the prosperity found within the Lord's royal garden, they moved eastward and created their own garden where they had access to the water of the Tigris and the Euphrates and thus ample food supplies. Babel became a center representing their national prosperity. There the intentions of the builders were revealed in the structure they started to build. The building brick materials they chose (Gen. 11:3) and the term *tower* (Gen. 11:4) made their structure sound very much like the ziggurats found in that portion of the Fertile Crescent. The ziggurat was built using a combination of kiln-baked bricks and bitumen (tar). The foundation of just such a structure can still be seen in Babylon.

Brick inscriptions dedicating ziggurat temples to the various deified kings and idols have been discovered on their foundations throughout the region. It is no surprise that ziggurats were built in this region as symbols of prosperity as the nations attempted to "make a name for" themselves (Gen. 11:4) and create their own counterfeit Garden of Eden that they could control. Given the intentions behind the tower, it is no wonder that

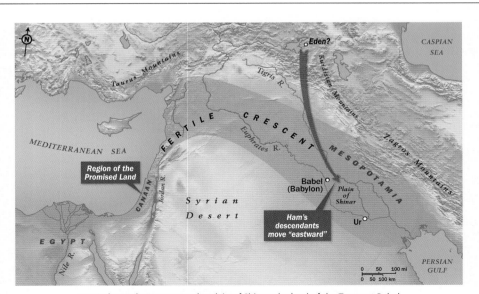

The partly restored ziggurat (temple tower) at Agur Quf, dating to about 1400 BC.
Courtesy of the British Museum

the true King of the Universe acted in a way so as to frustrate the construction of this building project and scatter the architects of this idolatrous tower over the face of the earth.

When humanity was removed from the Garden of Eden and traveled east to Babel, they did so for a reason. Their move to settle in the Fertile Crescent provided them with water from the Tigris and the Euphrates rivers. Here they could build towers in their own honor and create idols that they could manipulate. Here they could create their own pseudo-Eden.

Ham's descendants move to the plain of Shinar: the land of the Tower at Babel

ABRAM IS PROMISED THE LAND OF CANAAN

GENESIS 11:10–12:9

The ancient region of Haran (view looking northeast), where Abram lived before the Lord called him to Canaan.

*T*he Lord came to Abram when he was at Haran and delivered instructions for Abram to leave his home and father's household and travel to a land the Lord would show him. Although childless at the time, Abram received the Lord's promise that he would become the father of a great nation through which all peoples of the earth would be blessed (Gen. 12:1–3). In addition, Abram and his descendants would be given a land of their own (Gen. 17:3–8). These promises became the core of the Lord's promise to Abram that would cast a large and enduring shadow over all the subsequent books of the Bible.

With the mutiny of the world so often associated with people moving east (Gen. 3:24; 4:16), we breathe a sigh of relief when we finally find a man not moving east. When Abram takes his first steps out of Haran, we find ourselves focusing with increasing interest on Canaan. The land of Canaan will become the setting for the divine rescue mission—a mission that happened here for a reason. Canaan (now referred to as Palestine and Israel) is a narrow strip of land that runs north and south along the eastern shore of the Mediterranean Sea and functions as a land bridge connecting Africa, Asia, and Europe. As we pan away from this close-up view, we see that Canaan is located in the southwestern

Babylonian terra-cotta plaque from Ur (2000–1750 BC), depicting a loving couple.
© Dr. James C. Martin. The British Museum.

edge of the Fertile Crescent. Because the Tigris, Euphrates, and Nile rivers did not pass through the land, the availability of fresh water and agricultural land was not guaranteed. Canaan did, however, possess a major transportation artery, a route that would interconnect the commerce of Africa, Asia, and Europe.[8] We do not know what this road was called by the ancients, but we will refer to it as the "International Highway."

Although the term *Promised Land* is not in Scripture, it has become a term often associated with the land of Canaan because the Lord promised this land to Abram. The Promised Land presented those who lived there with many challenges, but one of the most daunting was the constant threat of invasion. The natural boundaries of the Syrian Desert and the Mediterranean Sea squeezed the International Highway onto a very narrow land bridge as it moved through Canaan. Since international commerce passed over this narrow land bridge, the superpowers of the ancient world sought to control Canaan and to gain wealth from the taxes levied on the merchants. As international superpowers wrestled one another for control of Canaan, these foreign invaders brought their idols into this Promised Land.

When the Lord pledged Abram and his descendants the land of Canaan, he did so for a reason. The passage of the International Highway through Canaan made the

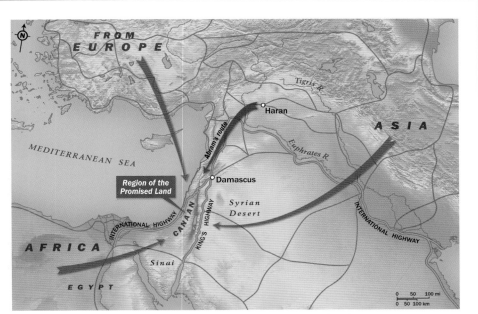

The Promised Land and its location on international roads

Promised Land a podium to an international audience. As the merchants moved their goods on this highway, they also carried the news of the day with them, depositing what they learned at every stop along their path. The Lord had chosen Abram and his descendants to serve, proclaim, and represent the one true God and thereby be a blessing to all nations. This could be accomplished by traveling to the far-flung reaches of the world, or the family of Abram could be placed on a podium to speak before travelers from every corner of the world. Abram and his descendants were to be God's messengers, and they were given the Promised Land to be used as a podium, so all nations could be blessed. Thus it is not surprising that Canaan, the land bridge connecting Africa, Asia, and Europe, became the podium known as the Promised Land.

Part of the International Highway that passed through the Promised Land (aerial view).

ABRAM HEADS FOR EGYPT

GENESIS 12:10–20

The Lord selected Canaan, the hub between three continents, to be the Promised Land. Our expectation is that Abram would remain securely settled in this land (Gen. 12:1–7). So we are surprised to read just three verses later that Abram is leaving the Promised Land (Gen. 12:10). Without apparent hesitation and without seeking the Lord's approval for his decision, Abram headed to Egypt. We will see why he left and why his reason for leaving was not justified.

The motivation for Abram to flee the famine in the Promised Land and move to Egypt was the Nile River. The land of Canaan had a much more austere and challenging natural environment than most readers might think. The water that matured the grain fields, filled the wells and cisterns, and turned the pasturelands green came from the heavens in the form of precipitation. If the cycles of seasonal rainfall were mistimed or failed to arrive altogether, the residents of Canaan were in for a very rough time. As this account opened, that was the reality, for a severe famine had come to Canaan (Gen. 12:10).

By contrast to Canaan, the well-being of those living in Egypt was not dependent upon a cycle of seasonal rainfall. Egypt enjoyed a river-based hydrology that tapped into the ever-flowing waters of the Nile. Gathering precipitation from lands as far as four

Wooden model of Pharaoh Senusret I (1971–1926 BC) of the Egyptian Twelfth Dynasty.
© Dr. James C. Martin. The Cairo Museum.

Scene from the tomb of Khnumhotep at Beni Hasan in Egypt of a group of Semite traders entering Egypt to sell eye paint (ca. 1890 BC).

thousand miles away, the Nile provided an environmental stability to those living in Egypt that was completely foreign to those living in Canaan.[9] Abram had originally come from southeastern Mesopotamia, a land that enjoyed hydrology similar to that of Egypt, so he knew the security that a river-based system like the Tigris and Euphrates rivers provided. But rather than walking toward his former homeland, he walked the shorter and well-worn path to Egypt to seek relief from the famine.[10] Along with that relief, he understood the potential of tapping into the benefits that were intimately linked to living on the Nile.

As compelling as these reasons might be to abandon the Promised Land, the reasons for staying in Canaan were that much more so. The first and most glaring reason for remaining was that Canaan, not Egypt, was the Promised Land that the Lord had chosen as the podium to proclaim the message of the one true God. When Abram left Canaan, and for as long as he was absent, the plan for the podium was on hold. Second, the security offered by the abundant natural resources of Egypt did not encourage trust in the Lord in the same way the famine-stricken land of Canaan could. The predictability and regularity of the water provided by the Nile River could foster independence from God, while the uncertainty and unpredictability of rainfall in Canaan encouraged dependence on the Lord. Finally, God had directed Abram to remain in Canaan so that his family might become a blessing to the world. This promise was in no way compromised by the famine at that time in Canaan. But Abram abandoned God's plan and chose to seek rescue from Egypt on his own terms (Gen. 12:13, 16).

When Abram left Canaan and traveled to Egypt, he did so for a reason. He sought security and wealth in the predictable land of Egypt. In doing so, he put himself, Sarai, and the greater plan of rescue and blessing the nations at risk. Abram rejected the Promised Land to find survival in a predictable environment. It would take time before Abram learned the Creator of the universe would fulfill all the promises made to him—but in very unpredictable ways.

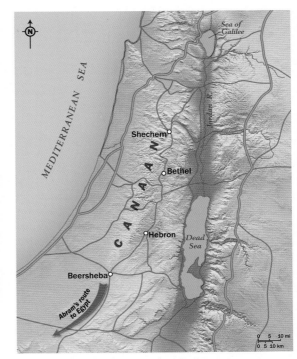

Abram travels to Egypt

The pyramids at Giza were already hundreds of years old before Abram and Sarai journeyed to Egypt.

ABRAM AND LOT SEPARATE IN CANAAN

GENESIS 13

Abram's unfortunate journey to Egypt in a time of famine leaves us certain that Canaan is the only land for Abram and his family (Gen. 12:10–20). Despite the fragility of its ecosystem, the Lord could and would sustain Abram's family there. But had Abram arrived at this same conclusion? That answer comes to us very quickly in the account that finds Abram and his nephew parting company (Genesis 13). The Lord had so richly blessed these two families that they were no longer able to live together. A dispute over grazing land had begun between Abram and Lot's herdsmen, requiring selection of separate regions in which to live. The question was, where would each family go and what was the reason behind their choice?

Byzantine chapel built over the traditional site of Lot's cave near Safi in present-day Jordan, which could be the ancient location of Zoar.

When it came time for Abram and Lot to choose their respective territories, Abram encouraged Lot to select first. Lot quickly turned his eyes toward the well-watered "plain of the Jordan" and made his choice of an area associated with Zoar, Sodom, and Gomorrah (Gen. 13:10).[11]

In relating the event, the biblical writer particularly emphasized the quality of the land selected by Lot. First, we learn that the cities were "well watered, like the garden of the Lord, like the land of Egypt" (Gen. 13:10). The Garden of Eden and the land of Egypt are both noted for their abundant and predictable water supply. All other matters aside, this would be the land to choose—a land rich in water. But Abram had just had an experience that suggested there was more to God's promises than fresh water. He had left the Promised Land, which had been stricken by famine, hoping

Pottery from the site of Bab edh-Drah, which some identify as Sodom.

© Dr. James C. Martin. The British Museum.

to find greater security and abundance in Egypt (Gen. 12:10–20). That trip nearly ended in disaster. The fact that he gave Lot the opportunity to select first, coupled with the fact that he had abandoned a quest for land rich in water, suggests that Abram had grown in his understanding that the Lord was sufficient, at least with the issue of survival. Lot elected to move to an area of land with predictable water resources, but Abram trusted the Lord to take care of him and his family on a land that did not have predictable water resources.

Note again that the land Lot selected required him to travel *east*. In the book of Genesis, this is never a good sign.[12] After the decision to mutiny, Adam and Eve moved east from the Garden of Eden (Gen. 3:24). Cain was forced to move east after murdering his brother (Gen. 4:16), and those who conspired to build the Tower of Babel did so after moving east (Gen. 11:1–2). So while this move of Lot seemed to be a logical move in the right direction of abundant fresh water, it proved decidedly to be a move in the wrong direction. The predictable water supply of the Jordan plain was used by a populace whose wickedness was so intense that the

The site of Numeira, which some believe to be ancient Gomorrah, on the southeast side of the Dead Sea.

Lord brought about their complete destruction within a short time (Gen. 18–19).

Abram had learned some lessons in Egypt: the Lord is faithful to his promises no matter what deterrents came upon the Promised Land. Abram would no longer pursue a life where abundant water and idolatry enjoyed one another's company. Instead he would remain in the Promised Land confident that his all-powerful King would provide for all his physical needs.

When Abram and Lot separated to their specific areas, they did so for a reason. Abram gave Lot the first choice. Lot walked by sight and mistakenly concluded that the water-rich areas of Zoar, Sodom, and Gomorrah would be to his benefit. Abram walked by faith and remained in the unpredictable and limited water resources of the hill country and Negev, trusting in the Lord's provision.

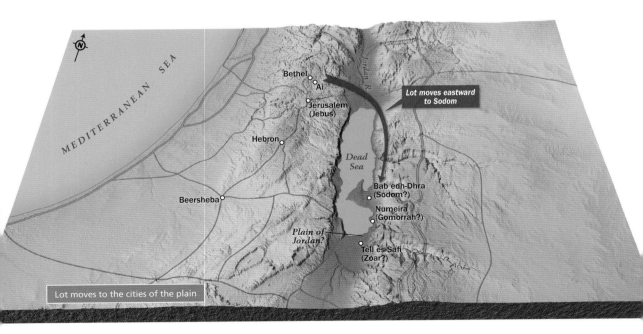

ABRAHAM'S PURCHASE OF LAND AT HEBRON

GENESIS 14–23

When Abram was ninety-nine years old, the Lord changed his name from Abram (exalted father) to Abraham (father of many, see Gen. 17:1–5). Soon after, the Lord appeared to Abraham at the great trees of Mamre (i.e., Hebron; Gen. 18:1–15; see also 23:19) to announce that Sarah would give birth to the promised heir. And so Isaac was born (Gen. 21:1–5).

Then the passing of Sarai, now called Sarah by God (Gen. 17:15), Abraham's beloved wife and the mother of the promised heir, Isaac, precipitated an unprecedented event (Genesis 23). Abraham purchased land in Kiriath Arbah (Hebron). While the need for a tomb is unquestioned in that culture at that time, the significant amount of space dedicated to the telling of this event begs for explanation. Why did the writer of Genesis give the location of this tomb with such precision? Why was the business transaction relayed in graphic detail? And why did Abraham choose property in Hebron? The answers to all these questions make it clear that it happened there for a reason.

Abraham and his family were nomadic. Since the animals they tended required water and fresh pastures, it meant they were a family on the move. The family living quarters was a tent. As the seasons changed, the stakes were pulled from the ground and reset in one location after another as this family sought fresh pastures for their flocks and more temperate climate. That is why Abraham described himself to Hebron's local landowning residents as a foreigner and sojourner in the land (Gen. 23:4). The Lord had promised Abraham that his descendants would inherit the land of Canaan. But for the moment, they pitched their tents and grazed their animals wherever they found space.

The death of Sarah brought about a change in circumstance. She was the first member of this family to die in Canaan, presenting the practical need for a tomb. Abraham identified a location to purchase and make his own—a field and associated cave owned by Ephron the Hittite near Mamre. The importance of this incident is indicated by the great amount of detail used in relating these events to the reader. We hear the bartering between Abraham and Ephron, the exact price that is paid, as well as the specific portion of Ephron's property that exchanged hands (Gen. 23:10–18). And lest anyone care to challenge the veracity of the contract, all of this took place in front of

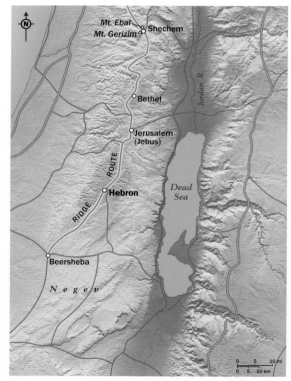

Hebron on the Ridge Route

This massive structure was built by Herod the Great over the burial cave of Machpelah at Hebron, which was purchased by Abraham in order to bury his wife, Sarah.

Remains of a palace built by Herod the Great at Ramat el-Khalil, identified with the site of Mamre.

the appropriate witnesses at the city gate. At the end of the encounter, Abraham legally owned a specific piece of the Promised Land.

The location of the property Abraham purchased indicates that he had larger plans for this tomb. Following the tradition of the time, this cave would also become the burial vault for other family members.[13] Ultimately the bodies of Abraham, Isaac, Rebecca, Jacob, and Leah joined Sarah's bones there. As the survivors visited this tomb, Abraham surely wanted them not only to remember those who had passed away but also to recall the promises made to this family and the great hope for all the world that was attached to them. First, the direct promise that Sarah would give birth to a son occurred at Hebron (Mamre, see Gen. 18:1–15). Second, the initial fulfillment of possessing the Promised Land occurred when Abraham purchased the cave in the field of Machpelah near Mamre for Sarah's burial (Gen. 23:19).

Abraham could have bought a tomb in many locations, but he purchased land in Hebron for a reason. Turning personal tragedy into an opportunity, Abraham purchased property at Hebron near the location where the Lord informed him of Sarah's child-to-be, Isaac. Thus Sarah's tomb at Hebron was not that of a childless woman but instead marked the initial fulfillment of the Lord's promise of numerous descendants in a land in which those descendants would proclaim the one true God.

The traditional cenotaph of Sarah, located inside the Machpelah at Hebron.

BUILDING MEMORIALS ON THE RIDGE ROUTE

GENESIS 24–36

The connection between events in the book of Genesis can be very subtle and, consequently, easily missed. That is the case with the memorials that were built by Abraham and his grandson Jacob along the Ridge Route. We will see how five events, three locations, and one roadway all came together in a way that reminds us that these memorials were built where they were for a reason.

In order to read about the five events, we must turn to four different chapters of Genesis. When Abram entered the land of Canaan, he built an altar to the Lord at Shechem (Gen. 12:6–7). Shortly after this we find Abram building another altar between Bethel and Ai (Gen. 12:8). After Abram and Lot went their separate ways, Abram traveled to Hebron and built an altar (Gen. 13:18). When Abraham's grandson Jacob used deception to steal the birthright of his brother, the burning anger of Esau sent Jacob fleeing in the direction of Haran. En route he stopped at Bethel, where he set up and anointed a stone in remembrance of the vision he had there (Gen.

28:18–19). And years later when he returned to the Promised Land from Haran, Jacob took his household to Bethel. There they rededicated themselves to the Lord and built an altar (Gen. 35:6–7).

While these accounts are scattered across many pages in Genesis, several points of similarity invite us to see them as connected to one another. First, the Lord spoke to Abraham and Jacob about the enduring plans that he had for their family, particularly reminding them that their descendants would become a great nation and inherit the land of Canaan. Therefore they

Standing stone of the Israelite temple at Arad. Jacob set up and anointed a standing stone to dedicate the site of Bethel.

built memorials, either altars or standing stones,[14] commemorating that experience.

Next, when we plot these memorials on a map, we find they were all built on the same roadway, the Ridge Route, a secondary road through the country. This eighty-five mile path stretched between the Negev and the Jezreel Valley, following the watershed line of the central mountains.[15] The most topographically trouble-free route was the International Highway, which ran down the coast along the western side of Canaan. At that time of history, however, it was under Egyptian dominance. The Ridge Route through the hill country of Canaan was more difficult to travel but more secure from Egypt's military. Shechem, Bethel, and Hebron, where the memorials were constructed, were along the Ridge Route.[16] When the Lord appeared to these men and when they built memorials, they did so along this Ridge Route.

When Abram and Jacob built memorials along the Ridge Route, they did so for a reason. As Abram and his descendants moved their livestock north and south through Canaan, they used the Ridge Route, which brought them into regular contact with these memorials. Each stop provided the opportunity for the members of this family to review, reflect, worship, and recommit to proclaiming the Creator's message of rescue to the nations of the world. Just as we might turn our eyes to the promises of God written in his Word, the family of Abraham turned their eyes to these places and memorials to see the words and promises of God.

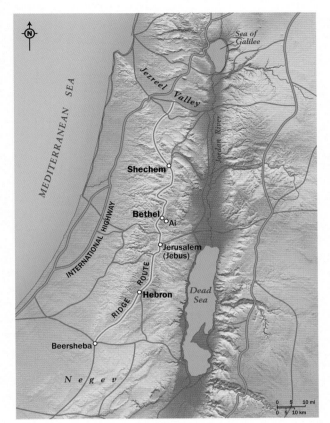

The Ridge Route

Bethel region.

◀ The standing stone from the temple at Shechem with Mount Gerizim in the background.

JOSEPH IS TAKEN TO EGYPT

GENESIS 37–46

The family of Abraham, his son Isaac, and Isaac's son Jacob had a purpose to accomplish in the Promised Land. By the time we reach Genesis 37, we have come to wince whenever we read that a member of this family is even thinking of setting foot outside the Promised Land (cf. Gen. 26:2). So when we read that Joseph has been sold as a slave and taken to Egypt, we expect misfortune and pain will follow. But in the end, we learn that this trip to Egypt precipitated a family migration that was part of God's plan rather than a diversion from it. The Lord allowed Joseph to be taken to Egypt for two important reasons that become apparent when we consider the circumstances in which this family found itself: first, to provide a place of refuge for the small number of Abram's descendants to increase numerically into a nation, and second, to provide a place to escape the wickedness of Canaan.

As the oldest son of Jacob's wife Rachel, Joseph was given the distinctive patriarchal coat—the symbol of authority worn by the head of the family. This position of authority fueled powerful flames of jealousy in his siblings, who were the children of Leah and of Jacob's concubines. They conspired to be rid of him by selling him into slavery to Midianite traders who were en route to Egypt (Gen. 37:17–28). At first, Joseph's stay in Egypt brought misfortune (Gen. 39). But in time, Joseph's God-given ability to interpret dreams brought him before the royal throne.

Pharaoh had become undone by troubling dreams that Joseph alone was able to interpret. The dreams were a message from God signaling seven years of agricultural abundance that would be followed by seven years of oppressive famine (Gen. 41:1–40). Working quietly behind the scenes, the Lord propelled Joseph from prison to prominence. Pharaoh placed him in charge of a massive public works project designed to store food during the years of plenty and to organize a distribution plan for the years of famine (Gen. 41:41–57).

Other famines had been mentioned in Genesis, but this one was particularly severe. The rainfall shortage did not just impact a region but a continent, causing the predictable flow of the Nile River to be compromised for successive years. Only with advance warning and the savvy leadership of Joseph was disaster averted for thousands who were at risk of starvation, including the family of Jacob.

Using Egypt like a lifeboat, the Lord brought the family of Jacob there and settled them in the fertile region of Goshen, located in the northeastern portion of the Nile delta.[17] Their location became a matter of importance to the writer of Genesis, who made formal mention of it eight times within two chapters (Gen. 46:28 [twice], 29, 34; 47:1, 4, 6, 27), noting in particular the high quality of this land (Gen. 45:18, 20). While this region was not part of the Promised Land, it was part of God's plan (Gen. 45:8–11).

Joseph was responsible for building the storehouses located adjacent to this mud-brick pyramid of Amenemhat III at Hawara in the vicinity of the Faiyum.

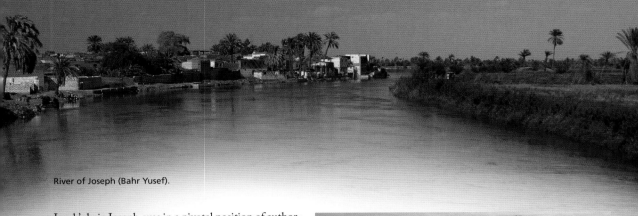

River of Joseph (Bahr Yusef).

Jacob's heir, Joseph, was in a pivotal position of authority in Egypt. The Lord used him to provide vital food supplies that would preserve Abraham's descendants along with all of Egypt during this famine.[18]

But Egypt was more than a physical lifeboat. The family of Jacob had other problems that needed to be addressed as well. After Joseph was taken to Egypt as a slave, the Bible interrupts the account to bring us a glimpse of life back in Canaan (Genesis 38). What we read is a tawdry tale that strongly suggests the family of Abraham had begun to assimilate into the idolatrous ideals and lifestyle of the Canaanites. Goshen provided food and a greater degree of cultural isolation (Gen. 43:32; 46:34), enabling this family to recollect their purpose as messengers of the one true God. So while the earlier chapters in Genesis led us to view Egypt negatively, the closing chapters of Genesis reveal the two reasons the Lord allowed Joseph to be taken to Egypt. There the Lord used him to preserve Abraham's descendants in the face of famine as well as to isolate them from the idolatry prevalent in the Promised Land.

Depressions surrounded by covered wall remains once functioned as a granary at Hawara, dating to the time of Joseph's rise to power in Egypt.

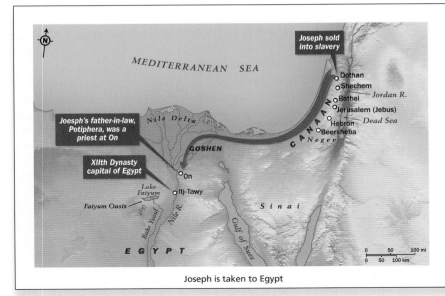

Joseph is taken to Egypt

GOD ASSURES JACOB AT BEERSHEBA

GENESIS 46

Jacob's long-lost son Joseph, whom he presumed dead, was alive, and only a few days travel stood between this moment of discovery and their reunion. Even more astounding was the news that Joseph had become a high-ranking official in the Egyptian government, responsible for the distribution of food that his family so desperately needed (Gen. 42:1–2). How could there be a question of what to do? Jacob and his family quickly accepted Joseph's invitation and migrated to Egypt. But while the trip to Egypt started quickly, it came to a pause at Beersheba (Gen. 46:1–7)—a pause that happened there for a reason.

God had not authorized Abraham or his descendants to leave the Promised Land for Egypt, even in the face of famine. The Lord had assured Abraham that his family would grow to become a great nation in Canaan. No doubt Jacob recalled what his grandfather Abraham and his father Isaac had told him about their own experiences with Egypt. Abraham had left Canaan for Egypt under circumstances similar to those now facing Jacob (Gen. 12:10–19). That unauthorized trip had nearly cost Abram his wife. Later, Isaac also elected to leave the Promised Land for Egypt under the duress of a famine. But before he had gotten to the Egyptian border, the Lord blocked his path and told him to return to the

Tell Sheva (ancient Beersheba).

land in which his family was supposed to live (Gen. 26:1–3). Now with famine in Canaan and his desire to see Joseph, Jacob was drawn toward Egypt. Perhaps previous commands of the Lord and the experiences of his father and grandfather caused Jacob to question the wisdom of travel to Egypt.

Beersheba marked the place for Jacob to answer this question as no other place could. For those living in the Negev like Jacob's family, Beersheba represented the natural starting point for a trip to Egypt. Perhaps, like his grandfather Abraham, Jacob had positioned himself at the start of a roadway to Egypt called the Way to Shur (Gen. 20:1). What is more, Beersheba represented the southern boundary of Canaan.[19] A step southward from Beersheba was a step out of and away from the Promised Land. And if that were not enough to give Jacob pause, Beersheba also was the site of a memorial altar built by Isaac. The Lord had appeared to Isaac at Beersheba recalling the promises made to Abraham and affirming Isaac's decision to remain in the Promised Land (Gen. 26:23–25). Isaac then built a memorial altar there—somewhere near the road that led to Egypt on the border of Canaan—that would challenge any member of his family thinking about a trip to Egypt to think again.

Tomb paintings of Semitic traders entering Egypt are reminders of Jacob's journey into Egypt.

When Jacob considered a journey to Egypt, the Lord assured him at Beersheba for a reason. If he was going to make a decision about leaving the Promised Land with Egypt as his destination, that decision had to be made at Beersheba. So Jacob stopped and "offered sacrifices to the God of his father Isaac" (Gen. 46:1). In contrast to the trips to Egypt initiated by Abram and Isaac, this one had divine approval. The Lord appeared to Jacob at Beersheba, assuring him that his departure from the Promised Land was sanctioned and promising that his family would return (Gen. 46:3–4). With these promises firmly established, a confirmed Jacob was ready to leave Beersheba to escape the famine and reunite with his son Joseph. Beersheba, formerly a stepping-stone of fear and doubt when Abram and Isaac sought security in Egypt, became a stepping-stone of faith as Jacob trusted and obeyed the Lord.

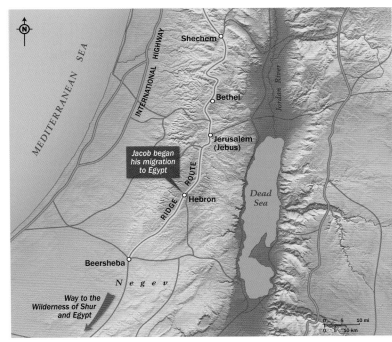

Jacob delays at Beersheba

The region of Beersheba toward the Way to Shur (view looking southwest).

JACOB AND JOSEPH ARE BURIED IN THE PROMISED LAND

GENESIS 49–50

Because of the threat imposed by a severe famine in Canaan, the Lord placed Joseph in Egypt and used him to save thousands from starvation. The grain he brought in during the seven years of abundant harvest was stored to feed the population during the seven years of famine, including Abraham's descendants—a family intimately connected to a much larger scope of rescue (Gen. 45:8–11). The famine came to a close, and in time, both Jacob and Joseph died in Egypt. But out of sight did not mean the land of promise was out of mind. Both Jacob and Joseph directed their families to transport their bodies to the Promised Land for burial (Gen. 49:29–31; 50:22–26).

The Bible makes it clear that the bodies of Jacob and Joseph were transferred to Canaan, the podium that linked their destiny (Gen. 46:4; 49:29–30; Josh. 24:32). And while both Jacob and Joseph were buried in the Promised Land, they were not buried in the same location. Jacob requested that his burial site be located with his grandparents, parents, and wife Leah (Gen. 49:29–33), so he was buried at Hebron in the family tomb that held their remains (Gen. 49:31). We might expect that Joseph would have requested burial in the same tomb, but he did not. He simply directed that his body be carried from Egypt when the Lord brought this family back to Canaan (Gen. 50:24–25). After Joshua led the Israelites into the Promised Land, they took the bones of Joseph, which the Israelites had taken with them out of Egypt, and buried them at Shechem (Josh. 24:32).

So why were Jacob and Joseph buried in these two cities? The answer is rooted in family history and in travel accessibility to these memorials. Both were located on the Ridge Route, which was the primary north/south roadway through the hill country of Canaan. Hebron was twenty miles south of Jerusalem, and Shechem was thirty miles north. Both Hebron and Shechem were significant urban centers throughout this period,[20] located at transportation hubs from which secondary roads radiated.[21]

Hebron was directly connected to God's promises to Abraham. After promising land and descendants, the Lord instructed him to walk the land. Abraham's immediate response was to move his tent to Hebron, where he built an altar commemorating those promises (Gen. 13:14–18). Thus it is no surprise that after the Lord promised Abraham a son though Sarah at Hebron (Gen. 18:1–15) and after the death of Sarah

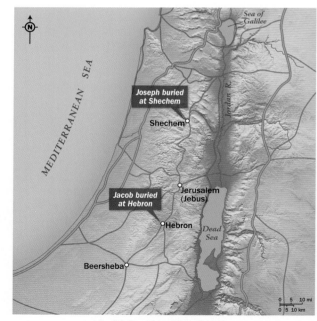

Burial sites of Joseph and Jacob

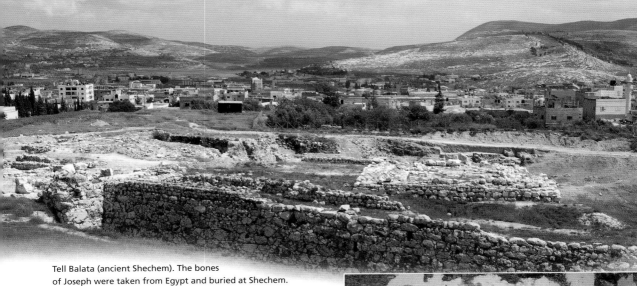
Tell Balata (ancient Shechem). The bones of Joseph were taken from Egypt and buried at Shechem.

at Hebron (Genesis 23) that Abraham purchased the cave at Hebron, which was the first and only real estate he personally owned in the Promised Land. Therefore, considering who was already buried there, it was clearly the perfect site for Jacob's burial.

Shechem was also linked to Abraham and Jacob, so the Israelites buried Joseph there. It was the place where his great-grandfather, Abraham, had received the Lord's promise of the land (Gen. 12:6–8), ground that later his father, Jacob, had purchased (Gen. 33:18–19; Josh. 24:32), thereby marking the second piece of property obtained by the patriarchs prior to the sojourn in Egypt. The burials of Jacob and Joseph stand like bookends on either side of this family's Egyptian experience. Jacob was carried from Egypt during the early years of that sojourn, and Joseph was carried from Egypt at the time of the exodus. In each case, their burial requests invited their family members to greater faithfulness as they remembered the promises of God—promises of a land and descendants to bless all nations with the message of the rescuing power of the one true God. The purpose for their life in that place could be kept vivid as parents traveled the Ridge Route with their children, pointing to the family tombs and reminding them that Jacob and Joseph were buried there for a reason.

Embalming illustration from the tomb of Tausert and Seth-Nakht (Nineteenth Dynasty). The bodies of Jacob and Joseph went through the process of Egyptian embalming.

Traditional cenotaphs of Isaac, Rebecca, Jacob, and Leah are located inside the Machpelah at Hebron.

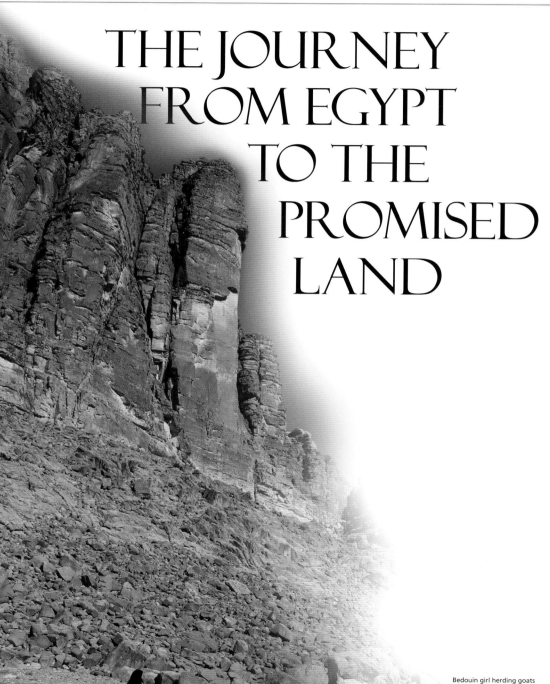

PART 2

THE JOURNEY FROM EGYPT TO THE PROMISED LAND

Bedouin girl herding goats in the region of Edom.

EXODUS, NUMBERS, DEUTERONOMY

Within the chapters of Genesis, the Lord had repeatedly promised Abraham and his family that they would come to possess the land of Canaan. But as Genesis comes to a close and the book of Exodus opens, the descendants of Abraham, Isaac, and Jacob are living in Egypt. With the exception of a dozen men, no one from that family will set foot in the Promised Land again until we reach the opening chapters of Joshua.

The book of Exodus reports a 430-year stay in Egypt (Exod. 12:40), and the book of Numbers records nearly forty years in the Wilderness of Zin (Num. 14:32–34). These books trace the footsteps of the fledgling nation of Jacob (i.e., Israel) on a lengthy detour around Edom that finally lands this people on the Transjordan plateau east of the Dead Sea. And all these events happened where they did for a reason.

Egypt provided the setting for the first chapters of Exodus. The Lord had used the natural resources and the political climate of Egypt to grow Jacob's descendants into a great nation. But the Hebrew people came under affliction and hardship in Egypt. They cried out to the Lord for deliverance, and God responded by marking the path for their return to the Promised Land. Many routes were available for this exit, but only one would do.

The Lord took Israel out of Egypt into the Sinai, where a harsh wilderness tested their resolve and a mountain served as the podium for divine encounter. When business at Sinai was complete, God directed the people north to the southern gateway of the Promised Land. But just when their hopes for entrance were brightest, they were dimmed by mutiny. Respected tribal leaders were sent into Canaan but failed to heed the Lord's explicit instruction through Moses. As a result, they returned with information that drained Israelite confidence in the Lord's ability to bring them successfully into the land (Num. 14:26–30).

With the coming of a new generation, the Israelites were eager for Moses to lead them into Canaan. But then a shocking event occurred in the Wilderness of Zin. When pressed to deliver water, Moses disobeyed the Lord by striking a rock rather than speaking to it. The depth of his mutiny only becomes apparent when we see his actions linked to their location.

Another surprise quickly followed. The Lord led Moses south rather than north. The Promised Land was again at their backs as Israel circumnavigated the hostile, Edomite forces. When the Israelites again drew near the Promised Land, they made their approach from east of the Jordan River in a region known as the Transjordan. This was Amorite territory about to be taken by the Israelites. Before the book of Deuteronomy ends, we come to Pisgah, an outcrop on Mount Nebo. There two men, Balaam and Moses, climb Pisgah for very different reasons. Yet both of their experiences recall the promises initially given to Abraham. And as we look back over those events, one thing is clear: God used locations outside of Canaan to prepare the nation of Israel for their entrance into the Promised Land.

Sarcophagus relief with depiction of Israelites crossing the Red Sea (dated AD 375–400).

Sinai mountains.

The Wilderness of Paran. The Lord led the Israelites through the Wilderness of Paran on their way to the Promised Land.

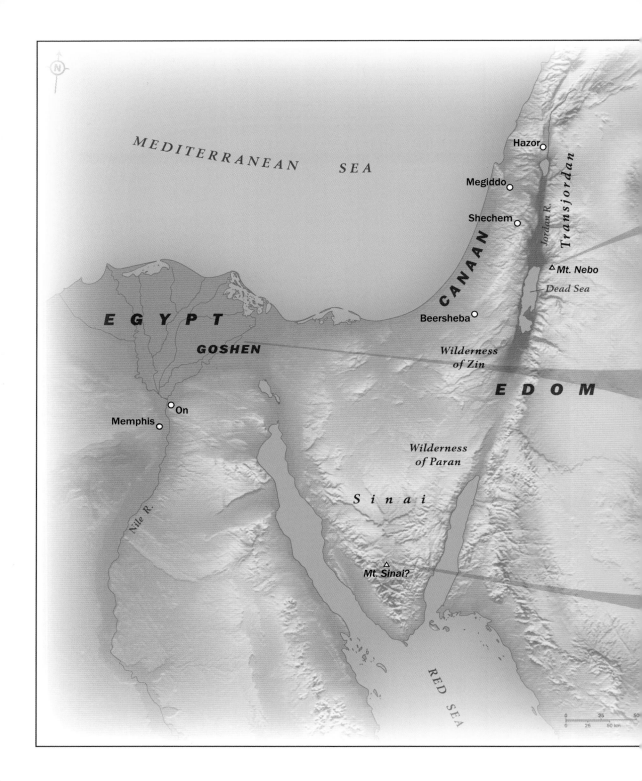

The Journey from Egypt to the Promised Land

Mount Nebo (view looking southwest). Moses looked over the Promised Land from Mount Nebo.

Goshen. This canal in the region of Goshen is near where the pharaoh's daughter found Moses.

Sinai Mountain. These mountains, positioned in the southern region of the Sinai Peninsula, are generally thought to be the location of Mount Horeb.

THE GROWTH AND AFFLICTION OF THE ISRAELITES IN EGYPT

EXODUS 1–12

The stay of Jacob's family in Egypt lasted hundreds of years longer than the famine that initially brought them there. Two things, both promised by God, were to happen before they would leave. The family of Jacob (i.e., Israel) was to multiply greatly in that land (Gen. 46:3–4) and be afflicted there (Gen. 15:13). Only when these events transpired did the Israelites leave. And they both happened in Egypt for a reason.

As Jacob worshiped the God of his fathers on the border of the Promised Land at Beersheba, wondering if he should leave Canaan for Egypt (even under the duress of famine), the Lord appeared to him and assured him that this journey to Egypt was part of a larger plan (Gen. 46:2–4). His family would return to the Promised Land but only after they had grown to become a great nation within Egypt. This was just the kind of place where that could happen. In contrast to Canaan, Egypt enjoyed a predictable supply of water from the Nile River, a more temperate climate, and less exposure to invasion than other countries within the Fertile Crescent.[1] Thus the natural setting of Egypt provided a place in which Israel's population could grow at an aggressive rate under the hand of their capable God.

Infant reed-basket coffin (First to Third Dynasty, Egypt). Moses's mother may have placed her son in a basket like this when she hid him among the reeds of the Nile River.

© Dr. James C. Martin. The Cairo Museum.

The political climate of Egypt was also favorable for such growth. Jacob's son, Joseph, had given Egypt an incredible life of public service. His contribution to the rescue and success of Egypt during the famine meant that his family enjoyed the political favor of Egypt for decades. That time came to a close, however, and the Hebrew people fell under oppression and servitude.

When Jacob, his sons, and their families originally went to Egypt they numbered only seventy people in total (Exod. 1:5). Through the years their numerical growth and prosperity became so great that it threatened the new king of Egypt.[2] This new pharaoh had no knowledge of Joseph, his relatives, or the contribution the Hebrew people had made to Egyptian society. As a result, the Israelite population was viewed as a political threat by Egypt's officials, so an edict was sent out that all Hebrew male infants should be put to death at birth.

Not everyone complied. When Moses was born, his mother hid him for three months. She then placed him in a papyrus basket coated with tar and pitch and hid him in that basket among the reeds along the Nile, near the pharaoh's residence.[3]

Tomb painting from the Egyptian nobleman Rekhmire, depicting forced labor (ca. 1450 BC).

Moses was discovered by the pharaoh's daughter and, after still being nursed by his own mother, was brought up in the pharaoh's court. Later he fled to Midianite territory for killing an Egyptian official. There he had an encounter with the God of Abraham, who instructed Moses to deliver the Israelites from Egyptian bondage. Through a series of plagues, Egypt's resolve to keep the Israelites enslaved was broken.

The Lord had informed Abram that his descendants would be enslaved and mistreated for four hundred years in a foreign land (Gen. 15:13–14). It was now time to leave. The challenge for Jacob's descendants was that Egyptian military power, which had put them into slavery, also controlled the road systems out of Egypt. This military power is illuminated by the historical records of Egypt that speak of seventeen military campaigns executed by Thutmose III (1504–1450 BC). Many of

Mortuary temple of Queen Hatshepsut. Some suggest she was the Pharaoh's daughter who discovered the infant Moses among the reeds.

those campaigns were targeted against Asian peoples who were subsequently brought to Egypt as slaves.[4] Given the powerful presence Egypt could project on the frontier, we can easily see that they presented more than enough intimidation to oppress the Israelites at home.

The growth and affliction of the Israelites happened in Egypt for a reason. The growth occurred during a period of time when Egypt functioned as a safe haven for the Israelites. Eventually their small population grew, making them a threat to Egypt, which now had a pharaoh who did not know Joseph.

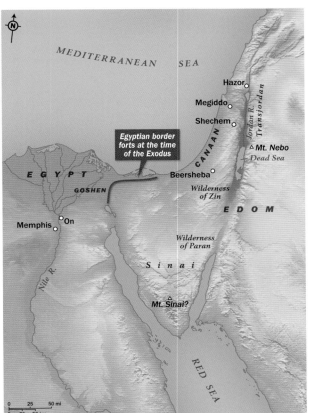

Egyptian border defenses, ca. 1450 BC

ISRAELITES ESCAPE THROUGH THE SEA

EXODUS 13–15

The oppressed Israelites desperately wanted relief from their misery. The Lord heard their cries and sent Moses to speak on their behalf to the Egyptian government. God's message for Egypt was brief and clear: "Let my people go" (Exod. 5:1). When the Egyptian pharaoh put his country as an obstacle in the path of God's plan, the Lord first warned and then opposed him with ten plagues. These plagues broke the arrogance and power of Egypt's pharaoh, and the Israelites were set free (Exod. 7–12). The route they took out of Egypt is described in some detail because it was selected for a reason.

At that time, the nation of Egypt was understood to be limited to the agricultural areas that could be irrigated by the Nile. The Israelites began their journey in the eastern delta of the Nile River. This was the general region where Joseph first settled the family of Jacob, near modern Tell ed-Dab'a. Recent archaeology has associated this area as the place called Rameses in the Bible,[5] which is located within the geographic region known as Goshen. The Israelites moved from here to Succoth, known today as Tell el-Maskhuta (Exod. 12:37), located at the eastern edge of the Nile delta. After leaving Succoth, the Israelites were directed by the Lord to a body of water near Pi Hahiroth, between

Wall remains of Tell el-Maskhuta, identified as biblical Succoth (Exod. 12:37), where the Israelites gathered to begin their exodus out of Egypt.

Migdol and the water opposite Baal Zephon,[6] which had to be crossed if they were to leave Egypt. This instruction placed them at the eastern edge of Egypt's fortified frontier. With the Egyptian army in pursuit, the Israelites found themselves blocked by the body of water the English translations call the "Red Sea" (Exod. 14:3–9).

There are a number of bodies of water between the Gulf of Suez and the Mediterranean that have been

The reeds on the edge of Lake Timsah, an area that some have associated with the Israelites' crossing of the Red Sea.

suggested as possible locations for the miraculous parting of the waters.[7] No matter what body of water it was, the Israelites were physically barred from continuing out of Egypt because the water functioned as a military "gate" preventing Israel's departure.[8]

The Lord led the Israelites on a route that gave the Egyptians the impression that they had wandered into a trap with no way of escape. In reality the Lord's route was designed to get Israel out of Egypt and away from Egyptian control in such a way that only he, the Lord Almighty, would be recognized as deliverer of the Hebrew people. So God himself miraculously opened the water blockade allowing the Israelites to flee Egypt, and then he quickly closed that door on the pursuing Egyptians. When that day was done, the Israelites were outside the borders of Egypt and safe from any military reprisal. The Lord's promise of rescue was accomplished in such a way that the reputation of the God of Israel was spread to the surrounding nations (see, e.g., Josh. 9:9–10).

It was a most memorable event that happened where it did for a reason. For centuries to come, nations of the world would hear of the power of the God of Israel because of what he had done in this miraculous water crossing. In generations to come, the Israelites would be reminded that they had been chosen to be messengers of Almighty God, who had rescued them from an oppressive and powerful nation. Safely crossing the impassable waters and escaping from the pharaoh was the evidence upon which they would be asked to base their trust when encountering future struggles. This deliverance was also a witness against those who turned to idolatry and questioned the Lord's authority, faithfulness, and power.

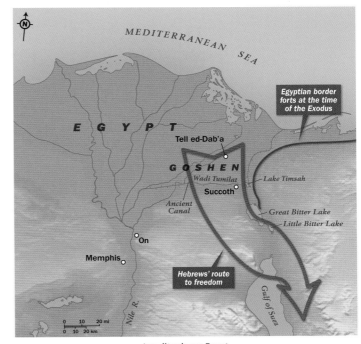

Israelites leave Egypt

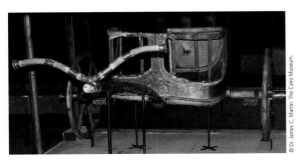

This wooden chariot was a gift from Pharaoh Amenhotep III.

© Dr. James C. Martin. The Cairo Museum.

THE LORD SENDS MOSES TO MOUNT HOREB

EXODUS 16–40

Following the dramatic exit from Egypt, our expectation is that the Lord would speed Israel on toward the Promised Land of Canaan. That was the land from which they had come many years earlier and the land promised to Abraham and his descendants. But rather than leading them on a direct route to Canaan, the Lord first instructed Moses to take the people away from the Promised Land to Mount Horeb for a reason.

The Israelites had personally experienced the Lord's deliverance out of Egypt. In the third month after leaving Egypt, Moses brought the people into the desert of Sinai and camped in front of Mount Horeb. It was there that the Lord provided Moses with special instructions and preparations for consecrating the people (Exod. 19:1–15). On the morning of the third day of the consecration process, Moses "led the people out of the camp to meet with God" (Exod. 19:17). Why would the Lord want Moses to take the people out

This bush, growing in the courtyard of Saint Catherine's Monastery, is traditionally thought to be the burning bush seen by Moses.

from Egypt to Mount Horeb before bringing them to the Promised Land?

Years earlier, when Moses killed the Egyptian overseer, he had fled to Midianite territory, married, and served his father-in-law. Some time later, while tending the sheep of his father-in-law, he came to Mount Horeb, which the Bible describes as "the mountain of God" (Exod.

Suggested site of Mount Sinai (Mount Horeb) is identified with Gebel Katherina, the highest peak in Sinai at 2,642 meters (8,668 feet) above sea level.

3:1). It was here that the Lord appeared to Moses in the form of a burning bush. At that encounter the Lord told Moses to remove his sandals, for the ground on which he stood was holy.

It was in this first encounter at Mount Horeb that the Lord revealed himself to Moses as "I AM"—the God of Abraham, Isaac, and Jacob. Moses was then instructed to bring the people out of Egypt (Exod. 3:1–14). The sign to Moses that the Lord had sent him for this task was this: "When you have brought the people out of Egypt, you will worship God on this mountain" (Exod. 3:12).

Thus, as instructed, Moses returned to Egypt. Upon meeting with the Egyptian royal family, his request was not to live in Egypt but rather to take the Israelites out of Egypt to worship the God of Abraham (e.g., Exod. 9:1). Because the pharaoh's heart was hardened, it ultimately took ten plagues before he allowed the Israelites to leave. After the plague on the firstborn and following the Passover (Exod. 11–12), Moses was finally able to lead the Israelites to Mount Horeb so they too could meet with "I AM" (Exod. 19:16–20) as Moses had done earlier.

Here in the rugged southern Sinai region the Lord used the uplifted mountains as a place from which to project his presence. When we stand among the lofty peaks of the Sinai mountains, we realize how fragile we really are. We know that the mountains of Sinai had that effect upon ancient people because their records indicate their belief that the southern Sinai was home to the Egyptian idols.[9] Their idols had no power before the one and only true living God, who revealed himself and provided the law to the Israelites at Mount Horeb.

The Lord sent Moses to Mount Horeb for a reason. One might think that Moses would have been assured of his mission by the rod used in the various plagues against Egyptian idolatry. But it wasn't the rod or the miracles that were Moses's sign that the Lord had sent him to deliver the people out of Egypt; it was his return to Mount Horeb where he had first met "I AM."

Saint Catherine's Monastery located at the base of Gebel Musa, adjacent to Gebel Katherina.

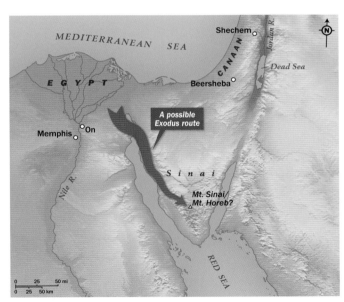

Mount Sinai/Mount Horeb in the Sinai

A DISCOURAGING REPORT: INVESTIGATING BEYOND THE NEGEV AND HILL COUNTRY

NUMBERS 1–14

After spending months at Mount Sinai with the laws of God in hand, the Israelites were ready to break camp. After traveling northward through the harsh and difficult terrain of the deserts of Paran and Zin, they arrived at the springs of Kadesh Barnea (Deut. 1:19), just south of Canaan. There Moses selected respected leaders[10] from each Israelite tribe, whose responsibility would be to explore the Promised Land and encourage the people about the land they saw. However, as it turned out, the investigation yielded a negative report by the majority, and that report happened for a reason.

The assigned investigation of Canaan was carefully described by Moses both in terms of where the leaders were to explore and what information they were to bring back. Moses appeared to have some advance knowledge of Canaan.[11] With this knowledge, he directed the explorers to search two subregions within Canaan: the Negev and the hill country (Num. 13:17). The Negev is a horizontal hourglass-shaped region with relatively flat terrain in the southernmost portion of the Promised Land. The hill country covers the central mountain spine traveling north and south through the heart of the Promised Land. Moses further directed these men to bring back answers to key questions about those two subregions.

What is the agricultural potential of the land? How densely populated are these regions? Are the communities undefended villages or cities with walled fortifications (Num. 13:18–20)?

Geographical and archaeological studies of the Negev and hill country lead us to a reasonable expectation of how their report should have sounded. The agricultural capability of the land might not equal that of Egypt, but in contrast to the wilderness regions in which they had been living, Canaan had much to offer the farmer and shepherd. After all, God was bringing Jacob's family of shepherds home. Thus the land was described to the Israelites as a land flowing with milk (shepherding) and honey (agriculture; Exod. 3:8). While a larger population and fortified cities existed in portions of Canaan that lay outside the parameters defined by Moses (that is, in the *Shephelah*, in the Jezreel Valley, and along the coastal plain),[12] the portion of the land to which Moses directed these men was thinly settled,[13] with very few fortified cities.[14] Knowing what we do about where these men were to look, we expect a positive if not glowing report that would have excited Israel about the days that lay ahead.

After forty days of exploration, these men returned, and with the exception of Joshua and Caleb, they

The Israelites chosen to bring a report of Canaan passed the remains of the ancient ruins of Arad (2600 BC). The fortress at the top of the tell dates to the period of the kings of Judah.

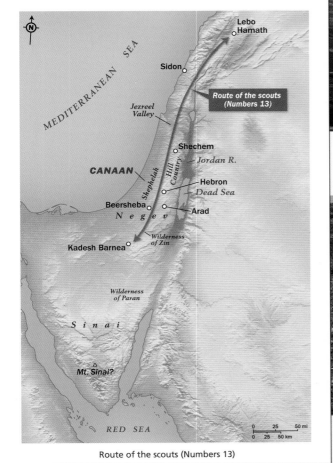

Route of the scouts (Numbers 13)

The Jezreel Valley. The Lord did not instruct the twelve Israelite scouts to go to regions such as the Jezreel Valley, which led to a discouraging report.

Vineyards in the Valley of Eshcol. A report of rich agricultural land was provided when the Israelite scouts returned to the camp with grapes from the Valley of Eshcol north of Hebron.

delivered a decidedly shaded report. It celebrated the agricultural capability of the Promised Land as expected (Num. 13:26–27), but ten of the twelve officials quickly shifted their tone. They spoke about the large and well-fortified cities that would resist Israel's entry (Num. 13:28), and they made it sound as though the land was full of people (Num. 13:29).

The reason the report was negative is because it was based on land outside of the area Moses instructed them to investigate—the land along the Mediterranean Sea and the Jordan River (Num. 13:29). Despite the protests of Joshua and Caleb (Num. 13:30; 14:6–9), it was

the misguided report of the majority that swayed the thoughts and feelings of the people. Calling for a return to Egypt under new leadership, these people incited a stunning message from the Lord: no one twenty years of age or older, except for Joshua and Caleb, would enter the Promised Land. These Israelites would remain for decades in the Wilderness of Zin until each of those participating in this mutiny had died. So the vision of the Promised Land that was to inspire hope and excitement was delivered in such a way as to instill dread and doubt. And that doubt brought to Israel not a blessing but disaster.

MOSES STRIKES A ROCK IN THE WILDERNESS OF ZIN

NUMBERS 20

It was springtime when the entire community arrived at the Wilderness of Zin, where Miriam died. The absence of water again stirred up a longing for the water-rich land of Egypt, and the Israelites decried the lack of water at their current location (Num. 20:2–5). Within verses of their complaint, we read that gallons of water came gushing from a rock. But as that water flowed, God informed Moses and Aaron that their actions had disqualified them from entering the Promised Land

Water seeping from a rock in the Wilderness of Zin.

(Num. 20:12). As we will discover, these actions happened where they did for a reason.

The first verse of Numbers 20 establishes the location of Moses and the Israelites as the wilderness called Zin. That placed the people south of the Promised Land between the Negev and the Wilderness of Paran.[15] This land resembles a moonscape, without significant vegetation or rainwater. But it is the geology of this region that promises us the most assistance in understanding the actions of Moses.

The stratified limestone structure of this region finds softer, more porous layers of stone rising above denser, less porous layers of limestone. When it rains, gravity carries the water downward, dissolving softer chalk of the upper layers and carrying it downward as a mixture. Eventually this descending water encounters a less porous layer of limestone and begins to flow laterally until such time as it exits the stone into the bright sunshine and warmth of the hillside. While the water may flow from this exit point for a time, eventually evaporation will leave behind a mineral cap that seals off the flow of water. Through the years, rainwater continues to collect

Moses may have used a rod like this rod of Pharaoh Khafre (ca. 2500 BC) to strike the rock to provide water for the people.

© Dr. James C. Martin. The Cairo Museum.

behind that cap under increasing pressure. If a water seeker is wise enough to read this geology well, one deft blow to the mineral cap promises a rush of fresh water.[16] In order to emphasize the importance of the geology in this narrative, the biblical writer purposely uses a special word for *rock* that is unique to this event and location in Zin.[17]

A similar event occurred at a different place with a very different geology. Earlier at Rephidim, Moses had been instructed to take the staff the Lord had given him to use during the course of delivering the plagues on Egypt and use it to strike a granite rock in order to provide water for the people. Striking such a rock in this location would not normally have produced water.[18] Thus the blow to the rock at Rephidim en route to Mount Horeb revealed Moses's obedience, which honored and gave credit to the Lord (Exod. 17:1–7).

When the Israelites were in the Wilderness of Zin, however, the Lord instructed Moses to *speak* to the rock. Zin was in a geographic region where any knowledgeable shepherd could strike a wisely placed blow that would produce water naturally. If Moses had spoken to the rock as instructed, the Lord would have been recognized as the one who provided water for the people. But

The Wilderness of Zin at En Avdat (aerial view). It was in the Wilderness of Zin that Moses struck a rock, rather than speaking to it as instructed, in order to provide water for the entire Israelite community.

Moses knew his staff would work as it had so many times before. So when Moses used his predictable staff rather than words to bring forth water, his actions replaced the Lord, and Moses became the provider for the people. From then on, who needed God when the people had Moses, Aaron, and the staff that always worked? Moses had stepped into the place reserved for the Lord alone.

A blow from his staff where a word would do sealed his fate in this place for a reason. Just before striking the rock, Moses cried out to the people, "Listen, you rebels, must we bring you water out of this rock?" (Num. 20:10). In times past, the people had complained and rebelled against God, Moses, and Aaron. But in this situation, when Moses struck the rock rather than speaking to it, he became the rebel. Therefore the Lord declared that he and Aaron would not enter the Promised Land because their actions replaced the Lord as the provider of the people (Num. 20:12)— something the Lord would not allow.

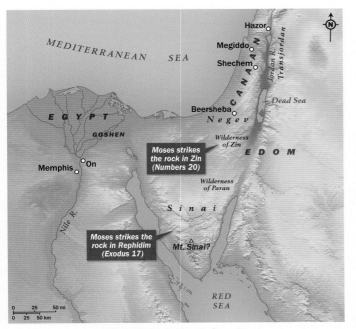

Where Moses struck rocks for water

ISRAELITES DENIED PASSAGE THROUGH EDOM

NUMBERS 20:14–21; DEUTERONOMY 2:1–8

The descendants of Abraham had lived in Egypt for centuries, and the people who left Egypt with Moses had lived in the wilderness for decades. With the stay in the wilderness coming to an end, our every expectation is that the Israelites will turn toward Canaan. But what we find is a turn in the opposite direction for a trip around Edom for a reason (Num. 20:14–21).

A glance at a map makes us wonder why Israel would want to pass through Edom in the first place. With their base camp at Kadesh Barnea, travel north into the Negev would have placed them in the Promised Land by the shortest possible route—the one used earlier by the Israelite explorers (Num. 13:1–25). But when the Lord spoke to Moses about the move from Kadesh Barnea into the Promised Land, he indicated they were about to pass through the land of Esau's descendants, Edom (Deut. 2:1–6). This meant that the Israelites were now to enter Canaan from the east rather than from the south.

Travel through Edom was the most direct route to the eastern side of Canaan. The Israelites would cross the Arabah (the valley that connects the southern end of the Dead Sea to the Gulf of Aqaba) and preferably ascend the western slopes of the mountains of Edom through Wadi Punon. From there they would continue to the plateau-like ridge that runs north and south along the watershed. There the Israelites would have had access to food and water and would have traveled more directly along the King's Highway.

With this plan in view, and knowing that the Lord had told Moses that he would not give the descendants of Jacob any of the Edomite hill country around Mount Seir (Deut. 2:5), we might well expect the people to pull up stakes and be on the move. So why did Moses pause to compose such a carefully worded appeal to the Edomites, requesting passage?

The answer lies in the geography. The mountains of Edom jut vertically out of the Arabah, reaching heights of over five thousand feet. The Edomites lived on the watershed of those mountains, with all the isolation and security of an eagle's nest (Jer. 49:16). Moisture received in the region cuts gorges down the western flank of the mountains. These gorges appear to provide natural walkways leading to the interior of Edom, but

The Israelites requested permission to enter Edom through Wadi Punon but were refused by the Edomites.

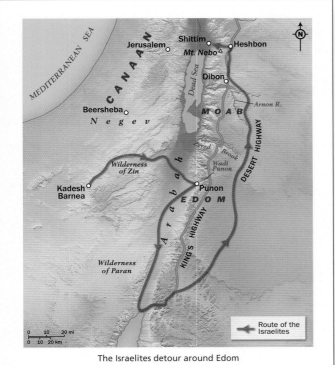

The Israelites detour around Edom

The mountains of Edom (view looking east from the Arabah).

virtually all of them end in abrupt rock walls.[19] Only a few gorges permit travelers to pass to the plateau above.[20] This terrain allows for a much smaller defending military force. Since the Lord had already told Moses to avoid war with the Edomites (Deut. 2:5), he had only one option: to request permission to pass through.

When Edom twice declined them access and sent its soldiers to guard the entrance routes, the Israelites had no choice but to go around Edom. They either had to fight uphill, disobeying God all the way, or they had to detour hundreds of miles to the south.

The next question is: why did Edom refuse the Israelites, even after such specific assurances from Moses that Israel would not trouble the Edomites (Num. 20:17–19)? The Bible does not directly record

a reason for the Edomites' actions, but the Lord had already told Moses, "They will be afraid of you" (Deut. 2:4). Why? Because the reputation of the God of Abraham had preceded them: "The nations will hear and tremble; . . . the chiefs of Edom will be terrified" (Exod. 15:14–15).

Edom's refusal to permit Israel to enter their land and Israel's detour around the southern and eastern fringes of Edom happened for a reason. It was not the Israelites who struck terror into Edom's heart, which led to denial of passage; it was the God of Abraham, Isaac, and Jacob, known to the nations by what he had done in delivering the Israelites out of Egypt. When passage was denied, the Israelites bypassed their relatives the Edomites in obedience to the Lord's instructions.

◄ Edomite religious shrine from En Hazeva, biblical Tamar (Ezek. 47:19), on the border between ancient Edom and Israel.

ISRAEL CLASHES WITH THE AMORITES ON THE TRANSJORDAN

NUMBERS 21; DEUTERONOMY 2:14–3:11

Since the children of Israel left Mount Sinai, their weapons had been used in only a few skirmishes. But starting in Numbers 21, those weapons were deployed more often and with different intentions. Israel became involved in battles of conquest designed to seize land from their opponents. The first of these military campaigns took place on the east side of the Jordan River—the Transjordan. While Israel was told not to harass, provoke, or make war with the Moabites (Deut. 2:9) or the Ammonites (Deut. 2:19), the Lord did direct Moses to seize the land that belonged to the Amorites (Deut. 2:24). This was the beginning of Israel's conquest of the Promised Land, and we will see that it started in the Transjordan for a reason.

When the Israelites arrived at the Arnon Gorge, they were on the verge of entering the Promised Land. At that point they were facing the Amorites, a nation that, according to the Bible, dominated Moab, Gilead, and Bashan—areas that were to be part of the Promised Land.

In Exodus 23:23 the Lord said, "My angel will go ahead of you and bring you into the land of the Amorites, . . . and I will wipe them out." It had been the Amorites who struck fear into the hearts of the explorers in Numbers 13. Now this new generation of Israelites was poised on the rim of the Arnon Gorge ready to take hold of God's promise and do what the Lord had instructed the generation before them to do.

In order to reach the Jordan River, the Israelites needed to travel through the region of Moab in the territory of Sihon, an Amorite king whose principal city was Heshbon. Moses sent messengers to request safe passage through Amorite territory in their move toward Canaan (Num. 21:21–22; Deut. 2:24–28). When Sihon refused that request and backed it up with a show of military force, the war of conquest began.

There was more to this battle than passage through the region. God had made it clear that the Amorites,

Mural of the Amorite ruler Shamshi-Adad (ca. 1780 BC) from the Mari royal palace.

both Sihon of Heshbon and later Og of Bashan, were to feel the full weight of the Lord's justice, putting an end to their reprehensible lifestyle (Gen. 15:16; see also Deut. 2:24–3:11; 2 Kings 21:11).

The military victory over the Amorites provided Israel with passage through the Transjordan. This victory also provided the Hebrew people with two benefits they would take with them in their conquest west of the Jordan River.

First, the campaigns against Sihon and Og were carried out so swiftly and successfully that they had a paralyzing effect on those living in Canaan. Well in advance of any Israelite battle in Canaan, news of this conquest east of the Jordan River shook the confidence of those who would resist Israel's invasion west of the Jordan (Deut. 2:25).

Second, the conquest of the Transjordan diminished the risk of a two-front war. Once the Israelites had entered Canaan, turning their backs on the Jordan River, they did not have to keep checking over their shoulders. The Edomites, Moabites, and Ammonites were all blood relatives of the Israelites, lessening imminent danger. That was not true of the Amorites, whose power in the

Tell Heshbon, the principle city in Moab of the Amorite ruler Sihon (view looking east).

Transjordan represented a threat that had required immediate attention. So the Israelites completely disabled the kingdoms of Sihon and Og, leaving Israel in control of the land from Mount Hermon in the north to the Arnon River in the south (Deut. 3:8) and ended the risk of a two-front war.

Thus the conquest of the Transjordan happened as it did for a reason. It provided the advancing army of Israel with safe passage and diminished the risk of a rear attack as they began the next stage of the conquest.

The southern portion of the Golan Heights, part of ancient Bashan (aerial view looking northeast).

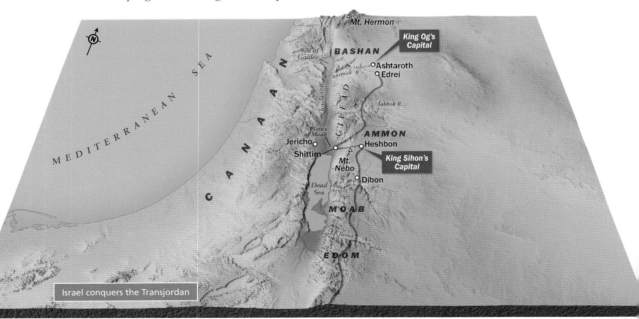

Israel conquers the Transjordan

THE VISITS OF BALAAM AND MOSES TO MOUNT PISGAH

NUMBERS 22–24; DEUTERONOMY 3:21–4:14; 34:1

*P*owerful moments in biblical history are often connected with rising terrain. The heights of Moriah witnessed the great test of Abraham (Genesis 22). The flanks of Mount Horeb were the stage for Moses's call to service (Exodus 3), and its thundering peak was the site of the giving of the law (Exodus 19–20). Despite this conditioning, it is still easy to miss the important yet obscure Mount Pisgah[21] at the close of Numbers and Deuteronomy. Two visits to Pisgah by two men, Balaam and Moses, are linked here for a reason.

The Israelites were camped in the plains of Moab, northeast of the Dead Sea, where they were preparing to make war on the Canaanites. But Balak, the king of Moab, was concerned that his cities were at risk, so he hired Balaam to put a curse on Israel (Numbers 22). Balaam could command a fee for such services because his employers believed that he could manipulate God's will and actions.[22] Toward that end, Balak ushered Balaam to various locations, all on or near Mount Pisgah, so that Balaam might fulfill his contracted obligation to curse Israel.

Although Balaam was called to curse the Israelites, he could only bless them again and again, at times using the very words the Lord had spoken to Abram, recalling God's promise to make his family a great nation (Num. 23:20–21; 24:9; cf.

Mount Nebo to the lower hill of Mount Pisgah, with the Dead Sea in the background (sunset view looking southwest).

Aramaic inscription (mid–eighth century BC) mentioning Balaam, son of Beor (Numbers 22–24).
© Dr. James C. Martin.
The Amman Archaeological Museum.

Gen. 12:2–3). Balaam even voiced the ultimate fulfillment of the promises given to Abram as he foresaw the coming Messiah (Num. 24:17). Thus on the heights of Pisgah, as Israel was about to enter Canaan, the Lord showed his authority. For "Balaam son of Beor, who practiced divination" (Josh. 13:22) could do nothing but confirm the Lord's promises.

As we turn through the pages of our Bible, it is not long before we glimpse one more individual climbing to the "top of Pisgah"—Moses (Deut. 34:1). His climb was motivated by very different circumstances. Moses would die on the heights of Pisgah and not enter Canaan because of striking the rock in the Wilderness of Zin (Num. 20:11–12). Before this popular leader of Israel died, he was given the opportunity to see the Promised Land. From this viewing platform that rises four thousand feet above the shores of the Dead Sea, Moses was able to see the land. "There the LORD showed him the whole land—from Gilead to Dan, all of Naphtali, the territory of Ephraim and Manasseh, all the land of Judah as far as the western sea, the Negev, and the whole region from the Valley of Jericho, the City of Palms, as far as Zoar" (Deut. 34:1–3). As the writer of

Deuteronomy directs our eyes to these details, he reminds us that this is the very land that the Lord had promised to give Abraham, Isaac, and Jacob (Deut. 34:4).

Moses and Balaam traveled to Mount Pisgah for a reason. From there Moses was given the opportunity to bless the Israelites' entry into the land. And from there Balaam's intended curse on the Israelites and their entry into the land was turned by God into a blessing. The Lord had promised Abraham that his family would become a great nation and that this nation would come to possess the land of Canaan. From his descendants in this land the Lord's appointed Rescuer would be born. The first five books of the Bible (sometimes referred to as the Five Books of Moses, the Pentateuch, or the Torah) close as they had opened: our attention is fixed on the promises of rescue—promises that were proclaimed on the summit of Pisgah in the words and experiences of Balaam and Moses.

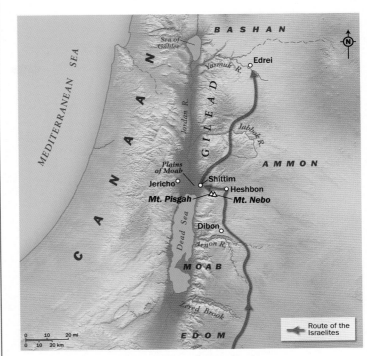

Mount Nebo and Mount Pisgah

Mount Nebo (view looking north).

PART 3

CONQUEST AND SETTLEMENT OF CANAAN

Tell es-Sultan (Jericho), with aerial view looking southeast. After crossing the Jordan River, the Israelites marched around the city of Jericho.

JOSHUA, JUDGES, RUTH

Eager expectation filled the air as Israel camped east of the Jordan River. This nomadic nation was poised to begin the next phase of God's plan: the conquest and settlement of Canaan. The books of Joshua, Judges, and Ruth chronicle this part of the Bible. In the context of these books, we find that geography is an important factor.

With recent victories in the Transjordan fueling confidence and trust in the Lord, Israel was ready to engage the Canaanites and Amorites in a series of world-changing battles over land ownership. The first obstacle Israel faced in its quest to enter Canaan was water, not warriors. When the Lord miraculously "piled up" (Josh. 3:16) the Jordan River, the Israelites were able to enter Canaan on dry ground. This miracle quickly led to another as the walls of Jericho proved as flimsy as swaying reeds before the powerful hand of God.

With the Jordan River and Jericho at their backs, the next battle at Ai gave the Israelites a powerful lesson in obedience. After Ai, Joshua did something unexpected. Rather than continuing in battle, he led the people of Israel to Mounts Ebal and Gerizim, a place selected to recapture the passion of their ancestors. There they read aloud God's blessings and curses (Josh. 8:34). As the last *amen* sounded, it was time for war once again.

When the local Gibeonites succeeded in their crafty deception and tricked Joshua into forming an alliance with them, a five-city coalition rose up to test Israel's resolve. They launched an attack that gave Israel and the Lord a further opportunity to surprise the land's inhabitants. The Lord led Israel in another amazing victory in which his power was shown in a striking new way.

Joshua led the Israelites from victory to victory until the major centers of power were brought low. Then he divided the land among the twelve tribes of Israel and instructed each to secure its hold on the land they had been assigned.

After Joshua died, no one leader was chosen to replace him. Rather the Lord used a series of temporary leaders called judges, who rose to the occasion when crises called for tribal militias to fight local wars. It was through leaders like Deborah, Gideon, and Samson that the Lord restored peace to the Promised Land.

With each cycle of judges, we see the faith of the Israelites and their leaders deteriorate until it seems to vanish. Against this darkening horizon, we capture a glimpse of hope shining through the life of Naomi from the book of Ruth. Famine, death, and uncertainty had taken their toll on her faith. Just when all seemed lost, the Lord quietly worked behind the scenes to bring the message of rescue and restoration to her, her family, the nation, and ultimately his entire creation.

The conquest and settlement of Canaan happened just as God said it would, accompanied by challenges, disappointments, battles, and miracles. One event after the other draws us in and forward. And as we shall see, one event after the other happened where it did for a reason.

Looking west down the Beth Horon Ridge toward the Aijalon Valley, where Joshua led the Israelite army in pursuit of the Amorites (Joshua 10).

Sea peoples such as the Philistines used anthropoid coffins in their burial practices (ca. 1150 BC).

© Dr. James C. Martin. The British Museum.

Like Naomi and Ruth, this woman is harvesting grain near Bethlehem.

MEDITERRANEAN SEA

△ Mt. Hermon

ASHER

NAPHTALI

EAST MANASSEH

Sea of Galilee

ZEBULUN

Kishon R.

ISSACHAR

Yarmuk R.

Beth Shan ○

MANASSEH

Jordan R.

Mt. Ebal △
Mt. Gerizim △

Jabbok R.

EPHRAIM

GAD

C A N A A N

BENJAMIN ○ — Jericho ○

DAN

Gibeon ○

Mt. Nebo △

Bethlehem ○

REUBEN

JUDAH

Dead Sea

Arnon R.

SIMEON

MOAB

Zered Brook

0   10   20
0   10   20 km

Mount Gerizim (left) and Mount Ebal (right). Joshua brought the Israelites to Mount Ebal and Mount Gerizim, where they proclaimed blessings and curses, as instructed by Moses (Deuteronomy 28; Josh. 8:33–35).

Jericho (view looking southeast). Joshua marched the Israelite army around the ancient city of Jericho prior to its fall.

Gibeon (view looking northeast). The rulers of five Amorite cities came against Gibeon after learning that the Gibeonites had made a treaty with Joshua.

ISRAELITES CROSS THE JORDAN RIVER

JOSHUA 1–4

The opening chapters of Joshua find Israel encamped east of the Jordan River on the plains of Moab at a place called Shittim (Josh. 2:1). We might want to dash forward to the well-known account of Jericho's fall, but for two chapters the Scripture focuses our attention on the banks of the Jordan River (Joshua 3–4). While there were other ways to enter Canaan, Joshua led the Israelites across the Jordan for three reasons, each sending a powerful message both to the Israelites and the inhabitants of Canaan.

First, the King of the Universe is faithful. Even though Jacob's journey to Egypt marked the beginning of a long sojourn outside the Promised Land, there was no question that the Lord would bring Israel back to this very land as a great nation (Gen. 46:3–4). After forty years in the desert and the passing of the generation who had escaped Egypt, the time had come.

Replica of the Ark of the Covenant. The flow of the Jordan stopped as the priests who carried the ark entered the water.

As the Lord led Jacob's descendants to enter Canaan and claim their promise, this new generation faced another water barrier, the Jordan River. Again, the Lord showed his faithfulness and power. He stopped the flow of the Jordan, and as they crossed the river, this generation of Israelites saw a reminder of the miracle given their parents. The association between these two crossings provided a visible and memorable encouragement that the Lord keeps his promises.

Second, this crossing of the Jordan River was used to mark a new chapter in Israel's continuing history. Just as the Lord had begun the previous chapter in Israel's history with a water crossing at the Red Sea, so a water crossing marked the start of this new chapter. Both miracles happened at the same time of year (Exod. 12:3; Josh. 4:19), both permitted Israel to cross the waterway on "dry ground" (Exod. 14:16, 22, 29; Josh. 3:17; see also Josh. 4:23), and both were associated with the journey to the land of promise.

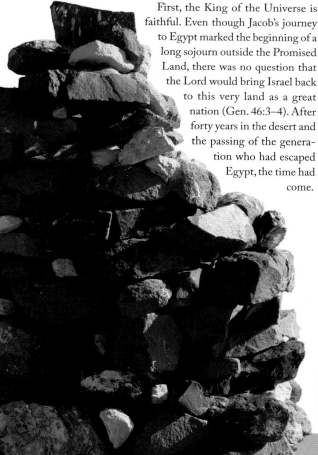

Stone pile. After crossing the Jordan River on dry ground, the Israelites took twelve stones from Jordan and erected a memorial to commemorate how the Lord cut off the waters of the Jordan.

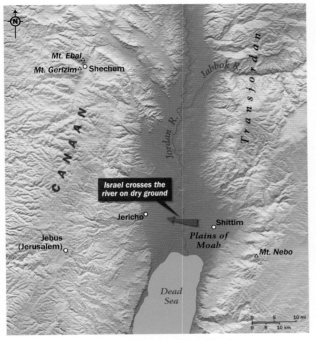

Israel encamps on the plains of Moab

Today, the Jordan River is much smaller in volume than during flood stage, when the Israelites crossed to enter the Promised Land.

Third, the miracle attending the crossing of the Jordan River sent a powerful message that the Lord would safeguard Israel's efforts during the coming conquest. Wading was the only way for them to cross the Jordan—a daunting adventure when the river was running at flood stage (Josh. 3:15). At that time of year the water at that location could be up to twelve feet deep[1] with currents so swift and fierce that they threatened the life of anyone who dared enter.[2] It is no wonder that such a crossing, particularly under the watchful eyes of hostile forces, was deemed an act of heroism in Bible times (1 Chron. 12:15).

Israel camped next to the water of the Jordan River for three days contemplating all that lay ahead. Then the priests carrying the Ark of the Covenant led Israel forward. As soon as the feet of those carrying the ark touched the water's edge, the water ceased flowing from upstream, and all the perils of that crossing went downstream with the rest of the water (Josh. 3:16). The Israelites walked across on dry ground, not only assured that the Lord was in the lead keeping his promises, but

also secure in the knowledge that he would safeguard their mission in the days ahead.

The Red Sea crossing had been a testimony of the Lord's power and faithfulness, but it was far away from Canaan. The Jordan River near Jericho was a border and significant gateway into the Promised Land. And the stone memorial placed by the crossing site became a ready reminder of the Lord's faithfulness (Josh. 4:4–7).

Great Bitter Lake, one of the possible crossings of the Red Sea. When the Israelites crossed the Jordan on dry ground to enter the Promised Land, they were reminded of how the Lord had opened the water for their parents to escape from Egypt.

THE LORD BRINGS DOWN THE WALLS OF JERICHO

JOSHUA 5–7

The Lord, who had opened the waters of the Jordan River before the advancing army of Israel, carefully orchestrated the attack plan that would bring Canaan under Israelite control. While camped at Gilgal, Joshua received a visit from the "commander of the army of the Lord" (Josh. 5:14). This commander-in-chief directed his field general to advance against Jericho and put the city under a divinely designed siege. The first military objective west of the Jordan River was Jericho, a target selected for a reason.

Numbers and Deuteronomy frequently mention Jericho when orienting their readers geographically. For example, the reader is told that the camp of Israel was located "on the plains of Moab by the Jordan across from Jericho" (Num. 26:3). The city made such a wonderful landmark because it was a strategic city and would continue to be so for thousands of years.

The long-lived legacy of this site is understood when we consider its unique geographic setting. Jericho had a tropical climate enhanced by an abundant supply of water. The archaeological site of Jericho lies just northwest of the Dead Sea in the dry, hot Jordan Valley about 820 feet below sea level with a lush oasis fed by springs (one of which pumps water at a rate of 1,200 gallons per minute).

A reminder of Rahab. A female figure attached to the top part of a juglet from Jericho (ca. 1500 BC).

© Dr. James C. Martin.
The Amman Archaeological Museum.

Jericho is considered one of the oldest cities in the world, as evidenced by this stone tower dating about 7000 BC.

Given these benefits, many generations of residents called the Jericho region home.

But abundant water and sunny skies would not have been reason enough for the military installation standing before Israel.[3] Jericho was uniquely positioned to control a critical ford across the Jordan River and regulate access into the central hill country of Canaan. This geographic asset provided anyone who ruled over Jericho a substantial source of wealth and military power. The city was built and fortified where it was for a reason, and it would fall at the Lord's command for that very reason.

Jericho was the gateway that opened up the interior of Canaan, a gateway that kept a watchful eye over the Jordan River. If Israelite soldiers fighting west of the Jordan River were to maintain contact with the tribes settled on the east side of that river, this ford had to remain uncompromised. Further, if the Israelites were to have ready access to the hill country on the roadways linking the interior of Canaan, Jericho could not remain in enemy hands. It did not. This powerful site would soon lie at Israel's back, neutralized because the Lord had brought down its walls.

Tell es-Sultan (Jericho), with a view looking toward Gilgal.

Throughout its long history, Jericho was an important city that was attacked, destroyed, and rebuilt many times, as evidenced by this destruction level, revealing fallen walls and burn layers.

In human thinking, it would have made sense to preserve and refortify this city-fortress in order to provide military cover for the development of the new Israelite nation. But the Lord had commanded that the city be destroyed, and a curse was placed on anyone who might seek to rebuild the city (Josh. 6:26). The Lord instructed the Israelites to destroy Jericho for a reason.

Joshua had experienced the miraculous escape from Egypt, the faithfulness of the Lord in the wilderness, and crossing the Jordan River on dry ground. He had seen the results of humanity's unfaithfulness in numerous events during the past forty years. He recognized what others did not grasp: the Lord is guardian, provider, and shield. No military fortress at Jericho or anywhere else could do what the Lord would do for Israel. In fact, trusting the Lord to guard their backs was far more effective. By refusing to rebuild Jericho, Joshua was true to the meaning of his name: *yeshua*, "the Lord will rescue."

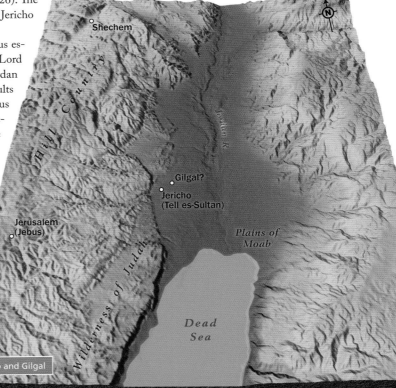

Jerico and Gilgal

READING THE BLESSINGS AND CURSES AT MOUNT GERIZIM AND MOUNT EBAL

DEUTERONOMY 27–29; JOSHUA 8:30–35

The defeat of Jericho opened the gate for the Israelites to enter Canaan's hill country. The second battle at Ai brought another victory and allowed them to begin the conquest of the entire region. Before continuing the military campaign, however, Joshua did something quite remarkable and unexpected from a military perspective: he ceased all military operations and led the Israelites to Mounts Ebal and Gerizim for a reason.

After the battles at Jericho and Ai, Joshua led the people of Israel north on the Ridge Route some twenty miles to the city of Shechem. This city, nestled in a pass between Mount Ebal (3,084 ft.) and Mount Gerizim (2,891 ft.), would host the rededication to the law given to Moses, a rededication that happened at God's direction (Josh. 8:30–35; Deut. 11:29; 27:1–28:68).

Here the Israelites built an altar of uncut stones on Mount Ebal. Joshua then had stones erected, coated them with plaster, and inscribed into them the words the Lord gave to Moses. Next he directed that the Word of God be read out loud so that everyone of that generation might hear the blessings the Lord had promised to those who heed his Word and the curses for those who do not.

Mount Ebal. The Israelites built an altar of uncut stones on Mount Ebal.

The design for this event and the selection of Shechem come to us from the time of Moses. While still east of the Jordan River, Moses spoke of blessings and curses that would naturally follow the obedience or disobedience of Israel. Moses directed that after they had entered Canaan, the Israelites were to speak to each other those words of blessings and curses, and they were to do so between the faces of Mount Ebal and Mount Gerizim (Deut. 11:29). He also told them to inscribe the words on stone monuments and to build an altar (Deut. 27:1–9).[4]

By placing the altar on Mount Ebal and by using the natural amphitheater provided by the valley between Mounts Ebal and Gerizim, the region of Shechem became the arena accommodating thousands of people where they could see, hear, and participate in the event Moses had commanded. But there was something even more important about this location than the topographical assistance it offered. Location can enhance the power of words and experiences when the setting recalls what had happened there before. That is true of Shechem as it is of many other biblical locations.

Replica of the Ten Commandments inscribed in Paleo-Hebrew in stone. Joshua instructed that the words the Lord gave Moses be inscribed on a plastered stone.

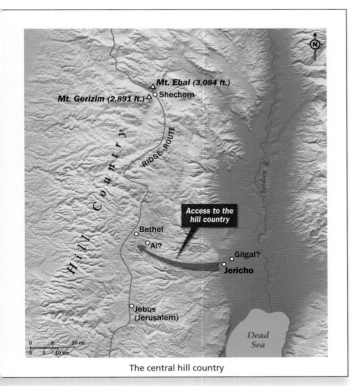

Mt. Ebal (3,084 ft.)
Shechem
Mt. Gerizim (2,891 ft.)

RIDGE ROUTE

Hill Country

Jordan R.

Access to the hill country

Bethel
Ai?
Gilgal?
Jericho

Jebus (Jerusalem)

Dead Sea

0   5   10 mi
0   5   10 km

The central hill country

When Abram had first entered Canaan, the Lord appeared to him at Shechem and affirmed that he had reached the land he and his descendants would inherit. So Abram built a memorial altar at Shechem to commemorate that momentous event (Gen. 12:6–7). Years later, Abraham's grandson Jacob purchased land in Shechem, dug a well, and built another memorial altar there (Gen. 33:18–20). Jacob then directed his entire family to rid themselves of their foreign idols at Shechem (Gen. 35:2–4).

Reading the blessings and curses at Mounts Ebal and Gerizim happened there for a reason. If there was any location in Canaan that connected the descendants of Abraham, Isaac, and Jacob to the Lord, the region of Shechem was it. So at the Lord's direction, Joshua brought Jacob's descendants and others among them to this area as Moses had instructed (Josh. 8:30–35). There Joshua reminded them in detail of God's promises to Abraham and Jacob. Before Israel moved forward in the difficult days ahead, taking over the land and resisting the temptations of idolatry, Shechem, located between Mounts Ebal and Gerizim, was the place to pause and be reminded of the Lord's purpose in bringing them back home.

View looking west toward Mount Gerizim (left) and Mount Ebal (right).

RESCUE OF THE HIVITES AT GIBEON

JOSHUA 9–10

After the Israelites had faithfully fulfilled the Lord's direction that they should honor him at Mounts Ebal and Gerizim, they returned to the assignment of conquering the land. To assure domination of the central hill country and protect themselves against attack from the major cities in the coastal plain, it was necessary for the Israelites to conquer the Hivite city of Gibeon.[5]

When the Gibeonites heard of Joshua's military victories (Josh. 6:27; 9:3), they surrendered without a fight. In an outlandish display of theater, complete with stage props of worn-out clothes, old wine skins, and stale bread, the Gibeonites sought out the Israelites at Gilgal. They claimed to be from a faraway place and pledged allegiance to Israel and the Lord. Without seeking God's counsel, Joshua and the elders perceived that these humble people posed no local threat and made a peace treaty with them. Shortly thereafter they discovered the Gibeonites lived only a short distance away in the very hill country the Israelites wanted to conquer. Still, since they had made a peace treaty with the Gibeonites (Josh. 9:19), the Israelites did not destroy the four Gibeonite cities or their inhabitants. Instead, in exchange for their testimony to God's greatness, Joshua directed that the Hivites serve the Lord as woodcutters and water carriers in the tabernacle (Josh. 9:23).

Old wineskin. The Gibeonites used cracked and mended wineskins to deceive the Israelites into making a treaty.

Meanwhile, word reached the Amorite city of Jerusalem detailing the early success of Joshua in defeating Jericho and Ai. Then messengers brought the Amorites more bad news: Gibeon had defected and made a treaty with the advancing Israelites (Josh. 10:1). Something had to be done and done quickly, for Joshua's strategy had become clear: to divide and conquer by taking cities in an east/west line running across the central mountains of Canaan. So the king of Jerusalem proposed an attack on Gibeon that would bring together the military assets of five Amorite cities: Jerusalem, Hebron, Jarmuth, Lachish, and Eglon (Josh. 10:3–5).

The defection of Gibeon called for such unprecedented action because its location in the land was critical to the security of southern Canaan. Jerusalem's greatest vulnerability was an attack from the north across the plateau that Gibeon guarded.[6] Further, no east/west road was as vital to movement through the heart of Canaan as the one that Gibeon and its allies controlled. For the Amorite cities in southern Canaan, the loyalty of Gibeon had to be reclaimed and Israel had to be repulsed. Geography determined the likelihood of the Amorite counterattack happening where and when it did.

As the Amorite forces assembled and began a siege of Gibeon, the Gibeonites appealed to Joshua for help. Marching all night from the Jordan Valley, Joshua and his army came upon the assembling Amorite armies and attacked. Surprised by the sudden appearance of the Israelites, the Amorites fled west down the road toward the coastal plain. At this point the Bible reports two miracles that enabled the Israelites to pursue and defeat the Amorite coalition. The first was a miracle of hailstones that struck the fleeing men on the road leading to the coastal plain.

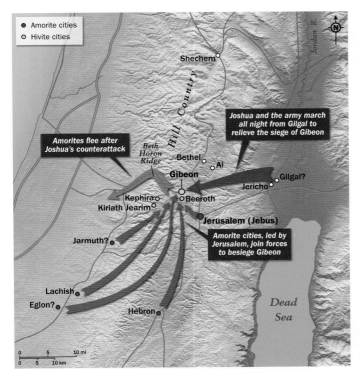

Amorite cities
Hivite cities

Shechem

Hill Country

Beth Horon Ridge

Amorites flee after Joshua's counterattack

Joshua and the army march all night from Gilgal to relieve the siege of Gibeon

Bethel
Ai
Gibeon
Gilgal?
Jericho
Kephira
Kiriath Jearim
Beeroth
Jerusalem (Jebus)

Amorite cities, led by Jerusalem, join forces to besiege Gibeon

Jarmuth?

Lachish
Eglon?
Hebron

Dead Sea

| 0 | 5 | 10 mi |
| 0 | 5 | 10 km |

The Amorite siege and Joshua's rescue of Gibeon

Beth Horon Ridge. Huge hailstones killed men of the Amorite army as they attempted to flee the Israelites down the Beth Horon Ridge.

The oval-shaped hill of Gibeon was once occupied by Hivites.

The second was a miracle in response to Joshua's prayer "when the LORD listened to a man" (Josh. 10:6–14).

The rescue of the Hivites and the Lord's defeat of the Amorite coalition happened where it did for a reason. The events surrounding Israel's peace treaty with the Gibeonites reflect God's graciousness, power, and faithfulness. The Lord graciously spared the Hivites of Gibeon twice. First, because of their testimony (Josh. 9:24), they were permitted to live harmoniously with the Israelites in the Promised Land throughout Bible history. Second, Israel responded to the Hivites' pleas for assistance, pursuing and defeating the Amorite army. In addition, the peace treaty allowed Israel to occupy a critical part of the hill country without having to militarily confront that powerful city (Josh. 10:2). God's power was also shown by the dramatic miracles he performed against the Amorites as they fled west along the Beth Horon Ridge toward the coastal plain.

ISRAELITE TRIBES ARE ASSIGNED TERRITORY IN THE PROMISED LAND

JOSHUA 15–21

At the Lord's direction and under Joshua's capable leadership, all of Israel had joined to break down the major Amorite and Canaanite opposition during their invasion of Canaan. While large portions of the Promised Land required further military attention (Josh. 13:1–7; 17:16), it was now time for Joshua to officially distribute parcels of land to tribes and individuals (Joshua 13–21). Woven into the details, we find a logic that suggests everyone received their portion of the Promised Land for a reason.

The language in the book of Joshua and earlier books of the Bible makes it clear that the Lord is the owner of Canaan and that it was provided to the children of Israel for a reason.[7] Under the guiding hand of the Lord, Joshua used topographical features and city lists to designate the land that belonged to each of the twelve tribes of Israel. He also assigned certain cities to individuals or subgroups within Israel. Hints found here and there suggest that there are very practical reasons behind the land distribution.

It is clear that size matters. While all Israel had grown to become a great nation, not every tribe within Israel had grown to the same degree. Recognizing that reality, larger tribes received more land while smaller tribes received less land (Num. 26:52–56).[8] Thus this distribution preempted a potential problem. Today good fences make good neighbors because families need to know where their kids can play and who is responsible for cutting what lawn. But in an earlier time the critical need to obtain water, plant grain fields, and graze flocks created a bond between land use and life. An appropriate distribution of the land by tribal size went a long way toward limiting internal fighting over land, which was necessary for unity within the tribes.

In at least one instance (Josh. 14:6–15), land was given specifically to an individual. After the first excursion of Israelite leaders into Canaan, when all but Caleb and Joshua came back to discourage the people

from following the Lord (Num. 13:30; 14:5–9; Josh. 14:8), Moses had promised Caleb "the land on which your feet have walked" (Josh. 14:9) for himself and his descendants. When it came time to distribute the land, Caleb laid claim to the Lord's promise and received Hebron along with a portion of the surrounding lands (Num. 14:24; Josh. 14:12–13).

One tribe, Levi, did not receive a contiguous tribal allocation of land but instead was assigned forty-eight cities distributed throughout the territories given to the other tribes. The Levites were the priests of Israel, and while they periodically served the Lord in the tabernacle

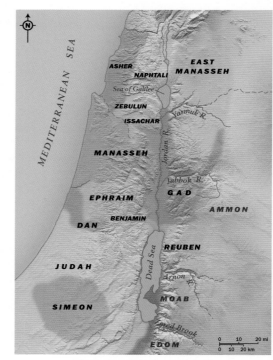

Distribution of the Promised Land

Territory of Asher (view looking south).

Territory of Gad and the Jabbok River (view looking northeast).

Region of West Manasseh, which later became associated with the northern part of Samaria.

at Shiloh in Ephraim, they were to live most of their lives among the other Israelites in order to encourage individual and national faithfulness (Josh. 13:33; 21:1–42).

Lest we miss the obvious, we take note of this simple fact: Joshua's assignments meant that every family received their own piece of the Promised Land. Whenever they shepherded the flock or scratched the soil with a plow, they were reminded that God had kept his promise to deliver into their hands this land flowing with milk and honey, a land suitable for both herding and agriculture (Exod. 3:17). Because the Lord had kept that promise, they could be confident that he would keep the overriding promise linked to the people and the land: the Promised Land would be a podium from which the Israelites were to proclaim the one true, loving God who offers rescue to the entire world.

Thus Israelite tribes were assigned territory in the Promised Land for a reason. Tribal population, meritorious service, and Levitical assignment all contributed to the designation of territory. There were no gaps in the distribution of the land. City by city, wadi by wadi, hill by hill the Hebrew people went to take possession of the land just as the Lord had promised.[9] Joshua concludes, "Not one of all the Lord's good promises to the house of Israel failed; every one was fulfilled" (Josh. 21:45). In that light, every family owned evidence that the Lord's promises for their tribal provisions had been accomplished.

ISRAELITES BEGIN WORSHIPING BAAL IN THE PROMISED LAND

JUDGES 1–3

The Lord had brought the Hebrew people out of Egypt, cared for them in the wilderness, taught them the dangers of faithlessness, and given them evidence of their purpose as the nation of Israel (Josh. 24:31). Yet in the very next book of the Bible, Judges, there is a description of Israelite life that is appalling. The people began to fall away from the Lord, choosing again and again to mutiny against him and participate in the abominable practices of Baal worship. Moses had warned against these self-destructive choices (Deut. 7:1–9; 32:1–47). In violating the very first commandment to worship no other gods, the Israelites commenced on a cycle of rebellion, oppression, deliverance, and rebellion that forms the core of the book of Judges (Judg. 2:10–23). Why did this happen? Israel worshiped Baal in the Promised Land of Canaan for a reason, although it was never a good one.

The climate and location of Canaan gives us an answer as to why Baal worship was such a draw to the Israelites. No food was more important to the residents of the ancient world than grain. They relied on wheat and barley to provide them with much of the protein and many of the calories in their daily diet.[10] Of course water was essential for bringing these field crops to the point of harvest. In Egypt that water was tapped from the Nile River, but in Canaan grain was matured and ripened by a cycle of seasonal rainfall. Without the rain the pastures would wither, wells and cisterns would sit empty, and no grain would find its way to the family table.[11] This reality was well known to the Canaanites, but Israel's most recent agricultural experience had been in Egypt. So when they entered the Promised Land, they learned local, rain-based, Canaanite farming methods. And while they were learning how to farm in Canaan, many Israelites also decided to worship the Canaanite idol, Baal.

In Canaanite theology, the phenomena that filled their days were explained by the presence of invisible beings whose action and inaction made life what it was.[12] Thunder, death, drought, and even war were manifestations of an imagined world and the activities of its unseen beings. Yet in the Canaanite mind-set, mortals were not completely helpless. They thought that through the informed use of rites, rituals, and incantations, they could manipulate the thinking and action of their idols to improve their daily lives.[13] That is where Baal and the rainfall cycle came together.

The Canaanites believed the rainfall that was so necessary to a successful grain harvest came from Baal. The manipulation of this idol took various forms, including the use of sexualized images and temple rituals involving male and female prostitution.[14] Canaanites taught the Israelites

Stela of the idol Baal from Ras Shamra.

© Dr. James C. Martin. Mus'ee du Louvre; Autorisation de photographer et de filmer—LOUVRE.

Bronze figurine of the Canaanite idol Baal.

Inspecting grain crops in the hill country of Judah. Israel was tempted to put their trust in the idol Baal rather than the Lord to provide the necessary rain for their agricultural needs.

that successful farming meant not only planting and harvesting their field crops according to the annual rainfall cycle, but they also seduced them into the abhorrent activities involved with the worship of Baal.

The Israelites began worshiping Baal in the Promised Land for faulty reasons. The Lord knew that he was sending his people into a detestable culture and had taken a strong stand against its destructive customs (Deut. 18:9–13). He also had forewarned his people that they were entering land with a new hydrology and a new way of farming (Deut. 11:10–15). In the Promised Land the Lord himself, not Baal, would provide the rainfall that would mature their wheat fields. But despite all the warnings, instructions, fulfilled promises, and marvelous signs, the Israelites again and again sought out the sexual allure of Baal worship, justifying such actions as a safeguard to successful harvests. Trusting the Lord in Canaan (Gen. 26:1–5), with its unpredictable water supply, would have shown great faith to the nations around them. Many Israelites, however, had chosen to put their faith in Baal.

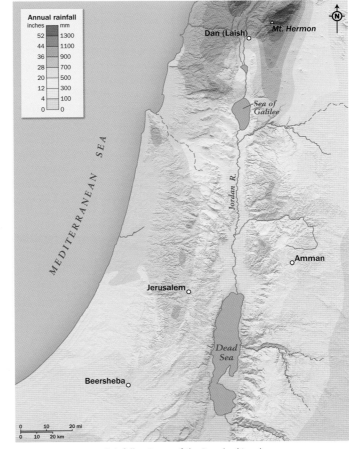

Rainfall patterns of the Promised Land

THE LORD DEFEATS HAZOR'S ARMY IN THE JEZREEL VALLEY

JUDGES 4–5

For twenty years the Lord allowed Jabin, king of the Canaanite city of Hazor, to terrorize and oppress the Israelites (Judg. 4:1–3). When Israel's pleas for help were joined with words of repentance, the Lord used the prophetess Deborah to initiate a battle that brought victory over Canaanite chariots in the Jezreel Valley. As we have so often seen, this victory happened there for a reason.

In advance of this engagement, both the Canaanite and Israelite forces organized themselves in places that favored their capabilities. In the ancient world women were not viewed as capable military leaders. Yet under the direction of Deborah and the command of Barak, the militia of Naphtali and Zebulun gathered on Mount Tabor. This mountain resembles a large dome, rising 1,929 feet above the Jezreel Valley. It was a natural meeting point for the soldiers joining Barak.[15] But more than that, its elevation and surface features favored the Israelite infantry. The higher elevation of Mount Tabor gave Barak command-and-control advantages unavailable to him on the plain below, while the steep and wooded sides of Mount Tabor kept the Canaanite chariots away from the lightly armed Israelite foot soldiers.[16]

When Sisera, commander of Hazor's army, saw Israelite soldiers gathering on Mount Tabor, he moved his chariots from Harosheth Haggoyim to a position that favored his capabilities (Judg. 4:7, 13; 5:19). Chariots were the battle tanks of the ancient world, providing superior speed and the ability to engage the enemy from a mobile firing platform. Their presence, particularly in the Jezreel Valley, had been a source of grave difficulty for the Israelites.[17] Of course that is exactly why the Canaanites mustered their chariots where they did. The Jezreel Valley is a sprawling plain that extends between the Nazareth Ridge to the north and the extended ridge of Mount Carmel to the south. In contrast to the mountains that surround it, the elevation of this valley across all quadrants does not change more than a few hundred feet. It is exactly where the Canaanites wanted the fight to be joined—on the level ground where chariots could do their worst to a poorly armed opponent.

With the Israelites on Mount Tabor and the army of Hazor in the Jezreel Valley, an uneasy tension held the day until the Lord revealed his plan. He directed Barak to charge off the flanks of Mount Tabor and carry the fight to the plains. From the human perspective, this plan seemed ludicrous. The Lord had asked the Israelites to abandon their high ground for risk on the plain. But in doing so, he allowed overconfidence to build in Sisera while calling the Israelites to trust in his power and wisdom.

As the Israelites charge off the mountain and onto the plain, our natural inclination is to look away from what is sure to be a slaughter. But as we turn our

The army of Hazor was using iron-plated chariots similar to this Hittite iron-plated chariot in their battle against the Israelites in the Jezreel Valley.

© Dr. James C. Martin. The Istanbul Archaeological Museum.

eyes to the battle scene, something quite unexpected happens. The Lord "routed" (the Hebrew word is *hmm*) the opposition (Judg. 4:15). This is exactly the same language used to describe what the Lord did in overcoming the Egyptians at the Red Sea (Exod. 14:24) and the Canaanite coalition at the time of Joshua (Josh. 10:10). In both cases, a miracle involving water made the difference.

The Lord defeated Hazor's army in the Jezreel Valley for a reason. Canaanite charioteers ventured out on the firm, dry ground for their expected victory over the Israelite infantry. But the Lord provided an unexpected downpour (Judg. 5:4, 21) that caused the Kishon River to overflow and flood the valley floor. When the rain began, Sisera and his soldiers quickly abandoned their worthless transportation and began to flee on foot (Judg. 4:15). Thus the Lord caused the defeat of the Canaanite army as Israelite soldiers, emboldened by the Lord, pursued their enemy. So God directed a victory for Israel at a most unlikely place, in a most unlikely way, at a most unlikely time, and with most unlikely leaders, revealing that the battle belonged to the Lord.

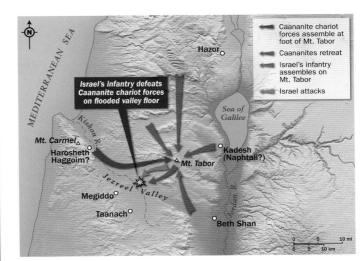

Israel defeats Canaanite chariots in the Jezreel Valley

The Jezreel Valley (view looking east), where the iron chariots of Hazor's army got bogged down in the mud.

THE LORD CONFIRMS HIS AUTHORITY ON A THRESHING FLOOR

JUDGES 6–8

"Again the Israelites did evil in the eyes of the Lord," and for seven years the Lord allowed Midianites and other intruders from the eastern wilderness to enter Israel where they seized or ruined the food supply (Judg. 6:1–6). The Israelites were so hard-pressed by these raids that they eventually cried out to the Lord for help. God chose to help Israel through Gideon (Judg. 6:11–18). In spite of Gideon's uncertainty and reluctance, the Lord confirmed that he was indeed calling Gideon and that he, the Lord, and not Baal, had ultimate control. This confirmation happened on a threshing floor for a reason.

With an unusual faith-building demonstration based on the provision of dew—moisture critical to the well-being of all in the Promised Land—the Lord convinced Gideon that Israel would be delivered under Gideon's leadership. During the summer months in Israel, warm, moist air is carried eastward from the Mediterranean Sea during the day, only to be cooled after sunset. If that moist air cools to dew point, the invisible moisture becomes visible, forming either fog or dew.[18] Since it usually does not rain in Israel during the summer months, this moisture is critical to the maturing of produce harvested at the close of summer. Grapes, figs,

Threshing floor.

The spring of Harod. The Lord instructed Gideon to choose his fighting men at the spring of Harod.

pomegranates, and melons all require dewfall in order to ripen.[19] No dew means no summer harvest.

Canaanites believed Baal to be the provider of this life-giving moisture, and his adherents pictured him with thunderbolt in hand, bringing both rain and "dew from heaven" to the fields of Canaan.[20] But the Lord, the Creator of the universe, taught that he is the one who provides everything, including rain and dew (Deut. 11:10–17; 1 Kings 17:1). The Israelites vacillated between obeying the Lord and assimilating into the Baal worship around them. In this event, the Lord elected to demonstrate his power over Baal on a common threshing floor.

The miracle grew out of the natural relationship between dew and the threshing floor. To take advantage of the wind, threshing floors were located on ridges. In the morning, exposure to the direct rays of the rising sun caused such higher elevations to warm more quickly than the valley floors, making them the first to lose their dew. In this account, Gideon placed a fleece on the

Midianites encamped in the Harod Valley between Mount Gilboa (left) and Mount Moreh (right).

threshing floor and asked the Lord to allow the highly absorbent fleece to be wet while the remaining floor was dry. This followed natural expectation. But then Gideon asked the Lord to demonstrate his power over Baal and the dewfall by allowing the fleece to remain dry while the threshing floor around it became saturated with moisture (Judg. 6:36–40). When it happened in just that way, Gideon knew that the Lord was faithful and that the Lord, not Baal, controlled both dew and the upcoming battle.

The threshing floor became a practical, visual reminder of the miracle for the men who came to fight with Gideon. By design the threshing floor was a large, open area that could provide an unobstructed view to the gathered forces and give encouragement to them about the outcome of the approaching battle (Judg. 6:33–36).

The Lord confirmed his authority on a threshing floor for a reason. Like dew, the threshing floor was a fundamental part of Israel's agricultural year, making it the ideal place for God to demonstrate his control over dew. It was the place that the Lord promised his blessing would be apparent (Lev. 26:3–5; Deut. 16:13). Ruined harvests and invasions had indicated God's absence (Judg. 6:7–10). What better place for the Lord to reaffirm his desire to bless Israel than the threshing floor—a place that speaks of a wider return during a time of blessing under God's hand.[21]

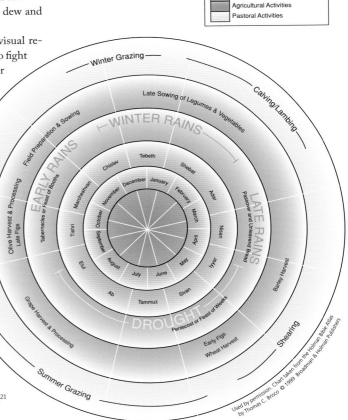

Agricultural cycles and rainfall in the Promised Land

SAMSON FIGHTS THE PHILISTINES IN THE SOREK VALLEY

JUDGES 13–16

As the Israelites were settling into their new land, the Philistines arrived.[22] They struck the Canaanite strongholds along the Mediterranean coast with a vengeance, destroying and then replacing the Canaanite presence there in about 1,200 BC. Five Philistine city-states rose from the Canaanite rubble: Gaza, Ashkelon, Ashdod, Gath, and Ekron.[23] From these powerful strongholds, the Philistine military experience and advanced weapons technology allowed them to press inland toward the hill country that was home to the Israelites.[24] In order to reach the Israelites, the Philistines could travel through the *Shephelah* (Hebrew for "humble hills"), which functioned as a buffer zone just west of the hill country of Judah. This is where Samson was born, in Zorah overlooking the Sorek Valley. Like other valleys of the *Shephelah*, the Sorek was critical to the success and security of the Israelites. Thus Samson fought the Philistines in the Sorek Valley for a reason.

The low hills and wide U-shaped valleys of the *Shephelah* marked the transition between the low, flat coastal plains to the west and the high mountains of central Israel to the east. Both the Israelites and the Philistines wanted to control valleys like the Sorek for the same reasons. The region's plentiful rain and rich soil translated into abundant grain and produce. Even more important than food was the access realized through such valleys. The security of the Israelites in the hill country of Judah and Benjamin depended on their ability to control this buffer zone of the *Shephelah* now being invaded by Philistine raiding parties. Thus Samson

Aerial view looking north, with Tel Beth Shemesh (bottom), the Sorek Valley (center), and Zorah, hometown of Samson (top center right of the ridge).

lived in the crosshairs of Philistine conquest (Judg. 13:1; 15:11) in a region critical to Israelite security.

As we trace the life of Samson against this landscape, a pattern emerges. The closer the Philistines got to the mountains of Israel, apparent Philistine success quickly gave way to increasing Philistine defeat. Samson's romantic interest in a Philistine girl from Timnah, at the west end of the Sorek Valley (Judg. 14:1–4), and their wedding precipitated a series of attacks. During the wedding celebration, Samson lost a contest he himself had proposed. Obligated to obtain thirty linen garments and sets of clothes, he traveled to Ashkelon and killed thirty Philistine men to pay the debt (Judg. 14:19). On a subsequent trip to Timnah to see his wife, Samson learned that she had been given to another man. Angry, he set fire to the standing grain in the valley, destroying it and compromising grape and olive harvests (Judg. 15:1–5). Hundreds of Philistines were impacted by this act, leading their soldiers to press eastward into Judah where a battle with Samson at Lehi left one thousand Philistines dead (Judg. 15:14–15). A pattern developed: as Samson's engagements with the Philistines moved

Philistine terra-cotta head figurine (Iron Age I, eleventh century BC) from Ashkelon.

© Dr. James C. Martin. The British Museum.

Scene reminiscent of Samson's death at Gaza, from a Philistine cult stand from Beth Shan (eleventh century BC).

farther and farther east toward the interior of Israel, God empowered Samson to take more and more Philistine lives.

But the greatest victory was yet to come as we retrace our steps back to the Sorek Valley and the Philistine Plain. Once again betrayal preceded Samson's violence. Samson fell in love with Delilah, who lived in the Sorek Valley (Judg. 16:4). With Delilah's help, the Philistines captured Samson and imprisoned him in Gaza. But there on the coast, as Philistine rulers made fun of him in their temple to Dagon, the Lord gave Samson one last burst of faith and power that brought the structure down on their heads. Thus Samson died, destroying the Philistine leadership and killing more Philistines in his death than during his life (Judg. 16:25–30).

Samson fought the Philistines in the Sorek Valley for a reason. As his encounters with the Philistines take us back and forth through this critical corridor, God's power on Samson brought greater security to the Israelites living in the hill country.

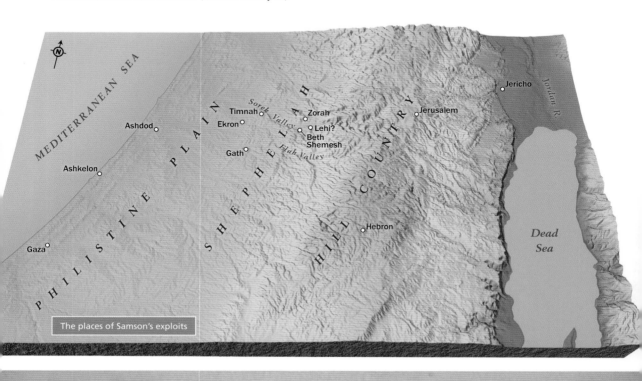

The places of Samson's exploits

NAOMI MOVES BACK TO BETHLEHEM

RUTH

The book of Ruth introduces us to Naomi and her family during the difficult and uncertain time of the judges in Israel (Ruth 1:1). Hardship forced Naomi to move from Bethlehem to Moab and back again. Although each move provided food, it was only the Lord who brought joy and restoration. And each move had a geographically related reason.

Bethlehem was home to Naomi, her husband, and two sons. In contrast to other villages in the hill country of Judah where deep, V-shaped valleys provided less area for produce, the terrain on the east side of Bethlehem provided large, fertile tracts of land for growing grain.[25] No wonder this village was named Bethlehem, the Hebrew term meaning "house of bread."

Bethlehem's agricultural advantages depended on rainfall at the right times in the right amounts. When rain stopped or came at the wrong time, crops failed and famine resulted. That is the setting for the events of Naomi's early life. A famine led her family to a difficult decision: Naomi's husband moved them east to the Transjordan plateau of Moab in the hope of finding food. Their travels took them beyond the Dead Sea to the sharp mountain wall rising from the Jordan Valley floor that

Winnowing grain near Bethlehem at sunset.

marked the western border of Moab. These mountains made Moab a desirable destination at the time because they rise higher than the mountains of Judah to their west, making them capable of extracting more moisture from the air masses passing over the area.[26] Once Naomi and her family reached the top of those mountains, they stepped onto a plateau that promised what Bethlehem was not providing—wheat fields and regular water supplies. But the satisfaction of living without famine evaporated for Naomi. There in Moab, her husband died, and about ten years later both of her married sons died. The pleasantness of Moab faded, so when she heard that the Lord had come to the aid of his people by providing food for them in Bethlehem (Ruth 1:6), she made plans to return home.

Swaying fields of barley with the promise of healthy harvest in Bethlehem greeted Naomi and her one accompanying Moabite daughter-in-law, Ruth (Ruth 1:22). Though the reasons for leaving Bethlehem earlier had been reversed, and despite the willing support of Ruth, Naomi asked to be addressed as "Mara," the

Young woman harvesting grain near Bethlehem. © Direct Design

bitter one. Thinking that the Lord was responsible for her past affliction, Naomi's hope had not yet returned (Ruth 1:20–21).

But the Lord was not against Naomi. Verse after verse in the remainder of the book of Ruth shows him gently and powerfully at work through Ruth, Boaz (who became Ruth's husband), and others in the village. Those gracious acts softened Naomi's bitter heart. But God had an even greater act of restoration in mind.

Naomi moved back to Bethlehem for a reason. Weaving together the laws, customs, locations, and background of these people, the Lord was preparing the way for the most profound event in human history. The child born to Ruth and Boaz continued a family line that would bring King David and ultimately the Messiah to the threshold of Israel's history. Bethlehem became the home of King David and the birthplace of Jesus. Bethlehem, house of bread and home of shepherds, became the home of the Bread of Life and the Good Shepherd. The Messiah, who would come to rescue all who called on him, counted in his ancestry a heart-broken grandmother, a foreign-born woman,

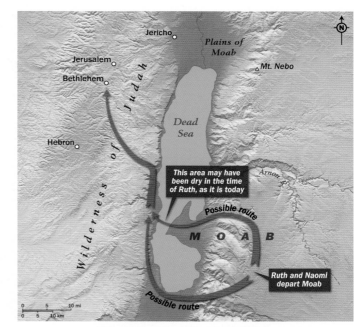

Ruth and Naomi leave Moab for Bethlehem

and a kindly farmer. The one true, loving God wove together rain, land, hunger, death, heartache, love, and a baby, revealing to us his character and establishing his plan of rescue.

The broad geographical terrain just east of Bethlehem was ideal for grain crops.

PART 4

THE UNITED MONARCHY OF ISRAEL

Relief of Assyrian slingers—
panel of Sennacherib's
attack of Lachish in 701 BC.

1 AND 2 SAMUEL; 1 KINGS 1–11

With Samuel, the last of the judges, a transition began that moved the nation of Israel from a loosely organized confederacy (Judg. 8:22, 23; 21:25) to a highly organized monarchy ruled by kings. This period is frequently referred to as the time of the United Monarchy or United Kingdom. And though uneven success marked the days of the first three kings (Saul, David, and Solomon), the descendants of Jacob were told that a royal descendant of David would sit on the throne forever (2 Sam. 7:1–16). Part 4 contains ten events that happened during the lives of the first three kings, events that happened where they did for a reason.

Following the rebellious days of the Judges, Samuel's presence brought hope. But before we read of Samuel's leadership, we read about the depth of Israel's apostasy. Israelites had come to believe that the God of Abraham could be manipulated through their possession of the Ark of the Covenant. However, to show them that no box could bind him, the Lord allowed the Ark of the Covenant to be captured and taken on an extended journey into the land of the Philistines.

Later, as Samuel's age advanced, the people demanded to have a king like all the other nations had. Samuel anointed Saul, who established his capital at Gibeah. Saul began to walk in the ways of the Canaanite kings, so the Lord chose David to replace him. Through a variety of geographic settings, including the Elah Valley and a cave near En Gedi, we have the opportunity to compare the leadership style, faith, and courage of these two men.

On David's slow and steady trip to Israel's throne, he spared Saul's life on more than one occasion. But in a confrontation with the Philistines on Mount Gilboa, Saul died with his army retreating around him.

The end of Saul did not mean the end of internal fighting for the throne (2 Sam. 2:10). The northern tribes rallied around Saul's son, while David had support in Judah. During those days Hebron became David's capital city, which he later moved to Jerusalem.

Solomon succeeded his father, David. Knowing the challenges that lay before him, Solomon requested guidance from the God of his father and received a gift of remarkable wisdom. He received this gift while praying at Gibeon.

David prepared to build the Lord's Temple in Jerusalem, and Solomon later built it among the matrix of other government buildings. We will see that the Temple was built in Jerusalem and associated with his palace complex for a reason.

Solomon also advanced the national security of the land and developed its economic potential. We will see how Gezer became a wedding gift from Egypt that brought idolatry into his government. And we will note how the size and location of Solomon's kingdom produced phenomenal wealth and power that he misused, and thereby he forsook the King of the Universe. From king to king and from place to place, the events of the United Monarchy happened where they did for a reason.

Tel Beth Shan. After Saul's death, the Philistines hung his body on the city walls of Beth Shan.

Remains of a Philistine temple altar discovered at Tel Qasile (inside Tel Aviv).

Originally, this rectangular stone tomb, which Solomon had hewn from bedrock in honor of the pharaoh's daughter, had a pyramid-shaped roof that was later removed.

© Dr. James C. Martin. The Eretz Israel Museum.

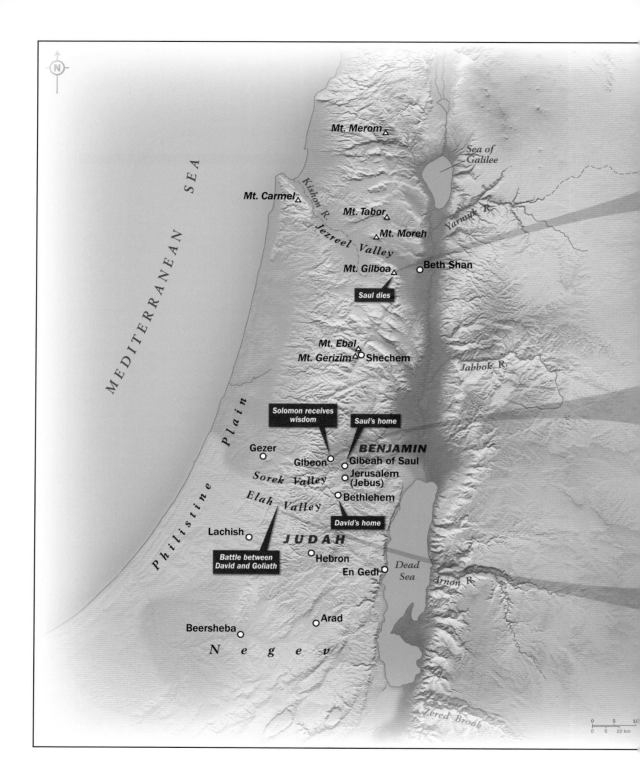

N

MEDITERRANEAN SEA

Mt. Merom △

Sea of Galilee

Mt. Carmel △

Kishon R.

Mt. Tabor △

Jezreel Valley

Mt. Moreh △

Yarmuk R.

Mt. Gilboa △ ○ Beth Shan

Saul dies

Mt. Ebal △
Mt. Gerizim △ ○ Shechem

Jabbok R.

Solomon receives wisdom

Saul's home

Gezer ○

BENJAMIN

Gibeon ○ ○ Gibeah of Saul

Sorek Valley

○ Jerusalem (Jebus)

Elah Valley

○ Bethlehem

Philistine Plain

David's home

Lachish ○

JUDAH

Battle between David and Goliath

Hebron ○

Dead Sea

En Gedi ○

Arnon R.

Beersheba ○

Arad ○

N e g e v

Zered Brook

0   5   10
0 5 10 km

Mount Gilboa (view looking southeast). Saul's death occurred on Mount Gilboa during a battle with the Philistines.

The great pool at Gibeon. This staircase led into the main water system for the Gibeonites, whose murders by Saul were avenged by David (2 Sam. 21:1–13).

The Elah Valley (view looking east). David battled with the Philistine warrior Goliath in the Elah Valley.

THE ARK TRAVELS FROM SHILOH TO PHILISTINE TERRITORY AND BETH SHEMESH

1 SAMUEL 1–7

When Israelite soldiers took the Ark of the Covenant from the tabernacle at Shiloh into battle as though it were a good luck charm, the Lord allowed it to be captured and taken to several Philistine cities. While the ark was in Philistine hands, it was moved throughout their territory until it was returned to the Israelites at Beth Shemesh (1 Sam. 4:1–6:13). And each event along the way happened where it did for a reason.

The first stop on the ark's itinerary was Aphek. This city was important to Israelite and Philistine alike because it marked the border between the Philistine Plain and Israelite territory. From there the Philistine army could follow the road system into the hill country and attack all the way to Shiloh, the Israelite city that housed the tabernacle and the Ark of the Covenant.[1] At Aphek, Israel's elders exposed their distorted thinking about the Lord. When the Philistines won the initial engagement at that location, the victory created a panic among the Israelites. They brought the Ark of the Covenant from Shiloh to their camp near Aphek, called Ebenezer, assuming its mere presence would "save us from the hand of our enemies" and force the Lord to provide the victory that eluded them before (1 Sam. 4:1–4).[2] At Aphek, however, Israel experienced not victory but defeat, and the ark of God's covenant was captured. As news of the tragedy reached Shiloh, Eli the priest died and his pregnant daughter-in-law gave birth—naming the child Ichabod, "the glory has departed from Israel" (1 Sam. 4:12–22).

The Philistines took the captured ark to the second stop, Ashdod, one of five large and imposing Philistine cities. They determined that their victory over Israel meant that Dagon was more powerful than the God of Jacob, and they placed the ark in Dagon's temple (1 Sam. 5:1–2). The Lord used that place and presumption to demonstrate his sovereignty. Twice the image of Dagon collapsed, breaking into pieces in front of the ark, while the city's residents suffered an affliction of tumors (1 Sam. 5:1–8). Consequently the Philistines moved the

The hill of Shiloh. The tabernacle and Ark of the Covenant resided at Shiloh.

Looking north from Aphek toward the plain of Ebenezer (1 Sam. 4:1).

Tel Beth Shemesh (view looking east).

ark from Ashdod to Gath and from Gath to Ekron, and as they did, plague and suffering accompanied the ark as long as it remained among these enemies of God.

After seven months the Philistines had experienced enough. They placed the ark on a new cart pulled by cows that had recently calved. With God-given motive, the cows left their calves and pulled their treasure through the Sorek Valley straight to the third stop, the Israelite town of Beth Shemesh.

This hilltop (Tell el-Ful) has been identified as Gibeah of Saul.

Beth Shemesh was no ordinary location because it was one of the Levitical cities set aside for Israel's priests (Josh. 21:8, 16). If anyone knew how to handle the ark properly, it would surely be the people living there, for they were Kohathites, descendants of Aaron (Josh. 21:4). But just as a pious welcome and appropriate sacrifice seemed to end the lessons God had to teach (1 Sam. 6:13–16), we find another presumption. Some men of the town opened the Ark of the Covenant to look inside. While the Kohathite priests had the right to carry the ark, they were strictly forbidden "to look at the holy things, even for a moment, or they will die" (Num. 4:20). The Lord's ways had not changed, and his Word was holy; the men were struck down (1 Sam. 6:19).

There are reasons the ark traveled from Shiloh to Philistine territory and on to Beth Shemesh. The Israelite army mistakenly believed that the presence of God would be with them because they had the ark at the battle at Aphek. The Philistines learned to fear God because their idols fell in front of the ark at the Philistine temple at Ashdod. And the population of Beth Shemesh, a Levitical city of Kohathite priests, was reminded that even the priests were bound by the Lord's instructions.

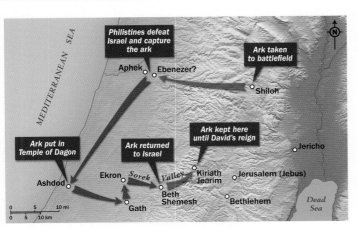

The travels of the ark

CHOOSING A KING FROM BENJAMIN

1 SAMUEL 8–14

The chaotic close of the book of Judges casts its long shadow into the early chapters of 1 Samuel (Judg. 21:25). For a time, the prophet Samuel was accepted as Israel's leader, but in his later years the people cried out for a king. Even though the Lord God was to be Israel's true and only King, and even with the Lord's warnings of excessive taxation, servitude, and wars brought about by a human king, the people still insisted, so their desire was granted (1 Sam. 8:1–20). Israel's first crowned monarch was Saul from the village of Gibeah, located in the tribal territory of Benjamin. And there were reasons a man from Gibeah became Israel's first king.

Benjamin "was the smallest tribe" (1 Sam. 9:21), so even if Saul's tribe had wanted to exert unfair influence on the affairs of state, the risk was very low given its limited size. The size of Gibeah is a product of sordid events reported at the close of Judges. There we read about a Levite who looked for hospitality in Gibeah. He had purposely avoided Jebus (i.e., Jerusalem, which at that time was an Amorite city) out of concern that the non-Israelites there would treat him poorly. Tragically, it was the men of Gibeah who stormed the house that night, demanded sex from him, then ended up raping and murdering his concubine (Judges 19).[3] The outrage of this atrocity spread throughout the other tribes of Israel and resulted in the tribes joining to wipe out both the city of Gibeah and the tribe of Benjamin (Judges 20). The battles that followed nearly annihilated this tribe from Israel's map and hung a bitter reputation over Gibeah. So Gibeah of Benjamin was a location over which no one would be jealous. Thus Saul's tribal affiliation and his hometown combined to stave off resentment that he had been anointed king.

Keeping in mind that neither the nation of Israel nor Saul had any experience in forming a national government, the place in which this first king lived was important. Geographically, Benjamin was the center of

Some suggest Tell en-Nasbeh to be the site of Mizpah, where Samuel anointed Saul as Israel's first king.

the nation. Joshua had focused his initial attacks in this area in part because the essential east/west and north/south road systems came together there. It was in the regions of Ephraim, Benjamin, and Judah that Samuel, as judge, had lived and led the people. Both the ark and the tabernacle were placed in nearby towns. And it was a high-profile location in terms of the Philistine threat.

As the nation of Israel sought to organize itself, the Philistines responded with new incursions, establishing strongholds deep in the heart of Israel's hill country. When Samuel prepared to anoint Saul, he directed him to travel to Gibeah of God—apparently located near Saul's Gibeah.[4] Even this special place hosted a Philistine outpost (1 Sam. 10:5).

Saul's Gibeah was located on the Ridge Route at an important internal crossroad from which one could travel north and south through the heart of Israel or east and west to the Jordan River or the coastal plain.[5] If the Philistines wanted to control the Israelites, this was the location from which to do it. If the new king, Saul, was going to remove the Philistine threat from the land, the area around his hometown was a good place to start, and battles soon were fought nearby at Geba, Micmash, and Beth Aven (1 Samuel 13–14). Saul lived at Gibeah in the midst of the conflict.

There were reasons for Gibeah to be the hometown of the nation of Israel's first king. It was the least likely place to arouse jealousy among the tribes. Also, it was improbable that the small tribe of Benjamin would be able to exert undue political influence. In addition, its location in the heart of the country provided the base for the new monarchy to strike its enemies. Sadly, the people soon forgot about Gibeah of God (1 Sam. 10:5) and looked to Gibeah of Saul for their protection (1 Sam. 10:17–19).

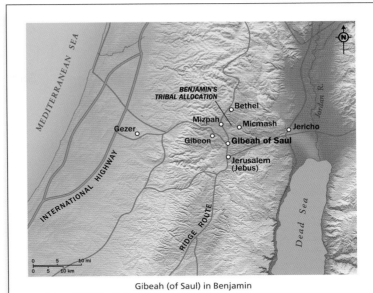

Gibeah (of Saul) in Benjamin

Saul's son Jonathan defeated the Philistine garrison controlling the pass at Micmash.

DAVID KILLS GOLIATH
IN THE ELAH VALLEY

1 SAMUEL 15–17

The hopeful start to the new monarchy faded with the passing months. Despite the Lord's desire to define the kingship of the nation as a unique institution (Deut. 17:15–20; 1 Sam. 10:25), Saul increasingly assumed the attitude of a Canaanite monarch. When Saul violated God's orders in a battle with the Amalekites, the Lord announced that he had rejected Saul (1 Sam. 15:11) and directed Samuel to privately anoint David to be the next king (1 Sam. 16:1–13).

Not long after David was anointed king, he was called into Saul's court to serve as harpist and armor bearer due to his reputation as a musician, brave man, and warrior (1 Sam. 16:18–23). Soon David began to take on the role of Israel's champion, a leader who loved and served the Lord. When the Philistines advanced up the Elah Valley toward Bethlehem, it was David who took on the decisive battle with Goliath—a battle that finds new depth of meaning when we see that it happened where it did for a reason.

The Elah Valley is part of the *Shephelah*, an area that provides the transitional buffer zone between the sprawling coastal plain and the high mountains of Judah. This transition zone is characterized by rounded foothills rising above wide, U-shaped valleys. The low hills and wide valleys made an important contribution to the economy and national security of Israel.[6] While the economic benefits of the Elah Valley made it desirable real estate, its role in Judah's security plan made it a strategic necessity. Israelites had to control the Elah

Ancient Gath (Tell es-Safi), hometown of Goliath the Philistine (view looking southwest).

Valley if those who lived in the mountains of Judah were to be secure.[7]

The early verses of 1 Samuel 17 depict a terrifying picture. The Philistines had made camp in the west end of the Elah Valley at a place called Ephes Dammim, between Socoh and Azekah. Saul and the Israelites were camped in the eastern end of the valley (1 Sam. 17:1–3). The map tells the story. The critical Elah Valley was not just threatened but fully occupied by the Philistine aggressors, who were using the route to get to Bethlehem. Thus the economic benefits and the security of this region were all but lost to the Israelites.

With the two key leaders now present at this geographic locale, we can compare the leadership skills of the ruling king, Saul, and the recently anointed king, David (1 Sam. 16:13). The Israelites had called for a king who would go before them and lead them in battle (1 Sam. 8:20). If there was a time to act, a time for valor, a time for inspired leadership, this was it. But we find Saul offering anything but leadership. The

Assyrian sling stones. David would have used similar stones in his battle against Goliath.

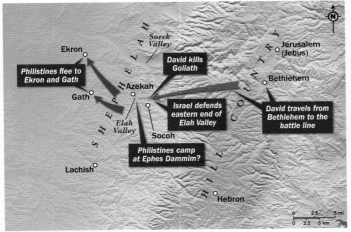

David meets Goliath in the Elah Valley

Wadi Elah (view looking southwest). David picked up sling stones in his battle with Goliath from Wadi Elah.

booming voice of Goliath had issued the same challenge twice a day for forty days (1 Sam. 17:16). The Philistine champion defied the Israelites to produce just one fighter willing to engage him in hand-to-hand combat. The only response they could muster and Saul could inspire was fear (1 Sam. 17:11, 24).

In contrast, David was everything that Saul was not. His words echoed across the valley with faith and power: "You come against me with sword and spear and javelin, but I come against you in the name of the LORD Almighty, the God of the armies of Israel, whom you have defied" (1 Sam. 17:45). Taking on his kingly role by proclaiming the Lord as King, with actions that matched his words David slew Goliath.

David killed Goliath in the Elah Valley for a reason. In a battle charge that protected Bethlehem and the hill country of Judah, David, the newly anointed king of Israel, and the Israelite army drove the Philistine menace from the Elah Valley. The Philistines fled back to their cities of Gath and Ekron with the Israelites in pursuit (1 Sam. 17:51–52). David had defeated Goliath in the name of the Lord and driven the Philistines from the Elah Valley, and the result was that David was elevated in the eyes of the people (1 Sam. 18:1–5; 23:16–18).

The Elah Valley with the mountains of Judah (near Bethlehem) in the background (view looking east).

DAVID HIDES NEAR EN GEDI

1 SAMUEL 18–25

After the victory over Goliath and the Philistines, David was riding a rising wave of popularity that offered him widespread support as Israel's leader (1 Sam. 18:5, 30). Of course, that position was occupied. The Lord had announced Saul's rejection as king, but Saul was of no mind to leave his throne quietly, and his changing moods could bring death to David at any moment. So David left Gibeah, Saul's headquarters, seeking refuge in places like Naioth at Ramah and Nob (1 Sam. 19:18; 21:1). But these villages were located within Benjamin, Saul's home tribal territory. For that reason David fled farther south near the crags of the Wild Goat, in an area called En Gedi (1 Samuel 24).

David found refuge from Saul in the oasis of En Gedi, about twenty miles southeast of Bethlehem.

En Gedi is located within the Wilderness of Judah, west of the Dead Sea and east of Judah's watershed line. The rugged and menacing terrain is dominated by narrow and deeply cut east/west gorges. Their stony hillsides show little sign of life since the Wilderness of Judah lies within a rainfall shadow.[8] Its canyons often accommodate torrents of water that speed toward the Dead Sea. But this is rainwater that has fallen elsewhere, water that enters and leaves the wilderness quickly, providing little life support.

Chalky soil, demanding terrain, and low humidity combined with the heat of summer made it difficult to travel or live there. But the Wilderness of Judah offered one thing that Benjamin and western Judah did not. This was the place to go to get away from everyone else—a refuge for rebels and a hideout for fugitives. Once a person left the road systems in this region, it was easy to hide from anyone. David was familiar with this area because he had lived in nearby Bethlehem, undoubtedly shepherding the family flocks in these hills. Life would not be comfortable here, but if one could find access to water, this wilderness could provide security.

That is what made En Gedi David's place of escape. It was located in the midst of a rugged landscape that provided dozens of caves and dry river beds (Arabic, *wadi*) where a fugitive could hide. Yet unlike most of the surrounding area, it had drinkable water. Due to the geologic contours beneath the earth's surface, rainwater had fallen on the west side of Judah around Bethlehem, traveled underground, and broken out as a spring in the wilderness oasis of En Gedi.[9] There a slash of green in an otherwise pale landscape signaled the spring's presence. David went there because it offered him both water and security while living on the run.

While David used this setting to hide, it became a proving ground for his character. Saul's hunt for David eventually brought him to En Gedi, to the very cave in which David and his men were hiding (1 Sam. 24:3).

As the unwitting Saul used the cave as a bathroom, David's men urged him to execute the defenseless man who stood between him and the throne. Many ideas must have crossed David's mind at that moment. Saul's vulnerability might spell the end of the running, waiting, and hiding. But when David wielded his knife, it was not to cut the flesh of Saul but to cut his garment. David later explained his actions: "The LORD forbid that I should do such a thing to my master, the LORD's anointed, or lift my hand against him" (1 Sam. 24:6). David would wait for God's plan to mature on its own. For David, not even more time on the run, living in the difficult landscape of the Wilderness of Judah, was enough justification to advance a plan without the Lord's approval.

There were reasons David hid near En Gedi. It became the stage for two very different events: David's escape from Saul and a demonstration of David's faith that the Lord would make him king at the right time in the right way.

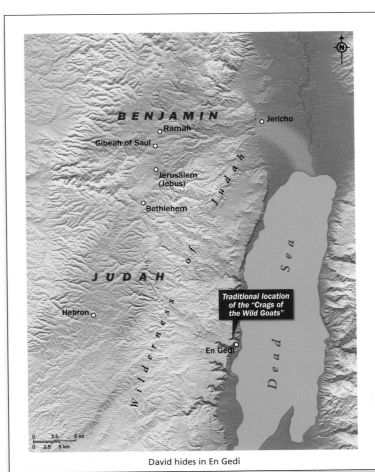

David hides in En Gedi

En Gedi, which in Hebrew means "spring of the wild goats," is known for the ibex (wild goats) that climb the rugged terrain around the En Gedi oasis. © Direct Design

SAUL FIGHTS AND DIES ON MOUNT GILBOA

1 SAMUEL 26–31

The area where Saul died had often witnessed significant Israelite victories. At the time of Deborah and Barak, the Canaanites filled the Jezreel Valley with their chariots but were defeated by the untrained and underequipped Israelite fighters (Judges 4). Gideon's limited army also won a victory in the Jezreel Valley even closer to the scene of Saul's defeat. In his day, Midianite raiders were camped in the Jezreel Valley near Mount Moreh and Mount Gilboa, not far from Endor.[10] At the Lord's direction, Gideon used extraordinary, faith-demanding tactics to win a great victory for Israel (Judges 7). These victories stand in stark contrast to the death and defeat of Saul, which happened on Mount Gilboa for a reason.

First of all, the defeat of Saul in this region would affect the Israelite economy. As its Hebrew name suggests, the Jezreel Valley was suited for field crops.[11] Rich soil combined with plentiful moisture made this valley a prized possession.[12] But the valley floor offered something almost as wonderful as grain. It provided ancient traders with the best convergence of east/west, north/south routes through the Promised Land. In most places, mountain ridges stood as roadblocks, requiring travelers to climb and descend thousands of feet for passage. By contrast, the Jezreel Valley could be crossed with only a few hundred feet of elevation change. It is no wonder that the International Highway traveled through this valley and that the one who controlled this valley would control the economy of the surrounding empires.

Even more important than agriculture and trade revenue was the matter of Israel's national security. Loss of the Jezreel Valley meant that the northern third of Saul's kingdom would be cut off from its capital, Gibeah, located farther south in the territory of Benjamin. And if the Philistines continued down the Jordan Valley, another part of Saul's kingdom would be severed.[13] Given all that was at stake, this was clearly the most significant battle of Saul's life.

Relief of captured Philistines on the walls of Madinet Habu of Ramses III near Karnak, Egypt.

Saul's defiance of the Lord came to a head when his old enemies, the Philistines, assembled their army at Aphek, moving their chariots through the Jezreel Valley to Shunem. Saul mustered his soldiers near a spring in the valley (1 Sam. 28:4; 29:1). When Saul saw the Philistine army, he was terrified and finally sought the Lord, but by then the Lord had stopped answering Saul (1 Sam. 28:5–6). Lost in fear and desperation, Saul completed his turning away from the God of his fathers and did a detestable thing in the sight of the Lord: he consulted the witch who lived at Endor, a village near the northern slope of Mount Moreh (1 Sam. 28:7).

Earlier in Israel's history Deborah's general, Barak, had led his troops from a mountain to the plain (Judges 4), but now Saul's army retreated from the plain to a mountain. And while the Lord had provided

Mount Gilboa, where King Saul died in a battle against the
Philistines (view looking south).

Gideon with victory over the Midianites in the region
near Endor (Judges 6–7), Saul now went to consult a
medium there. As the Philistines advanced against him,
Saul's outmatched army was soon forced up the sides
of Mount Gilboa, where Saul was killed, his rebellion
and life at an end.

   Saul fought and died on Mount Gilboa for a reason.
At just the moment when geography and history called
for Saul to step out in faith and trust the Lord, he sought
advice from a medium, fled to a mountain, and fell on
his sword. He died, and his body was hung on the walls
of the nearby Philistine-held city of Beth Shan (1 Sam.
31:8–10). The act mocked both Israel's independence
and their God. The Israelites had wanted a king to lead
them. The Lord wanted a leader with a submitted heart
to the King of Kings. Saul had become neither.

Only a small mound and a few trees near Mount Tabor mark the
ancient site of Endor (En Dor), where King Saul consulted a medium
prior to his battle with the Philistines on nearby Mount Gilboa.

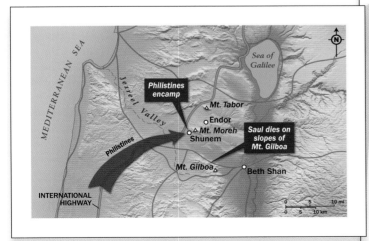

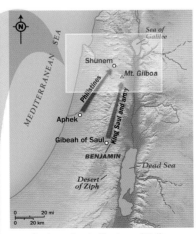

Saul marches to the Jezreel Valley
to fight the Philistines

DAVID MOVES FROM HEBRON TO JERUSALEM

2 SAMUEL 1–6

Saul's death meant that David could stop running and that Israel's new king could establish his own capital. For seven and one-half years, the United Monarchy was split, leaving Judah isolated from the rest of the tribes who looked to Saul's son Ish-Bosheth for leadership (2 Sam. 2:10). It was during those days that David designated Hebron as his capital. In time all twelve tribes of Israel came to acknowledge David as king. Therefore David retired Hebron as capital, captured Jebus, renamed it Jerusalem, and proclaimed it capital of a reunited nation. These changes happened where and when they did for a reason.

Although David was born in Bethlehem in Judah, it was Hebron where he first established his headquarters. The Hebron region was the place where Saul's defectors had come to David to make him king, and it became the hub from which David's army operated (1 Chronicles 12). Consequently, tribal loyalty had an effect on where David located his capital city in Judah.

Hebron had much to offer its residents, including a significant amount of moisture for agriculture[14] and transportation routes that radiated into Judah.[15] But more importantly, Hebron was a place that nurtured the faith of its residents. Abraham built an altar there, heard the promise of his coming son Isaac, and purchased a cave that became the tomb for family members (Gen. 13:18; 18:1–15; 23:17–20). Both altar and tomb served as reminders of the promises the Lord had made. In addition, Caleb,

Aramaic inscription (ninth century BC) with reference to the house of David.

© Dr. James C. Martin. The Israel Museum.

who had faith like David, was given this city as his inheritance (Josh. 14:13–15; Judg. 1:20). Since Israelites found their national identity in the promises given to Abraham and found an example of faith in Caleb, Hebron was more than just a place to live; it was a place that reminded the Israelites of relationship with the one true God. In addition to all that, Hebron was also a priestly village and a city of refuge (Josh. 21:13). As a result, Hebron gave David protection from Saul's dynasty, a faith-nurturing history, and support from the priesthood.

After the country was united under David, he could have kept Hebron as his capital or used Saul's old capital, Gibeah. Neither place forwarded David's desire to heal and unite the nation. Consequently, he turned his attention to Jebus.

Geographically, this location had some problems and one big advantage. The narrow valleys that flow around the thirteen-acre ridge on which Jebus sat offered very little room for agriculture. The Gihon Spring at the base of the ridge could support only a limited population. And Jebus was not only far from international trade routes, it was also off the main internal roadways of Judah. But because it was buried deep into the hill country and perched on an isolated ridge, any aggressor might hesitate to attack the city, knowing that considerable time and loss of life would be sacrificed to obtain a site promising little in return.

What made Jerusalem important to David was its location relative to the tribal boundaries. It shared a

Jerusalem (aerial view looking north). The white box denotes the ancient Jebusite city conquered by David, which was renamed Jerusalem and became Israel's capital of the United Monarchy.

The late Roman emperors attempted to remove the memory of the Davidic dynasty by quarrying the tombs of its kings, which were located in the southern section of the City of David.

border with both Judah and Benjamin. Joshua 18:28 records Jerusalem as belonging to the tribe of Benjamin, and Joshua 15:63 notes that the city is associated with the sons of Judah. Thus Jerusalem seemed to be the connecting point not only between two tribes but between the two kingdoms David wanted to unite.

David moved from Hebron to Jerusalem for a reason. Judah had been the first to proclaim David king, but in time "all the tribes of Israel" came to recognize David as their leader (2 Sam. 5:1). How could David's choice of a capital win the hearts of the other tribes without dismissing the loyalty of Judah? The answer was not in

Hebron or Gibeah but Jebus, a city acceptable to followers of David and those who had served Saul's family. During this fragile time when the selection of a capital site could reignite old jealousy or foster loyalty, Jebus became Jerusalem, the capital of united Israel, the city assigned to acknowledge the Lord as King (Deut. 12:5; 2 Sam. 7:8–9, 21, 26; 1 Kings 8:16–18; Psalm 87; 132:13–14).

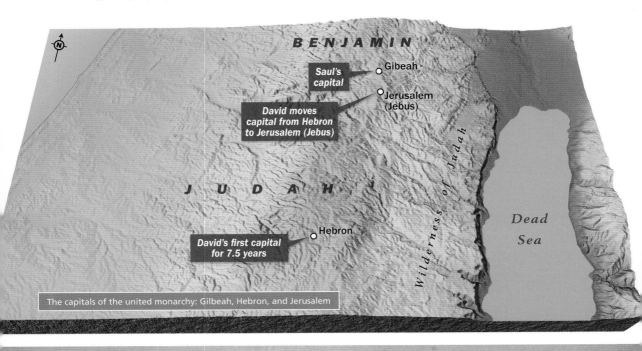

Saul's capital · Gibeah

Jerusalem (Jebus)

David moves capital from Hebron to Jerusalem (Jebus)

BENJAMIN

JUDAH

Wilderness of Judah

Hebron

David's first capital for 7.5 years

Dead Sea

The capitals of the united monarchy: Gilbeah, Hebron, and Jerusalem

SOLOMON PRAYS AT THE TABERNACLE IN GIBEON

1 KINGS 1–4

By the end of the second chapter of 1 Kings, the writer tells us that the kingdom and its capital city, Jerusalem, were "firmly established in Solomon's hands" (1 Kings 2:46). Yet when Solomon went to worship, he traveled to Gibeon, the place where the Lord gave him his incredible wisdom (1 Kings 3:5–14; 2 Chron. 1:7–12). Here we will see that Solomon ruled from Jerusalem but worshiped the Lord in Gibeon for a reason.

At one level, it makes perfect sense. The Temple had not yet been built in Jerusalem, so the Israelites were using various high places like Gibeon for worship.[16] During the early days of Samuel, the tabernacle was erected at Shiloh (1 Sam. 1:3). We find it at Nob during David's early years (1 Sam. 21:1–9). But now this important structure had been moved to Gibeon, only a few miles north of Jerusalem. Thus the high place at Gibeon was deemed the "most important" because the tabernacle and the great altar were there (1 Kings 3:4; see also 2 Chron. 1:3) representing the Lord's presence.[17]

While this begins to explain why Solomon traveled to Gibeon to pray and make sacrifices, it raises another question. David had moved the Ark of the Covenant to Jerusalem (2 Samuel 6). Why had he not brought the tabernacle there also so that the ark and the tabernacle might be reunited? Part of the answer may lie in the fact that Gibeon, not Jerusalem, was designated as a Levitical city—one of forty-eight such cities staffed with priests (Josh. 21:8, 17). And of these Levitical cities, Gibeon had a very centralized location. It was in Benjamin, where the internal north/south and

The small Palestinian village of Jib lies on the northern edge of the ancient site of Gibeon.

east/west roadways crossed one another, making travel to and from Gibeon more easily accomplished by those wishing to worship there.

But Israel's early history may provide a more penetrating answer to the question of why David left the tabernacle in Gibeon rather than bringing it to Jerusalem. Looking back at the initial contact of Gibeon with Israel, we are reminded of the ruse employed by the Gibeonites to save themselves during Joshua's conquest (Joshua 9). They knew that the Lord had given Israel permission to spare people who lived far away from Canaan (Deut. 20:10–15), so they wore old clothes and shoes to a meeting with Joshua, claiming that they had

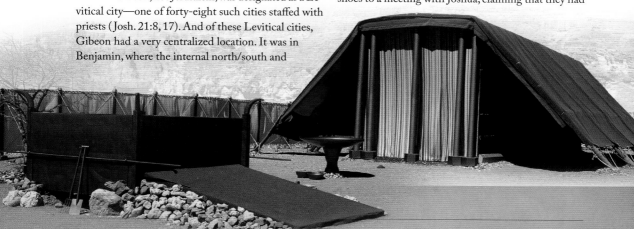

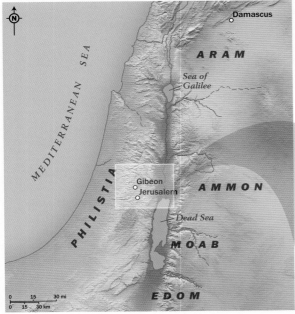

The regions of Solomon's kingdom and the central location of Gibeon

The great pool at Gibeon.

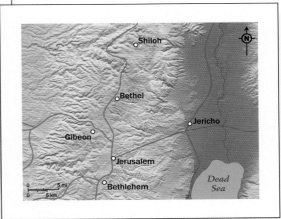

come from a distant land. Joshua and the elders believed them and granted them safety (Josh. 9:15). When the deception became known, Joshua was pledged to honor his word to them but also declared that the people of Gibeon would always be servants to the Lord's altar, carrying water and cutting wood "at the place the LORD would choose" (Josh. 9:27).

Though the Gibeonites had lied, they had recognized the power of Israel's God and were willing to cast their lot with the Lord, who not only rescued them but put them to work tending his holy altar. Some time during his reign, Saul had inflicted a horrible massacre upon the Gibeonites (2 Sam. 21:1–6), violating Joshua's promise.[18] King David had been faced with making amends for the atrocity. As Solomon received God's blessing, the Lord apparently chose that the tabernacle and the great altar would remain in Gibeon to reward the Gibeonites for their faithfulness.

There were reasons Solomon prayed in the tabernacle in Gibeon. The Lord brought together many participants on the day Solomon went to Gibeon to pray and make sacrifices. There was Solomon, Israel's king, who at the time seemed to sincerely approach the Lord with a desire to rule with discernment. There were the Israelite priests of the Levitical city, descendants of the same family as Moses and Aaron. There were the Gibeonites, non-Israelites who believed in Israel's God, serving the Lord in his tabernacle by bringing water and cutting wood for his altar. And the Lord himself came to Solomon, bringing gifts of wisdom, peace, and hope.

Storage pits for the royal wine vessels at Gibeon.

◄ Replica of the altar and tabernacle that Solomon visited at Gibeon.

SOLOMON BUILDS THE TEMPLE IN JERUSALEM

1 KINGS 5–9; 1 CHRONICLES 21:18–26; 2 CHRONICLES 2

The Bible is very clear about where Solomon was to build the Temple for the Lord. David's desire to build that Temple (carried out by Solomon) resulted in a massive public works project that consumed the hill located just north of the wall that had enclosed David's thirteen-acre Jerusalem. This hill had come into royal possession years earlier when David bought it and built an altar on the threshing floor of a Jebusite named Araunah (1 Chron. 21:20–26). He did this to build an altar to the Lord in order to stop a plague (2 Sam. 24:18–25). This area, sometimes referred to as the Temple Mount, was the area where Solomon built the Temple complex—for a reason.

From Abram to the time of David and into the early years of Solomon there had not been a centralized, permanent worship building for the Hebrew people.[19] So why build a permanent Temple for the Lord on the northern hill bordering David's Jerusalem? Geographically, the location is reasonable. It is immediately adjacent to David's capital city. Its location is protected on all sides except the north by the same valley system that surrounds the City of David, yet it is somewhat higher and can be seen from a great distance by approaching visitors. Topographically, it was an impressive site for the location of the Lord's Temple. In addition, there is no indication that the hill was associated with any of the high places that had been used for either legitimate or corrupted worship.

The building of the Temple at Jerusalem may be associated with Abram.

The earliest biblical reference to Jerusalem goes back to when Abram visited the city of Salem (i.e., Jerusalem) after he had rescued Lot's family (Genesis 14). The rescue complete, Abram returned home through the hill country, where he passed through Salem and was met by the king, Melchizedek, who was also the "priest of God Most High" (Gen. 14:18; see also Hebrews 7). In this encounter, Melchizedek proclaimed, "Blessed be Abram by God Most High, Creator of heaven and earth. And blessed be God Most High" (Gen. 14:19–20). Thus it was in Jerusalem that Abram was blessed by God and the Lord was blessed by the priest of the Most High. Moreover, Mount Moriah (i.e., the Temple Mount) was associated with the location where the Lord instructed Abraham to sacrifice Isaac (Gen. 22:2; see also 2 Chron. 3:1). So when the Temple was completed, it was understood as the site of the Lord's choosing (1 Kings 8:29) where the Israelites were to appear three times a year to worship the God of Abraham (Deut. 16:16–17).

Worship ceremonies for the Temple were designed to focus on the Lord, the goodness of his character, and the Israelites' relationship with him. Following the plans and preparation of his father, David, Solomon constructed the Temple in Jerusalem "so that all the peoples of the earth may know your name and fear you" (2 Chron. 6:33).

Silver amulet (ca. seventh century BC) written in paleo-Hebrew script and containing the priestly blessing (Num. 6:24–26). © Dr. James C. Martin. The Israel Museum.

The Temple built by Solomon once stood on the mount where the gold Dome of the Rock and El-Aqsa Mosque now reside.

This Israelite temple sanctuary at Arad (tenth century BC) measured 60 by 45 feet. The Temple built by Solomon in Jerusalem was 90 feet long, 30 feet wide, and 45 feet high (1 Kings 6:2).

Solomon built the Temple in Jerusalem for a reason. The Lord God could have located this Temple in other significant places in Israel, but he chose a specific hill in Jerusalem for its construction. He directed David to prepare for the building of the Temple and confirmed the choice by sending fire down from heaven to consume the sacrifice that David offered (1 Chron. 21:26–30). Once completed, it was no coincidence that fire came down from heaven and consumed the sacrifices Solomon offered at the Temple's dedication (2 Chron. 7:1–3).

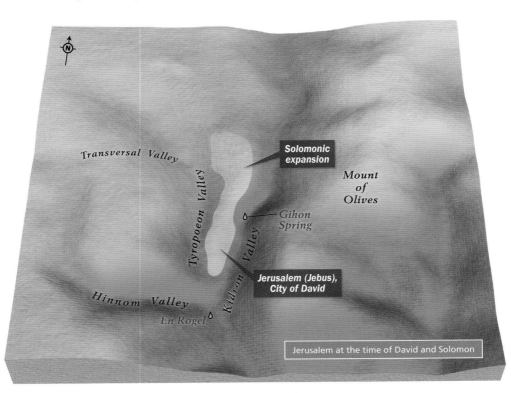

Transversal Valley

Solomonic expansion

Mount of Olives

Tyropoeon Valley

Gihon Spring

Kidron Valley

Jerusalem (Jebus), City of David

Hinnom Valley

En Rogel

Jerusalem at the time of David and Solomon

THE COST OF THE WEDDING GIFT OF GEZER

1 KINGS 9

The Temple-palace complex in Jerusalem was the most magnificent of Solomon's architectural achievements, but Solomon's passion to strengthen the security of his kingdom motivated him to initiate other construction projects outside Jerusalem. Hazor, Megiddo, Lower Beth Horon, Baalath, and Tadmor all experienced design enhancement during the reign of Solomon (1 Kings 9:15–19).[20] Yet no fortified city may be as important to the enduring security of Jerusalem as Gezer, a city Solomon received as a wedding gift (1 Kings 9:16) for a reason.

During the early days of Solomon, Egypt was politically divided and struggling to assert power beyond its own borders. During the reign of Pharaoh Siamun, the Egyptian army advanced against the Philistines. As is often the case, the dispute motivating this incursion may have been money. Since the Philistines controlled the International Highway in this sector of the world, a dispute over trade rights or taxation is what likely brought Egyptian soldiers to Philistine soil.[21] It is somewhat uncertain whether Israel participated with Egypt in this war against the Philistines or was merely an additional target on their agenda. In either case, Pharaoh Siamun formed an alliance with King Solomon and offered one of his daughters in a marriage designed to seal this international treaty. During the campaign mentioned above, Siamun captured Gezer, burned it, and gave it to Solomon as a wedding gift.[22]

Geography suggests this was an invaluable gift. Gezer promised its residents an abundance of water, fields for growing grain, and green pastures for their flocks. But beyond natural

The site of ancient Gezer (view looking northeast).

resources, it was Gezer's position astride the International Highway and at the mouth of the Aijalon Valley that promised a greater reward. The Aijalon Valley is so wide that it resembles a plain much more than it does an enclosed valley. It departs the coastal area as an inviting roadway heading east toward the Beth Horon Ridge, a natural ramp leading into the central mountains and onto the plateau of Benjamin. From there, a turn south and a short walk led directly to the northern edge of Solomon's Jerusalem. The natural east/west roadway that connected Jerusalem with its seaport at Joppa and with the International Highway flowed right past Gezer. It was the gateway that created an international trade market for the residents of landlocked and mountain-enclosed Jerusalem.

If one of the armies of the ancient world wished to bring their weapons rather than trade

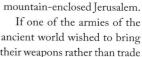

Agricultural calendar (eleventh to tenth century BC) discovered at Gezer.

© Dr. James C. Martin. Istanbul Archaeological Museum.

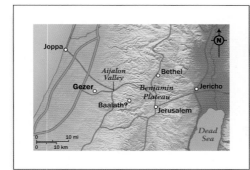

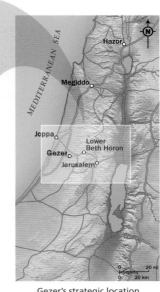

Gezer's strategic location

goods to the capital of Israel, they too would march right past Gezer on that very route to attack Jerusalem. In fact, the future history of this city bears out that fact again and again. From ancient to modern times, an attack against Jerusalem consistently pursued its course on the Gezer–Beth Horon–Benjamin route.[23] An attack from this direction was particularly threatening to ancient Jerusalem since it brought the invader to the northern, most vulnerable side of Jerusalem where the topography offered the least defensive assistance to the city.

Solomon received Gezer as a wedding gift for a reason. He captured many cities, fortified them, and enhanced the security of his country in the process. No gift would seem more important than Gezer. But in making a treaty with Egypt, Solomon took the pharaoh's daughter as a wife. In this act, Solomon turned his heart away from the ultimate Gift Giver (1 Kings 11:1–2). The Lord, for whom he built the Temple, had expressly warned against Israel's idolatry. This treaty and its accompanying gift, along with Solomon's other transgressions, ultimately cost Solomon the kingship of the United Monarchy of Israel and severed his relationship with the living God.

Jerusalem's "Hill of Corruption" (view looking east), where Solomon kept his foreign wives and enabled their idol worship.

SOLOMON BUILDS UP HAZOR, MEGIDDO, AND GEZER

1 KINGS 9–11

As Solomon's kingdom developed, there was the possibility of forgetting his intended relationship with the Lord. Moses had expressed this concern both for the people in general (Deut. 8:17–20) and for the king in particular (Deut. 17:16–17). Samuel also warned of this (1 Sam. 8:10–18). Thus building up Hazor, Megiddo, and Gezer (1 Kings 9:15; see also 10:23) became a test of Solomon's faithfulness—a test related to these cities for a reason.

Two geographic factors produced the wealth of Solomon's kingdom: the size of the area he ruled and the location of the land he controlled. In the first case, Solomon had obtained economic control over a region that far exceeded the size of Israel at the time of either Saul or David. Solomon's kingdom extended from the Red Sea to the Euphrates River and from the Syrian Desert to the Mediterranean Sea (1 Kings 4:21–24; 2 Chron. 9:26). For non-Israelite inhabitants of these regions, that meant paying tribute. Tribute resembled a tax but was more like protection money. Residents of Aram, Moab, Edom, and Phoenicia were required to pay tribute. In exchange, the army of Israel would not invade their land to demand additional payments from them. The tribute collected from this enlarged kingdom was the significant amount of twenty-five tons of gold Solomon received each year (1 Kings 10:14).

The second and more important geographic factor that produced Solomon's wealth was the location of the land he controlled. Merchants wanted to bring their goods to market as quickly as possible. Because of Israel's unique position between the Mediterranean Sea and the Syrian Desert, it became a land bridge that supported the movement of trade between Asia, Africa, and Europe. During the time of Solomon, Israel controlled long stretches of both the International Highway and the King's Highway—international trading routes that moved across this land bridge. In addition, Solomon also tapped into the maritime skills of the Phoenicians, building two trading fleets. One sailed from Joppa into the Mediterranean Sea and the other sailed from Ezion Geber into the Red Sea (1 Kings 10:22; 2 Chron. 8:17–18).

By controlling so much land and building up cities along the International Highway such as Hazor near Lebanon, Megiddo in the Jezreel Valley, and Gezer on the Philistine Plain (1 Kings 9:15), Solomon was uniquely positioned to become extraordinarily wealthy. These three military stations established by Solomon required traders to pay a fee for passage. Markets for Israel's surplus agricultural products like wheat and olive oil flowed north and were exchanged for construction-grade lumber in Lebanon (1 Kings 5:10–11). Every time products passed through Israelite land or hands, there was a profit to be made (1 Kings 10:28–29). Thus the size of Solomon's landholdings and their location turned Solomon's Israel into a wealthy country. It was said that in Jerusalem silver became as common as stones (1 Kings 10:27).

Megiddo. The gate complex of Megiddo is located at the bottom of the photo.

The inhabited section of Hazor during the reign of Solomon ▶ (view looking northeast).

Building up Hazor, Megiddo, and Gezer (1 Kings 9:15; see also 10:23) became a test of Solomon's faithfulness for a reason. These cities, located along the International Highway, could be strategic centers to advance the message of the God of Israel. However, Solomon used Hazor, Megiddo, and Gezer to accumulate vast wealth for himself in direct violation to the Lord's instruction to Israelite kings (Deut. 17:16–17). Instead of using these cities to represent the Lord accurately and to be a blessing to all nations, Solomon built his own kingdom, promoted his own fame, and built high places for the detestable idols of his many wives (1 Kings 11:7–8). In the process of acquiring foreign wives and such enormous personal wealth, Solomon turned away from the Lord. This man, to whom the Lord had given unmatched wisdom, became foolish when he abused the blessing of the land and cities such as Hazor, Megiddo, and Gezer.

Gezer gate complex at the time of Solomon.
© Dr. Dan Warner

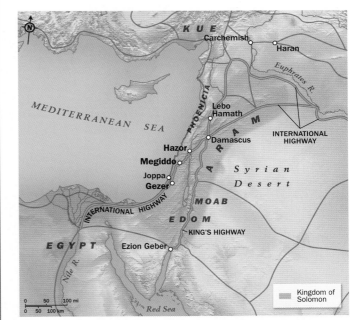

Kingdom of Solomon and major trade routes

PART 5

THE DIVIDED KINGDOM AND ASSYRIAN INVASION

Relief of Assyrian battle scene.
© Dr. James C. Martin. The British Museum.

1 AND 2 KINGS, JONAH, ISAIAH

Solomon chose to turn away from the Lord. Consequently the kingdom David so recently united would be torn apart (1 Kings 11:11–13) during the period referred to in Israel's history as the Divided Kingdom.

After the days of Solomon, the northern tribes declared their independence from David's family and retained the name "Israel," while the southern tribal territories of Benjamin, Judah, and Simeon controlled by David's heirs adopted the name "Judah." Israel and Judah each had their own king, capital city, army, and way of responding to the Lord.

The Lord had told Solomon that his kingdom would be taken away because he had turned to the worship of idols. Nevertheless, Rehoboam, Solomon's son, made a bid to keep the union intact. The location of his coronation was the first sign that this plan was in trouble. We would expect the venue to be Jerusalem, but it happened in Shechem for a reason.

When the northern tribes of Israel declared their independence from Rehoboam, Jeroboam became king of the newly formed Northern Kingdom of Israel, and a civil war began. Aware that his new kingdom was less than secure, Jeroboam established worship sites designed to bypass and compete with God's Temple in Jerusalem (1 Kings 12:26–33). Jeroboam's worship sites introduced perversion that tainted each succeeding king and dynasty that ruled the Northern Kingdom. King Ahab and Queen Jezebel were among the most corrupt of those leaders.

Through the prophet Elijah, the Lord called for the subjects of the Northern Kingdom to make a choice.

Either they would follow Jezebel and the prophets of Baal or they would return to the Lord. In that light, the prophet Elijah summoned the false prophets to demonstrate the power of God in an event that takes on new meaning when we see that it happened on Mount Carmel.

Despite the efforts of prophets like Elijah, the call to repentance did not lead to a broad and sustained reformation in the north. The result was that the Northern Kingdom was taken into exile more than one hundred years before the Southern Kingdom fell. We will see how geography expedited Assyria's defeat of Israel and their corresponding deportation from the land.

The Lord had originally called Abraham and his descendants so that all nations would be blessed through them. But their special calling was misunderstood by many, as evidenced by Jonah, the prophet. His response to the Lord's instructions and particularly his response in choice of travel itinerary provide an illustrative and corrective message as to the purpose of Abraham's descendants.

The Southern Kingdom withstood the first Assyrian invasion of the Promised Land that brought on the demise of the Northern Kingdom. Yet a few decades later the Assyrians returned with a lesson for Judah. Although King Hezekiah held out in Jerusalem, the invaders besieged and captured all other fortified cities of Judah, including Lachish. And finally, we will see why Lachish was the second most important city in Judah and trace the series of events that led to its fall to the Assyrians.

Tel Dan (view looking northeast).

Storm idol riding a bull.

Phoenician ivories. Assyrian spoils taken from places such as Ahab's palace at Samaria.

© Dr. James C. Martin. The Israel Museum.

© Dr. James C. Martin. The British Museum.

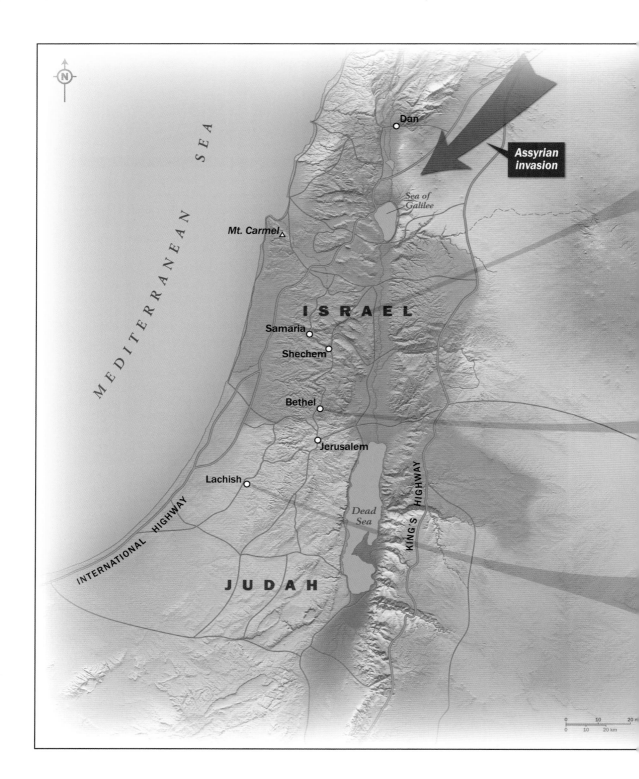

Dan

Assyrian
invasion

MEDITERRANEAN SEA

Sea of
Galilee

Mt. Carmel

I S R A E L

Samaria

Shechem

Bethel

Jerusalem

Lachish

Dead
Sea

KING'S HIGHWAY

INTERNATIONAL HIGHWAY

J U D A H

| 0 | 10 | 20 m |
| 0 | 10 | 20 km |

Samaria palace. Excavated remains of Ahab's palace in the city of Samaria.

Bethel region. Jeroboam I built an idolatrous worship site at Bethel.

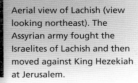

Aerial view of Lachish (view looking northeast). The Assyrian army fought the Israelites of Lachish and then moved against King Hezekiah at Jerusalem.

REHOBOAM TRAVELS TO SHECHEM

1 KINGS 11–14

Though Solomon had ruled a largely expanded kingdom, by the time of his death small fissures had broadened to lethal cracks. As Rehoboam aspired to sit on his father's throne, the United Kingdom split apart beneath his feet during his coronation that was planned at Shechem for a reason (1 Kings 12:1–17).

The inspired writer of 1 Kings warns his readers that a split in the kingdom is on the horizon. Solomon took new brides to solidify foreign alliances even though the Lord had commanded Israelite kings not to enter into such entanglements. He rejected the ways of the God of his father (1 Kings 11:1–4), so God announced to Solomon that the unity of his kingdom would collapse with his passing (1 Kings 11:11–13). This was fulfilled during the days of Solomon's son Rehoboam. The people of Israel's northern tribes met with Rehoboam at Shechem to offer their loyalty in exchange for a royal concession. They asked that the heavy yoke of taxation and forced labor,[1] imposed on them by Solomon, be lightened. When Rehoboam refused, the northern tribes seceded, rejecting the leadership of David's royal family (1 Kings 12:1–17).

This took place at Shechem for several reasons, including accessibility and history. Shechem had a number of roadways radiating in and out from it, providing ready access to attendees from across the region. Residents of the kingdom traveling from the north or south could walk the well-worn Ridge Route. East/west travelers could take the Wadi Faria Road, the most important lateral road bordering Ephraim and Manasseh (a region later known as Samaria).[2]

Ancient Shechem (Tell Balata) with Mount Gerizim in the background.

Shechem also had a memorable history for the Hebrew people. This was the location of some of the most transformative encounters and decisions of their forefathers. When Abram entered the Promised Land, the Lord appeared to him at Shechem and spoke a powerful set of promises that detailed an identity and assignment for him and his descendants (Gen. 12:6–7; Acts 7:15–16). Jacob purchased land there, dug a well, built a memorial altar, and led his family in a reformation that purged false gods from their midst (Gen. 33:18–20; 35:4). Later, Joshua led the Israelites to Shechem on two separate occasions to renew their commitment to the Mosaic covenant (Josh. 8:30–35; 24:1–32). Here Joshua's single-hearted and

El-Amarna letter from Labayu, ruler of Shechem and ally of the *Hapiru*.

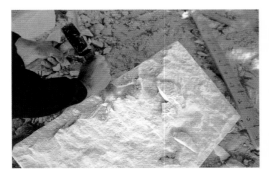

Stone cutting. Solomon placed heavy labor burdens on the population.

Jacob's well near Shechem.

now famous words echoed across this valley: "As for me and my household, we will serve the LORD" (Josh. 24:15).

As fitting as this location might seem to be, Shechem was not Jerusalem, the city of the Lord. And that fact subtly but powerfully betrays a new reality. A strong king—one who was going to follow the Lord—would expect his subjects to come to Jerusalem for a coronation.[3] Only a weak candidate would travel away from Jerusalem to negotiate for their loyalty.

So Rehoboam traveled to Shechem for a reason. The tribal rifts that happened during the days of David's reign (2 Sam. 20:1–2) may not have disappeared altogether. Although the entire country had been affected by Solomon's heavy tax and labor burdens, the northern tribes seemed to be most fully prepared to pursue a change of circumstances (2 Chronicles 10). A few well-placed concessions would have gone a long way toward forestalling civil war, but Rehoboam's harsh words did not resonate with the tone of the promises to Abraham earlier proclaimed at Shechem. Not only was he outside of Jerusalem, but it seemed as if he was reasoning from outside the realms of reality. Rehoboam must have wanted his power to remain over the northern tribes, but

his human reasoning, self-sufficiency, and rejection of God's guidance resulted in political weakness. The Lord had warned Solomon that the kingdom would be divided. Rehoboam's actions at Shechem confirmed the time was at hand.

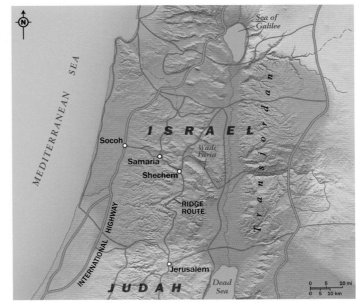

Shechem of Israel

JEROBOAM SETS UP SANCTUARIES AT DAN AND BETHEL

1 KINGS 11–12

The end of Israel as a united kingdom was at hand. The Northern Kingdom of Israel turned to Jeroboam, son of Nebat, and anointed him as their first king. Through the prophet Ahijah, God offered Jeroboam an enduring dynasty, just as blessed and enduring as the one he had promised David, if he would only stay true to the Lord (1 Kings 11:38). But Jeroboam didn't agree. Allegiance to the Lord would mean support of the Temple in Jerusalem. Since that city and the Temple had a close relationship to David's family, Jeroboam feared that such a policy would present the possibility of reunification and would remove the kingdom from him as quickly as he had received it (1 Kings 12:26–27). So Jeroboam rejected the Lord's offer and instead acted in a jealous way toward the King of Kings. He developed direct competition with his Maker, establishing worship centers at Dan and Bethel for a reason.

Jeroboam's high place at Dan.

The first order of business was to pick an idol that might serve as the focus for Jeroboam's new state religion. His kingdom was both ethnically and religiously mixed; there were Canaanites who worshiped Baal and Israelites who maintained their connection to the God of Abraham. So Jeroboam designed a state religion for his young government that was hybrid. He made Baal-like bull calf images, set them up at Bethel and Dan (1 Kings 12:28–33), taught counterfeit beliefs about God's Feast of Tabernacles, and lied to his constituents (saying that the bull calves he made were the ones who led the descendants of Jacob out of Egypt!).[4]

The most northern worship center was located at Dan on an important regional road.[5] Jeroboam's southern worship site

Beersheba to Dan

in the Northern Kingdom was built at Bethel on the Ridge Route, only a few miles north of Jerusalem. Each of these sites had an older tradition associated with them. The book of Judges recounts that the sons of Dan went to Laish (later known as Dan) and set up for themselves a graven image and appointed a corrupt priest who would officiate over their idol worship (Judg. 18:29–31). Thus when Jeroboam set up the calf worship at Dan and appointed false priests, he did so in a place that had been used as a worship site before, albeit a corrupt one. Bethel had also been a place to remember the Lord's loving-kindness from the time of Abraham and Jacob (Gen. 12:8; 28:16–19; 35:1) to the time of Samuel (1 Sam. 7:16). So Jeroboam was hoping the descendants of Abraham would make this historical connection to Bethel and think there was no need to continue a few more miles south to the Temple in Jerusalem.

Finally, the selection of Dan and Bethel marked the northern and southern borders of Jeroboam's kingdom.[6] By placing sanctuaries at these two administrative centers, Jeroboam could retire a phrase he no longer wanted to hear. For centuries, the united tribes were known as the kingdom that extended "from Dan to Beersheba" (Judg. 20:1; 1 Sam. 3:20; 2 Sam. 3:10; 17:11; 24:2, 15; 1 Kings 4:25). So Jeroboam had staked his own claim for himself, replacing the phrase "from Dan to Beersheba" with the phrase "from Dan to Bethel."

Jeroboam set up sanctuaries at Dan and Bethel for a reason. He believed that the selection of Dan and Bethel as worship sites would unify and strengthen the borders of his own new kingdom. But these cities would serve as examples of disloyalty to the Lord, symbols of idolatrous syncretism (2 Kings 10:29; Jer. 48:13; Hosea 10:15). Jeroboam took the Lord's gift of a kingdom, separated himself from the Lord and his blessings, and misrepresented the God of Abraham, Isaac, and Jacob by the idolatry established at Dan and Bethel.

Fields at ancient Bethel (Beitin).

High place at Dan.

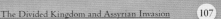

Bull statuette.

© Dr. James C. Martin. The Israel Museum.

AHAB BUILDS AN ALTAR TO BAAL AT SAMARIA

1 KINGS 16

Whether ruling the Northern Kingdom of Israel or the Southern Kingdom of Judah, the kings were to lead with a fervor that accurately represented the one true God. But that calling went completely unfulfilled in the Northern Kingdom. The mutinous leadership of Jeroboam seemed contagious, as one northern king after the other slipped into the same behavior of idolatry. One of the most infamous successors to Jeroboam was Ahab. He was a builder with construction projects under way in many cities. His reputation is described in this powerful critique: "Ahab son of Omri did more evil in the eyes of the LORD than any of those before him" (1 Kings 16:30). One reason for his tainted reputation is that Ahab built an altar to Baal in the city of Samaria.

To understand the life of Ahab is to begin with the account of Omri, Ahab's father. Although he too is criticized for walking in the rebellious footsteps of Jeroboam (1 Kings 16:25–26), Omri's political decisions advanced the security and economic well-being of his country. Political instability in the fifty years prior to Omri had seen the capital city of the Northern Kingdom moved from Shechem to Tirzah (1 Kings 12:25; 15:33; 16:8, 15, 23). But during his reign Omri purchased a prominent hill and there established his capital city, Samaria.[7] It would remain Israel's capital city in the Northern Kingdom for the next 150 years. This site was perched on a hill rising three hundred feet above the

Remains of Ahab's palace at his capital city of Samaria.

surrounding valleys, which produced abundant agricultural products for the city. Additionally, strong defensive walls built on this natural fortress allowed the city of Samaria to withstand multiple sieges.[8]

This secure city was also a prosperous one. Established near natural roadways that radiated to the west and north, the location of Samaria allowed Omri to pursue a trading relationship with the Phoenicians. At this time the Phoenicians were the most powerful seafaring people on the Mediterranean, with trading colonies as far away as Spain and Africa. By selling surplus agricultural goods and brokering products, Omri created an economic relationship that showered his kingdom with new money.[9]

Stela with a figure of a bull's head (ninth to eighth century BC), discovered in Bethsaida and possibly associated with the conquests of Tiglath-Pileser III in 734–732 (2 Kings 15:29).

Phoenician ivory depicting a woman looking out a window, reminiscent of Jezebel's actions just prior to her death. © Dr. James C. Martin. Mus'ee du Louvre; Autorisation de photographer et de filmer—LOUVRE.

In order to confirm their economic alliance, the Sidonian king sent his daughter, Jezebel, to wed Ahab, Omri's son. As Jezebel packed up her personal belongings for the trip to Samaria, she brought along her great love for Baal (1 Kings 16:31). With a passionate Baal worshiper in the royal court of Ahab, it was not long before he embarked on a building project. He founded a sacred precinct complete with altar and temple in the heart of the city of Samaria. Unlike the sacred precinct in Jerusalem, this worship center was not designed for the Lord. And unlike Jeroboam's worship centers at Dan and Bethel, this one made no effort to even blend the worship of the Lord with the worship of Baal. This sacred center was for Baal only.

Ahab built an altar to Baal at Samaria for a reason. It is certainly possible that he built the sanctuary to give his bride a place to worship, much as Solomon had built high places for his foreign wives to worship (1 Kings 11:7–8). Or it is possible that the altar and temple to Baal were only there as a visible symbol of Israel's commercial ties with Phoenicia.[10] In either case, Ahab was persuaded that great economic success would come to the northern tribes of Israel through an alliance with the Phoenicians and Baal. Thus he went to the unprecedented step of establishing an altar and temple to Baal in Samaria, his capital city. By doing so, he replaced the Lord's authority with that of Phoenicia and sought favor from Baal by establishing Baal worship as the state religion of the Northern Kingdom.[11] It is no wonder that the Scriptures say Ahab did more evil than any ruler before him (1 Kings 16:30).

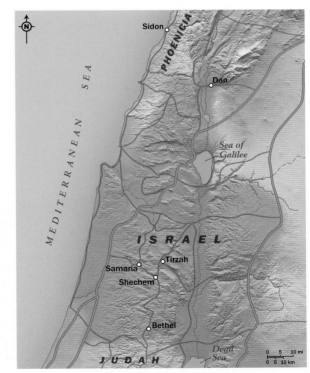

The capitals of the Northern Kingdom

A CONTEST ON MOUNT CARMEL

1 KINGS 18

King Ahab sponsored construction of a temple and altar to Baal in his capital city, Samaria, worshiped Baal, and provided food for the prophets of Baal (1 Kings 16:31–32; 18:19). Consequently, the Lord unleashed a three-year famine that ravaged the fields within Ahab's kingdom. Since Baal worshipers believed their idol was responsible for producing rainfall, this famine demonstrated his impotence. But instead of repentance, the famine brought violence when Jezebel ruthlessly hunted down and murdered many of the prophets of the Lord (1 Kings 18:4). Elijah, a prophet of God, challenged the prophets of Baal to a contest that would reveal the one true God—a contest that took place on Mount Carmel for a reason.[12]

Elijah challenged King Ahab and his subjects to witness a demonstration that put the power of Baal on trial. Elijah called on Ahab to gather his 450 prophets of Baal at a prominent landmark, Mount Carmel. There Elijah and the Baal prophets separately prepared sacrifices on two different altars. Wood and a butchered bull were placed on each altar, but no one was permitted to ignite their pyre. The plan was that each group of worshipers would call on whom they worshiped—Elijah to the

Mount Carmel (view looking southwest).

Lord and the prophets of Baal to their idol. The first to respond by sending down fire would be acknowledged as the real God.

The ridge of Mount Carmel points in a northwesterly direction for thirty miles, ending in the Mediterranean Sea. Egyptian sailors knew of this mountain from earliest times and gave it a name that meant "strong, mighty."[13] What may be most remarkable about this mountain is its thick vegetation, something that the biblical writers often note (Isa. 35:2; Jer. 50:19; Amos 1:2; Song of Sol. 7:5). This extravagant greenery is a product of Mount Carmel's unique geography. Near the Mediterranean Sea, the rising terrain extracts rainfall from the marching air masses at a rate that far exceeds that of the lower elevations

surrounding it. In addition, its proximity to the sea guarantees that it will receive a regular and heavy dewfall.[14]

A place this water rich and lush in a country so dry was destined to receive attention. The Egyptian leader, Thutmose III, called it the "Holy Headland."[15] Thanks to the Assyrians we further know that this mountain was used by Phoenician worshipers of Baal.[16] The Phoenician princess, Jezebel, could not have hoped for a more favorable venue for this competition. Elijah had challenged her prophets on what amounted to the Baal prophets' home field. If Baal existed, this was the spot where one would expect him to provide a flawless performance.

The contest took place on Mount Carmel for a reason. Despite the territorial advantage and the desperate efforts of the prophets of Baal, there was no fiery response. When Elijah stepped forth to call on his King and his God in Baal's territory on the heights of Mount Carmel, he made his sacrifice to the Lord even more difficult to ignite by dumping water over it. Yet with just a brief prayer and powerful faith in the one true

Kishon River (view looking southwest).

God, Elijah called on the Lord to reveal himself as the one true God. With that prayer, fire poured from the heavens consuming the sacrifice, the wood, the stones, the soil, and the water. This event reminds us of when the Lord sent fire and consumed David's sacrifice when he built the altar where the Lord's Temple was to be built (1 Chron. 21:26). It also brings to memory when, similarly, the Lord consumed Solomon's sacrifice at the Temple's dedication (2 Chron. 7:1). So it was that the Lord publicly demonstrated that worship of Baal was a fraud. The God of Abraham is the one true God, whether worshiped at Jerusalem's Temple Mount or on Mount Carmel.

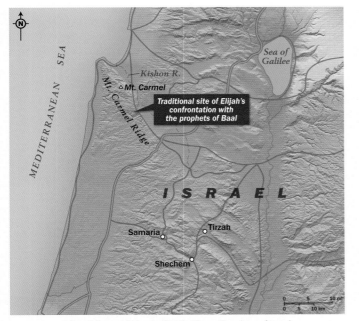

Mount Carmel Ridge in the Northern Kingdom of Israel

◀ This monastery on Mount Carmel is built over Elijah's cave, which functions as the crypt.

ASSYRIA INVADES THE NORTHERN KINGDOM

2 KINGS 17

The victory of the Lord at Mount Carmel over the prophets of Baal did little if anything to persuade the Northern Kingdom of Israel to return to the God of Abraham. Instability continued to rock the region until its defeat and exile at the hand of the Assyrians in 722 BC under Tiglath-Pileser III (745–727 BC).

During the history of the Northern Kingdom, there had been nine dynasties that ruled the country. Eight were violently overthrown when the kings and royal families were assassinated. The revolving door of leaders in the north had one thing in common: they had remained unfaithful to the Lord. Not one king of the north escaped the designation "evil"—a reality that infected king and citizen alike.[17] In connection with the historical, political, and religious realities, we will see that the geography of the Northern Kingdom also was a reason why it was invaded and fell many years before the Southern Kingdom.

Years earlier when the United Monarchy split, the largest amount of land and the greatest number of people went to the Northern Kingdom of Israel. Included among those citizens were many of the land's original occupants—Canaanites. Accommodation to their various religious beliefs became the norm. Adapting to Baal worship started with Jeroboam's calf idols at Dan and Bethel (1 Kings 12:25–33) and escalated into a broader acceptance and participation in idol worship. This included the use of Asherah poles, astrology, sorcery, and human sacrifice (2 Kings 17:16–17).

We also find Canaanite influence occurring within a government that found itself increasingly isolated from the influence of the Lord's priests and the Temple that Solomon had built at Jerusalem (1 Kings 6). Representatives of each family were to travel to the Temple three times a year where sacrifice, festivals, and readings from God's law would remind them of the Lord's

Assyrian relief of Tiglath-Pileser III's campaigns, depicting captives being deported into exile.

love, faithfulness, and power and of the mission that encompassed all the Hebrew people. But from the start, the leaders in the Northern Kingdom schemed to isolate its citizens from the Temple in Jerusalem (1 Kings 12:25–33). When this happened, legitimate and believing

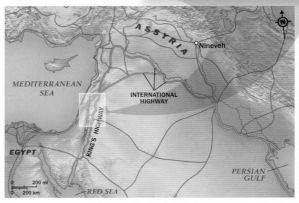
Fall of the Northern Kingdom

The Black Obelisk of the Assyrian ruler Shalmaneser III (858–824 BC) is thought to depict Jehu, king of Israel, paying tribute to the Assyrian ruler.

© Dr. James C. Martin. The British Museum.

priests who had been strategically placed by God in Levitical cities throughout the northern part of the Promised Land fled to the Southern Kingdom of Judah, taking their influence with them (2 Chron. 11:13–15).

Moreover, the Northern Kingdom of Israel controlled portions of the Promised Land that could generate much wealth. Compared to the Southern Kingdom of Judah, the north enjoyed the best agricultural land that supported its citizens and provided crops to be sold to others.[18] The Northern Kingdom also inherited geographic regions open to the two international trading routes—the International Highway and the King's Highway—with their tax and trade revenues. As a result, the northern tribes developed a wealthy upper class.[19] But the blessings of wealth became used for social injustice and self-reliance rather than for God's ways (1 Kings 21; Amos 2:6–8).

Finally, the same international trade routes that promised a wealth of tax revenue also attracted the attention and interest of power-hungry invaders. Assyria needed money to make its empire function, and there was no better place to generate revenue than the land bridge of the Promised Land that connected Africa, Asia, and Europe. Thus the very transportation routes

that provided the Northern Kingdom with lucrative income also provided Assyrian armies, which were eager for revenue, with motivation to seize the land of Canaan.

Assyria invaded the Northern Kingdom of Israel for a reason. The people of this kingdom would go into exile because they had spurned the Lord and plunged into horribly evil practices. Its own demise was facilitated by its proximity to Assyria and its topographically open access to invaders. Mutiny, wickedness, rejection of the opportunity to hear God's teaching in Jerusalem, and invasion vulnerability all contributed to the assault and destruction of the Northern Kingdom by the Assyrians.

© Dr. James C. Martin. The British Museum.

The annals of Tiglath-Pileser III (744–727 BC) include his Assyrian military campaigns during the reign of King Ahaz.

JONAH RESISTS GOING TO NINEVEH

JONAH

As the Northern Kingdom of Israel spiraled downhill toward its exile, the Lord sent one prophet after another to the people with words of warning and guidance. Powerful messages delivered by men like Amos and Hosea are preserved for us in books of the Bible that bear their names. Jonah was also among those prophets, but his message was delivered in his life's actions rather than in a sermon—actions that happened where they did for a reason.

Jonah was from the village of Gath Hepher, located in the Northern Kingdom of Israel in the tribe of Zebulun. This tribal location was part of a larger territory known as "the district of the Gentiles" (i.e., "Galilee of the Gentiles," Isa. 9:1). He addressed the northern tribes during the heady days of Jeroboam II, some fifty years prior to the fall of Israel's capital, Samaria (2 Kings 14:23–29). During the reign of Jeroboam II, a lull in Assyrian intrusion allowed this king to expand both the territory and the wealth of his kingdom in ways not seen since the time of Solomon.[20]

In a brief but clear directive, the Lord pointed his prophet in the direction of Nineveh (Jonah 1:1), a city that would later serve as the capital of Assyria. But at the time of Jonah, it was a sprawling, Assyrian administrative center located on the banks of the Tigris River in the northern portion of modern Iraq.

The Lord had ordered Jonah to Nineveh for a reason. He intended to change both the residents of Nineveh and the residents of Israel via Jonah's mission there. On the one hand, God had a message for Nineveh. The wicked behavior of its people was so appalling that the Lord determined to visit a horrible destruction on it.[21] Out of the Lord's love and mercy, Jonah was sent to give the Assyrians a message for repentance and guidance (Jonah 3:4).

Jonah's prophetic message delivered hundreds of miles from the Promised Land was also meant to reshape the thinking of Israel as well. Centuries earlier the Lord had promised Abraham that he would be blessed in order to become a blessing to the nations (Gen. 12:3). Jonah's trip to Nineveh reminded all Israel that their original assignment as messengers of the God of Abraham had not changed. Thus that trip sent two powerful messages in the direction of two very different audiences.

Roman marble sarcophagus (AD 300) with a scene from the life of Jonah.

The delivery of both messages nearly failed because of Jonah's fear and disdain of the Assyrians, as evidenced in his itinerary. We can understand his fear since Jonah may have known firsthand about the ruthlessness of Assyria because he lived in the district of the Gentiles frequented by the Assyrians. But that did not excuse his travel plans. He proceeded to Joppa, located on the shore of the Mediterranean Sea where the graceful curve of the coast is interrupted just enough to allow a small, natural harbor to develop (Jonah 1:3).

We know that the shortest and most direct route to Nineveh would have taken Jonah along the overland routes north through Israel and then east to Assyria. Jonah began his trip by heading south and west to Joppa.[22] From that seaport he booked passage for Tarshish—a destination that would take him about as far away from Assyria as one could get.[23] As the Lord was saying something to Jonah by sending this prophet to Nineveh, Jonah was saying something to the Lord. From Jonah's perspective, the Assyrians were not only cruel, they were not Israelites and did not deserve a warning or any other form of assistance from the God of Abraham.[24]

The Lord had sent Jonah to Nineveh for a reason; Jonah had traveled to Joppa for a reason. It would take a violent storm, time within a great fish, a worm, withering heat, and a failed shelter to bring Jonah to a better understanding of the God of Abraham, Isaac, and Jacob.

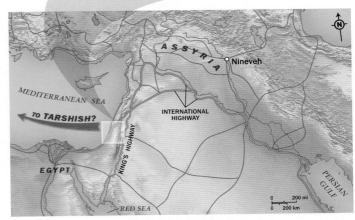

Jonah, Joppa, and Nineveh

The hilltop of the site of Gath Hepher (Kh ez Zurraa), home of Jonah the prophet.

THE LESSON OF THE SONG
OF THE VINEYARD

ISAIAH 5:1–7

*T*he destruction and devastation of the Promised Land by the Assyrians raised a troubling question. Why had all this happened? The answer came to the descendants of Abraham from prophets of the Lord like Isaiah. One powerful piece of poetry in Isaiah includes a word picture drawn from everyday life in the Promised Land: the Song of the Vineyard (Isa. 5:1–7). We can better appreciate its message as we learn about ancient family vineyards. And we will see that this song relates to a vineyard for a reason.

The Song of the Vineyard illustrates what almost every family in Israel and Judah knew: the care and keeping of a vineyard required sustained and intense attention. In this song, the farmer who represents the Lord has done everything possible to guarantee the success of his vineyard. At least five separate dimensions of that care are noted.

The first has to do with the field in which the vine was planted. The "fertile hillside"

In Bible times, grapevines grew on the ground.

for planting (Isa. 5:1) did not occur naturally but entailed years of work. In the hill country of Judah most valleys were too narrow to produce sufficient crops, so farmers built terraces on the hillsides to increase the acreage of their arable land. This was a time-intensive process. Since the best topsoil had already washed downhill into the valley, this meant lugging bag after bag of good soil up the hill to build the terrace.[25]

Second, while smaller stones were strategically left on the surface of the field to collect and preserve the moisture from vital dewfall, the larger stones were removed and used to construct walls around the terraced fields (Isa. 5:5). These walls protected the vineyard against soil erosion. As the crop matured, nonproducing vines were pruned and placed on the wall, creating a hedge to protect the vines against destructive animals (Ps. 80:13). Thus the caring farmer in this song described in Isaiah surrounds his precious vines with a wall and hedge to protect them.

Third, with the field and its defenses in place, the farmer took pains to obtain the choicest stock for planting (Isa. 5:2). The highest quality grapes were not grown from seeds but cultured from the cuttings

Agricultural watchtower.

of successful vines. In this case, the farmer used what are called, in Hebrew, *soreq* cuttings—the most celebrated grape in the Promised Land—to assure the finest harvest imaginable.[26]

Fourth, despite the quality of the stock, it would be six years before this vineyard produced high-quality fruit. During those years the farmer carefully cultivated and pruned his vines (Isa. 5:6). Cultivation removed weeds that competed with the vine for nutrients and water. Pruning the previous growth meant that vital nourishment would be directed to the most promising portions of the vine.[27]

Finally, since the family home was usually some distance from the terraced field, the farmer also built a watchtower in his vineyard (Isa. 5:2). This one- or two-story fieldstone structure provided the farmer and his family with temporary living quarters during the time of year when grapes were nearly ripe and at greatest risk to human and animal theft.

Isaiah's imagery in the Song of the Vineyard is provided for a reason. As the farmer did everything possible for his vineyard, so the Lord had done everything possible for the descendants of Abraham. He brought Israel as "a vine out of Egypt" and planted it in the Promised Land (Ps. 80:8–9). God had meticulously blessed and cared for the Hebrew people, and he had every reason to expect good grapes. But when he examined the vine, he saw only bad fruit (Isa. 5:4). The unimaginable had happened, and so the Lord removed his "hedge" of protection (Isa. 5:5). Israelites no longer sat in peace under their own vine and fig trees. The people went into exile for the most tragic reason: continued unfaithfulness to the Lord Almighty.

Drying grapes.

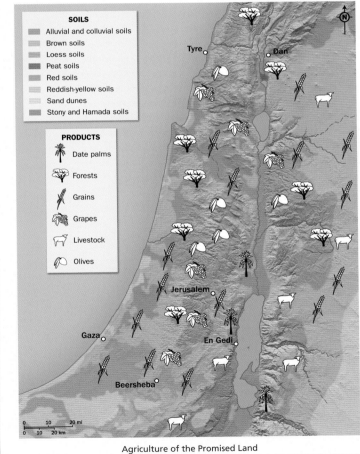
Agriculture of the Promised Land

THE ASSYRIAN SIEGE OF LACHISH

2 KINGS 18–19

After the Assyrians destroyed the Northern Kingdom of Israel, they proceeded south into the Southern Kingdom of Judah. In their advance against Judah, the Assyrians decided to conquer Lachish before they took Jerusalem. The Assyrian siege occurred at Lachish for a reason.

Lachish was located in the *Shephelah* (i.e., humble hills) of Judah. This region functioned as the geographic transition between the low, flat coastal plain and the dramatic elevations of the hill country of Judah. Like its companion valleys to the north (e.g., Elah, Sorek, and Aijalon), the valley in which Lachish lay was most cherished for its geographic setting as a buffer for Jerusalem's security. The city of Lachish was established on a small hill that guarded the route from the Philistine Plain into Judah's hill country leading to Hebron. Since this city attended roadways that provided access to Jerusalem,[28] the security of Jerusalem was intimately linked to the security of the Lachish fortress (2 Chron. 11:5, 9).

Judah had become a vassal to Assyria during the days of King Ahaz (2 Kings 16:7–8). But King Hezekiah reversed that policy and withheld tribute when he learned that the invaders were distracted by internal political turmoil.[29] Once he stopped paying tribute, Hezekiah

Assyrian relief of Sennacherib's siege of Lachish in 701 BC.

© Dr. James C. Martin. The British Museum.

hurriedly prepared his city for the inevitable return of the Assyrian army, knowing that this window of opportunity would soon close.[30] When the Assyrian ruler, Sennacherib, brought his army back to the Promised Land, he conquered dozens of other cities, including the fortresses protecting the Aijalon, Sorek, and Elah valleys, before turning his attention to Lachish.[31]

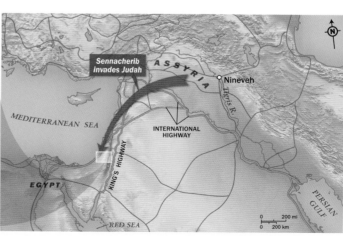

Sennacherib's attack of Lachish and seige of Jerusalem

Tel Lachish (Tell ed-Duweir), with a view looking east.

As we might expect, the siege and fall of Lachish also shook the foundations of Jerusalem. Hezekiah immediately recognized the peril that his capital, Jerusalem, faced. Consequently, the king sent messengers from Jerusalem to Sennacherib, the king of Assyria, urging him to withdraw. As an incentive for him to do so, Hezekiah offered the king of Assyria eleven tons of silver and one ton of gold, emptying the Temple and palace treasuries in a bid to prevent a siege of Jerusalem (2 Kings 18:14–15).

With Lachish securely in Assyrian hands, Sennacherib knew he had a bargaining chip of indisputable value. While he appreciated the significant sum of money Hezekiah had sent, Sennacherib knew he could demand more. Consequently, he dispatched envoys to Jerusalem demanding the surrender of the capital city (2 Kings 18:17–36; 2 Chron. 32:9–19; Isa. 36:1–22).

Sennacherib had planned his campaign well. The northern tribes were in Assyria's possession. Sennacherib had conquered the coastal cities south into Egypt and major fortifications of the *Shephelah* leading into the mountains of Judah (2 Kings 18:19–25). With the capture of Lachish, Sennacherib was as confident in himself as ever. The Lord, however, proved himself more powerful than the human king holding Lachish.

The Assyrian siege occurred at Lachish for a reason. It was the last defense protecting Jerusalem from the Assyrian army. As Lachish fell to the Assyrians, the residents of Jerusalem were terrified, and King Hezekiah tore his robes, pacing the palace in sackcloth. King Hezekiah and the prophet Isaiah actively brought the people before the Lord. The reforming king who had placed all his hope in the Lord was not to be disappointed.

At just the moment when everything seemed lost because Lachish was lost, the angel of the Lord struck down 185,000 soldiers in the Assyrian camp, causing Sennacherib to retreat back to Assyria (Isa. 37:36–37).

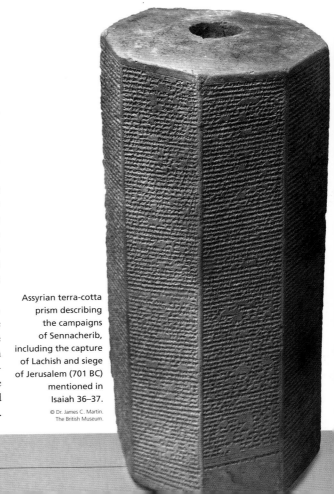

Assyrian terra-cotta prism describing the campaigns of Sennacherib, including the capture of Lachish and siege of Jerusalem (701 BC) mentioned in Isaiah 36–37.

© Dr. James C. Martin.
The British Museum.

PART 6

THE BABYLONIAN INVASION, EXILE, AND RETURN TO THE PROMISED LAND

Susa palace capitals of Darius I (ca. 510 BC).

2 KINGS 21–25; EZRA; ESTHER; JEREMIAH; EZEKIEL; DANIEL; OBADIAH

The Lord delivered Judah from Assyrian aggression because the nation returned to faithful living at the urging of the prophets. The last of the reforming kings of Judah was Josiah. After his death came the closing years of the Southern Kingdom. Josiah died in an unnecessary battle—a battle that he fought at Megiddo for a reason.

Josiah's death resulted in Judah growing increasingly disloyal to the Lord. This, in turn, brought divine judgment on Judah and Jerusalem in the form of an invasion by the Babylonians, who were engaged in trying to reduce the power of the Assyrian Empire. Though warned not to, Judah rebelled against their Babylonian rulers. Consequently the Babylonian army returned to the Promised Land. Although the city of Jerusalem had little to offer these invaders in compensation for their efforts, the Babylonians came with another purpose in mind: complete destruction of the Southern Kingdom.

The Lord had sent prophets to exhort the people to return to him and trust in his power and faithfulness. Foreign nations had ravaged, beaten, and exploited Judah, but these abuses would not go unaddressed. In the book of Obadiah, the nation of Edom faced God's stern judgment. In language that highlights the topography of Edom, Obadiah explains how they had become proud in a mountain home that would not give them the expected protection when the King of Heaven brought them down.

Ezekiel also encouraged hope for Israel through reference to the Dead Sea. In his vision he saw this salty, lifeless lake turn to freshwater teeming with fish. The Lord used the geography of the Promised Land and its environs to warn the people and at the same time establish hope for the future.

Despite God's direction to the contrary, when the Babylonians invaded, some from the Southern Kingdom fled to Egypt. There they hoped to find safety and security. When King Jehoiachin of Judah surrendered to Nebuchadnezzar, king of Babylon, many citizens of Judah were taken captive, and Temple articles were seized and taken to Babylon. Only the poorest residents were left (2 Kings 24:13–14). Shortly thereafter, even greater devastation was visited on the people as Jerusalem and the Temple were destroyed (2 Kings 25:1–17).

After decades of living in foreign lands, some of the Jewish exiles returned to Jerusalem following the liberating decree of Cyrus the Persian. Their plan was to live in Jerusalem and rebuild the Temple. The Persian government had a vital interest in supporting the project at this location, but it happened where it did because God's plan was even more pressing. A third group of exiles never returned from Persia. As we shall see, their motivations varied.

As the history of Judah continued to unfold in the events of its fall and captivity, not all Judeans went to the same place. But when we look carefully at the evidence, we find that they lived where they did for a reason.

Bullae of Gemariah ben Shaphan, thought to belong to the scribe mentioned in Jeremiah 36:10.

Ptolemy I (Soter I), successor of Alexander the Great, captured Jerusalem around 320 BC and established his rule over Egypt from 305 to 282 BC.

Lachish letter #4. The inscription reads, "And let (my lord) that for the beacons of Lachish we are watching . . . for we cannot see Azekah."

© Dr. James C. Martin. The Israel Museum.

© Dr. James C. Martin, Musée du Louvre; Autorisation de photographer et de filmer—LOUVRE.

© Dr. James C. Martin. The Israel Museum

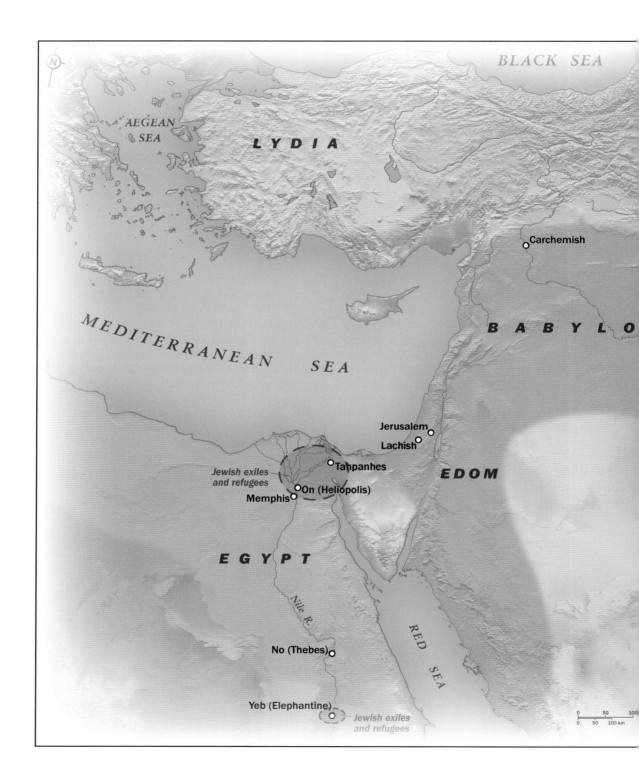

N

BLACK SEA

AEGEAN
SEA

L Y D I A

Carchemish

MEDITERRANEAN   SEA

B A B Y L O

Jerusalem
Lachish

EDOM

Jewish exiles
and refugees

Tahpanhes

On (Heliopolis)
Memphis

E G Y P T

Nile R.

RED
SEA

No (Thebes)

Yeb (Elephantine)

Jewish exiles
and refugees

0   50   100
0   50   100 km

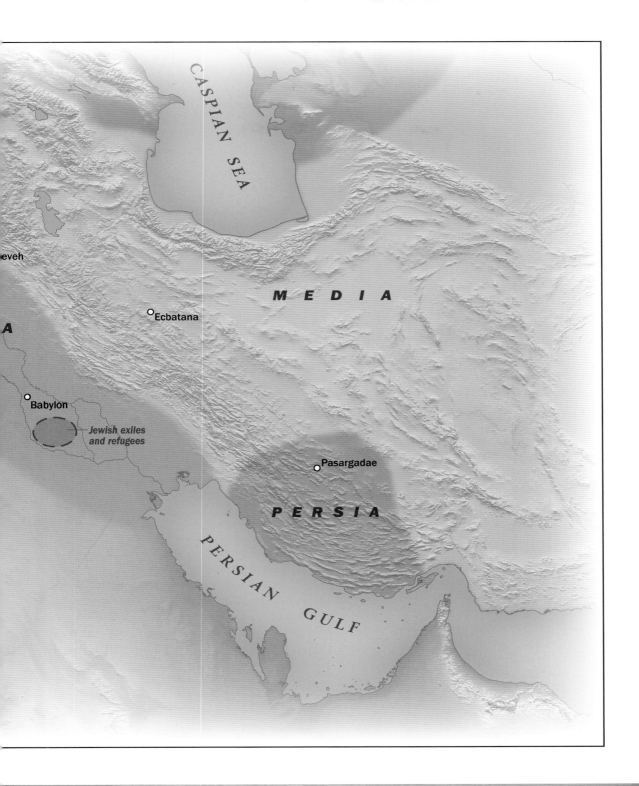

CASPIAN SEA

eveh

MEDIA

○ Ecbatana

A

○ Babylon

*Jewish exiles
and refugees*

○ Pasargadae

PERSIA

PERSIAN

GULF

JOSIAH KILLED AT MEGIDDO

2 KINGS 23:1–30; 2 CHRONICLES 34–35

As the residents of Judah heard the news, we can expect that some shook their heads in disbelief while others wept quietly. At age thirty-nine, King Josiah was dead, struck down by an archer near Megiddo. Josiah represented all that the Promised Land could be and all that a leader of the people of God should be. Taking advantage of Assyrian weakness in the north, he had expanded the size and influence of his country. More importantly, Josiah had brought the people to trust in the Lord in a way not experienced since the time of Hezekiah.[1] There was so much more that he could have done. But the news of his death left the country stunned and facing an uncertain future. Josiah was killed at Megiddo in battle against the Egyptians—a battle that happened where it did for a reason.

Josiah had received word that Neco, king of Egypt, was on the move, pressing north along the International Highway (2 Kings 23:29–30; 2 Chron. 35:20–26). On this campaign, Neco's destination was not Judah but Carchemish. His goal was to prop up a flagging Assyrian army in their war against the Babylonian Empire. Since the days of Sennacherib (701 BC), Assyrian power and influence had waned. But a new and powerful player was emerging on the international stage—the nation of Babylon. Under the leadership of King Nabopolassar and assisted by the Medes, Babylon had crashed the gates of Nineveh, taking the Assyrian capital city in 612 BC. As the Babylonians and Medes advanced, the Assyrians kept backpedaling west. By 609 BC they were in Carchemish, eager to counterattack but in desperate need of Egyptian reinforcements.

The balance of world power was tipping, and Pharaoh Neco wanted to make his contribution at the earliest possible moment. But Josiah of Judah was not eager for the Assyrians to receive support because they had earlier ravaged the Promised Land and deported citizens of the Northern Kingdom of Israel. Therefore Josiah took

Relief of Egypt's military activities—a reminder of Pharaoh Neco's battle at Megiddo.

it upon himself to call out his army with a plan to turn back the Egyptian forces at Megiddo.

Josiah chose Megiddo, knowing that there were few locations where he stood a better chance for success.[2] As the land bridge between Asia, Africa, and Europe, the Promised Land hosted an important segment of the International Highway. The north/south route of the International Highway between the Sharon Plain and the Jezreel Valley was blocked by the perpendicular ridge of Mount Carmel. This ridge had to be crossed, and several valleys that cut through the ridge offered promising access. None, however, offered the modest elevation change, gentle slope, and soft, chalky surface of the Wadi `Iron, a valley that cut through Mount Carmel and was

Tel Megiddo (view looking northeast). Josiah was killed ▶ on the plains near Megiddo.

controlled by the city of Megiddo at the valley's northern exit.[3] This is the one place along Neco's travel route where the smaller army of Judah had a chance. And that is why Josiah engaged the Egyptian army near Megiddo.

Josiah was mortally wounded in a battle that happened at Megiddo for a reason. Neco had no quarrel with Judah (2 Chron. 35:21), but Josiah came to resist the Egyptian advance because of his desire to influence international politics. Perhaps he recalled previous Israelite leaders, like Barak and Gideon, who had won great victories for the Lord near Megiddo (Judges 4–7). But these earlier fighters had the Lord's direct mandate—something Josiah lacked for this engagement. In fact, Neco had been commanded by the Lord to hurry to the battlefront against Assyria (2 Chron. 35:21). Josiah's opposition to Neco actually interfered with God's plan and thus was destined to fail.

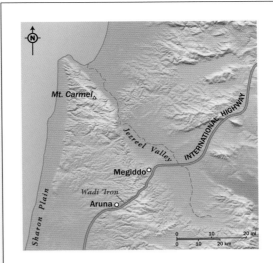

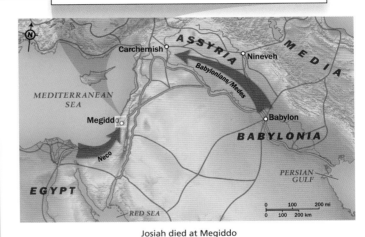

Josiah died at Megiddo

THE BABYLONIANS DESTROY JERUSALEM

2 KINGS 23–25; 2 CHRONICLES 36; JEREMIAH

The Babylonians under King Nebuchadnezzar had the capacity to put an incredible army in the field. They were of a mind to build an empire that would rival that of the Assyrians, and they had the military strength to do so. During the first quarter of the sixth century BC this war machine took aim at Jerusalem. When the dust settled, administrative buildings were leveled, beautiful homes were burned down, and the Temple lay in ruin. The Babylonian assault had taken place at Jerusalem for a reason.

The collapse of the Assyrian Empire created a power vacuum that both Egypt and Babylon wanted to fill. In all the twists and turns of this struggle, Judah was central. At first the Egyptians required money and loyalty from the Southern Kingdom during the days of King Jehoahaz (2 Kings 23:31–35). When the Egyptian campaign against Babylon failed at the critical battle of Carchemish (605 BC), Nebuchadnezzar's soldiers chased the Egyptians back to the mouth of the Nile and made Neco's vassal, Jehoiakim, their vassal (2 Kings 23:34; 24:1).

That might have ended the story had it not been for two revolts—revolts that the Lord (through the prophet Jeremiah) warned the people against. As a result the Babylonian army came crashing down on Jerusalem. In time, Egypt wanted to test the resolve of Babylon and encouraged Jehoiakim to revolt. Shortly after Jehoiakim died, his son Jehoiachin became king. It was in 597 BC, during the first three months of his reign, when Babylon entered

Excavated remains of Jerusalem's "Broad Wall" (eighth century BC), about twenty-three feet thick.

the city gates of Jerusalem and ransacked the Temple. The first of what would be three deportations skimmed off the leading citizens of the land (2 Kings 24:8–16; Jer. 52:28–30). Nebuchadnezzar set up Zedekiah as a puppet ruler in Jerusalem. Despite swearing allegiance to Babylon, this king of Judah initiated a revolt, which the Lord informed Zedekiah would end in defeat (Jer. 34:1–7).

The Babylonians had had enough. Nebuchadnezzar directed his army to annihilate the country and destroy Jerusalem. Dozens of cities and forts were leveled. And by the close of 586 BC, a multiyear siege left Jerusalem and the Temple a smoking ruin.[4]

Jerusalem had been founded as Israel's capital

Babylonian text mentioning Nebuchadnezzar's victory at Carchemish and his later capture of Jerusalem in 598 BC.

© Dr. James C. Martin. The British Museum.

City of David
(view looking southwest).

by David. The Lord had promised David that he would always have a son to rule on Israel's throne (2 Sam. 7:11–16). The Southern Kingdom assumed this enduring lineage of David would always express itself from Jerusalem. David's son Solomon had built the Temple of God in this city. The yearly festivals and the daily sacrifices in Jerusalem's Temple recalled God's call to a specific life and destiny for Israel (1 Kings 9:1–7). The Lord had warned his people through Jeremiah that the Temple structure would be of no help (Jer. 7:4). When it fell, what the Hebrew people assumed about themselves was put into question. That was the point proclaimed by the prophet Jeremiah.

The Lord used Babylon to remove the messengers, the descendants of Abraham, from the land where they had turned from him and become loyal to idols. They had misrepresented and rejected the King of the Universe. As a consequence, they were taken from their land for seventy years (Jer. 7:24–34). It was better to remove these intended messengers of God from the podium of the Promised Land than to allow them to misrepresent the Message Giver while on that

podium. Perhaps during their time of exile they would come to remember why they had received the land in the first place—to worship the Lord their God and be a blessing to the nations (Gen. 12:1–3).

The Babylonians destroyed Jerusalem for a reason. Jerusalem was the nation's capital, the location of all the public buildings that validated Judah's political identity. Once Nebuchadnezzar had taken Jerusalem, matters of state came to a close, and the people of Judah were removed from the podium.

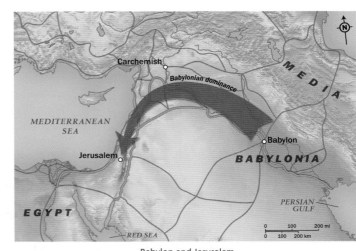

Babylon and Jerusalem

LIFE IS PROCLAIMED FOR THE DEAD SEA

EZEKIEL 47:1–12

This mosaic map (sixth century AD) from Medeba, Jordan, depicts fish swimming up the Jordan River to avoid entering the Dead Sea.

zekiel was among those taken captive by Nebuchadnezzar during the Babylonian invasion of Judah in 597 BC (2 Kings 24:14; Ezek. 1:2). While in Babylon, he became a spokesman for the Lord (Ezek. 1:1–3). Into the despondency resulting from the destruction of Jerusalem and the Temple, God poured hope. So what would come next? The exiles would return to the Promised Land to meet the dawning of a new era. Ezekiel described Jerusalem's restoration in terms of a life-giving change in the ecosystem of the Dead Sea for a reason.[5]

The Dead Sea is a large, elongated oval, inland body of water that lies south of the Sea of Galilee at the southern end of the Jordan River. The Dead Sea is about 1,300 feet below sea level, so considerable surface water flows into this natural depression.

It is the geological characteristics of the region, however, that make the Dead Sea one of the most mineral-rich bodies of water in the world. There is no natural outlet, so the only way that water escapes this basin is via evaporation. Yet unlike other bodies of water with no outlet, evaporation at the Dead Sea can occur at amazing rates due to its low elevation and summer

temperatures that reach 125 degrees Fahrenheit. This evaporation increases the salt-to-water ratio, producing a body of water higher in salt content than any other lake or ocean. While oceans have a salt content of around 3.4 percent, the Dead Sea has a salt content that rises to 30 percent at the surface and 33 percent at depth.[6]

The water of the Dead Sea looks inviting from afar, and its high salt content provides great fun for those floating atop its surface (one is unable to submerge or sink). Yet this water will burn the eyes; it is undrinkable, is unsuitable for irrigation, and means nothing but death for the kind of marine life we find in other waters. The intense salinity of this body of water was well-known in antiquity—a point aptly made by artists of the Medeba Map (sixth century AD). On that map, the lifelessness of this lake is illustrated by depicting fish approaching the Dead Sea at the Jordan River's inlet that turn back to escape the brackish water!

As Ezekiel described the new era dawning before his eyes, he saw water cascading from the Temple in

Ibex (wild goats) with the Dead Sea and the mountains of Jordan in the background. © Direct Design

Jerusalem, down the Wadi Kidron, and into the Dead Sea (Ezek. 47:1–8). What is absolutely shocking is what happens when this water gets to the Dead Sea. In Ezekiel's vision, the water becomes fresh (in Hebrew *npr*, "it heals"), turning the sterile and lifeless Dead Sea into a freshwater lake teeming with fish. Instead of swimming away, fish were swimming into it and reproducing so aggressively that commercial fishermen worked their nets near En Gedi and En Eglaim (Ezek. 47:10).[7]

Life was proclaimed for the Dead Sea for a reason. Jerusalem and its Temple had been destroyed, but healing and restoration would come. Things would be turned right side up by the dawn of the new era. The change would be so dramatic and bring such good news that it was depicted by a lifeless Dead Sea becoming filled with life brought about by waters from a new Temple. This forbidding body of water became symbolic of the fulfilled promise of the return of the exiles to the Promised Land. Just as river water brought life in the Garden of Eden (Gen. 2:10–14), so this river

flowing from the Temple would bring hope for new life to come out of the ruins and ashes of Jerusalem. The Dead Sea would come to life—a picture that aptly reveals the new era of hope for the exiles who returned to the Promised Land to rebuild Jerusalem and the Temple.

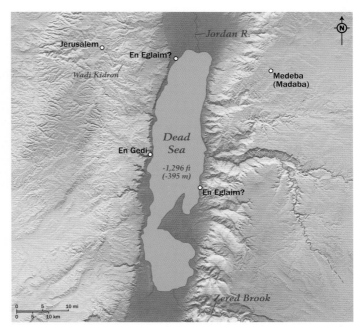

The Dead Sea

The Dead Sea (around 1,300 feet below sea level), with a salinity of about 30 percent, gives one the ability to float without aids.

ISRAELITES FLEE TO EGYPT AGAIN

2 KINGS 25; JEREMIAH 41–46

The Promised Land had seen its fill of Babylonian soldiers and violence. Its fortified cities were battered and beaten. The best and brightest of its citizens had been uprooted from their land and deported to Babylon. Only a small, destitute group was left in Judah. When the army of Babylon withdrew from the Promised Land, they appointed a Jewish governor, Gedaliah, and charged him with ruling what was left of Judah. But within weeks of the day Gedaliah took office, other leaders from Judah assassinated him, his entourage, and some of the remaining Babylonians (2 Kings 25:22–25; Jer. 41:1–3). This act was sure to provoke Babylonian anger, and the remaining inhabitants of Judah were filled with the fear of another reprisal that would set the land ablaze. So for this reason some of the Israelites fled to Egypt.

It was not long before the remnant in Judah was frantically packing everything they could carry. It was time to get out while the getting was still good (Jer. 41:16–18). Even Jeremiah was seized and carried to the city of Tahpanhes in northeastern Egypt (Jer. 43:6–7).[8] Other Israelites settled all along the Nile River from Upper to Lower Egypt in places like Migdol, Memphis, and even Yeb (Elephantine).[9]

What was it that drew these Israelites to Egypt even in the face of the Lord's clear prohibition against such

Excavations at Elephantine, where Israelites built a temple during the time of Jeremiah (view looking west).

a trip (Jer. 42:19)? The abundant natural resources of Egypt made the trip south appear attractive. When displaced from home and country, their first impulse from a human perspective was to go to the closest place that had a rich supply of food and water. This is what had drawn the families of Abram and Jacob to Egypt in an earlier age when famine coursed through the Promised Land (Gen. 12:1–20; 46:1–7). What is more, while Israelites had been suffering the pain of foreign invasion from Babylon, Egypt had been prospering under the leadership of Pharaoh Hophra.[10]

In addition to strong natural resources, these Jewish families were attracted to what they thought was a greater sense of personal security. While Egypt had

View from Elephantine, with the Nile River in the background (view looking southwest).

been an on-again, off-again ally throughout Israel's history, public perception was now guided by this motto: "The enemy of my enemy is my friend." Since Egypt had regularly opposed Babylon and could still field a strong army, the refugees began to trust in Egypt for some type of security. Following the assassination of Gedaliah by Ishmael (Jer. 41:2), a group of Israelites came to Jeremiah. They were inclined to leave for Egypt but asked him to consult the Lord on their behalf. Should they go to Egypt or remain in the Promised Land? The Lord's answer was crystal clear. He promised these trembling people of Judah that if they stayed in their homeland, they would live much better lives and actually receive those things they wished to gain in Egypt (Jer. 42:10). Of course in doing so, the Lord asked his people to step out with faith that looked beyond the current circumstances. These same people who had asked for God's input rejected his direction and assurances. They seized Jeremiah and headed into Egypt, where they further immersed themselves in the idolatry they had been warned against (Jer. 44:7–19).

Fearing another Babylonian attack, some of the Israelites fled to Egypt. The Lord had called these terrified Israelites to remain in Judah—the land God had promised Abraham and his descendants. But rejecting his promises, they fled to Egypt seeking prosperity and security among the idols of foreign rulers. So it was that the Israelites went down to Egypt again—rejecting the giver of true security for a temporary reprieve.

Judeans flee to Egypt before Babylonian army, ca. 560 BC

This alabaster sphinx from Egypt's Eighteenth Dynasty had been here at Memphis approximately one thousand years by the time Israelites settled in the area during the time of Jeremiah.

OBADIAH EXPOSES EDOM'S PRIDE
OBADIAH

While many people were either fleeing to Egypt or being deported to Babylon, the Edomites were adding to Judah's misery by taking advantage of their national crisis.[11] God's response to Edom comes in the book of Obadiah. Its inspired writer was aware of the significance of the geographic setting of the events of which he spoke. Edom's exceeding pride, its cruel treatment of the Hebrew people, and its coming judgment all had a connection to where its citizens lived.

The Edomites were related to the Israelites through Abraham's grandson Esau.[12] While the Lord had given the Promised Land to the descendants of Abraham, Isaac, and Jacob, he had also given Edom to Esau. The Lord's land gift to Esau was one the Israelites were instructed to respect (Deut. 2:2–6). This homeland God had given the Edomites offered strong security and lucrative trade. Their homes were nestled in the mountains of Edom that stretch 110 miles from the Zered River to the Gulf of Aqaba. Looking upward and eastward from the Arabah (i.e., the valley that extends from the southern end of the Dead Sea to the Gulf of Aqaba), our eyes see the mountains of Edom rise from the plain,

The area of Petra in the region of Edom.

reaching elevations that exceed 5,600 feet. From the perspective of those who lived below, these were people who made their homes with the eagles (Jer. 49:16). In antiquity, those who held the high ground had a strategic advantage, particularly when the high ground stretched miles and miles in either direction.[13] When its residents wished to deny access to the interior of Edom, their decision was nearly impossible to challenge (Num. 20:14–21). The homeland of Edom also connected to the markets of the world since the King's Highway traveled along its central ridge.[14] As

The mountains of Edom.

owners of this land, the Edomites were able to tax and/or market with the traders following various caravan routes over the mountain passes.

Due to their geographic setting, the Edomites had developed a false confidence. We see this as Obadiah began his prophecy against Edom:

> The pride of your heart has deceived you,
> you who live in the clefts of the rocks
> and make your home on the heights,
> you who say to yourself,
> "Who can bring me down to the ground?"
>
> Obadiah 1:3

The Edomites had been treating their extended family, the Israelites (Num. 20:14), with contempt. They "stood aloof" while Jerusalem was plundered by the Babylonians; they looked down on her misfortune and on her calamity (Obad. 1:11–13).

In the context of the Babylonian invasion, these highlanders celebrated Judah's demise, seized the assets they could carry off, and even blocked the roads on which refugees were trying to flee (Obad. 1:11–14). These attitudes and actions did not go unnoticed by the Lord. Earlier Edomites had denied Moses passage through their land during the Exodus (Num. 20:18). Now the Israelites were being attacked by Babylon, but that did not mean the Lord had invited Edom to participate in the process! So the Edomites' behavior would result in their destruction (Ezek. 25:12–14; 35:15).

The Lord gave Obadiah a message for the Edomites, who lived in their secure mountain fortress for a reason. This high-living people were reminded that the Lord held an even higher position. God's message was clear:

> Though you soar like the eagle
> and make your nest among the stars,
> from there I will bring you down.
>
> Obadiah 1:4

And he would do so by giving support to those living at lower elevations so they might find success against those living above. "People from the Negev will occupy the mountains of Esau" (Obad. 1:19; see also v. 21).

Wadi Rum in the region of Edom.

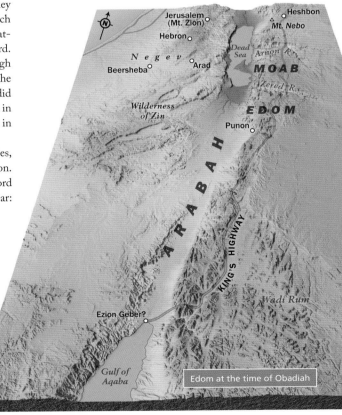

Edom at the time of Obadiah

REBUILDING JERUSALEM'S TEMPLE

EZRA

The Edomites had celebrated the Babylonian destruction of Jerusalem's Temple (586 BC) and the exile of many inhabitants of the Southern Kingdom. The sons of Esau even took advantage of the sons of Jacob, who were in misery, by taking away their goods while they were helpless. In contrast, the conquering of Babylon by Persian King Cyrus in 539 BC opened new opportunities for the Israelites. The Lord had informed the Southern Kingdom that its captivity would be limited to seventy years (Jer. 25:11–12). The time had come for the Lord's promise to be fulfilled. Within two years of Babylon's defeat by Cyrus, a group of exiles returned to Jerusalem. Within three years the foundation of the Temple had been laid, and the new Temple itself was completed in 516 BC (Ezra 6:15).

The Persians, who at the time controlled the world from modern Greece to India and south to Ethiopia, wanted the Temple rebuilt in Jerusalem. From the Persian perspective, the return of the exiles and rebuilding project was consistent with their larger national strategy. While the earlier invaders, Assyrians and Babylonians, had made a practice of deporting residents of conquered territories and despoiling their worship centers, the Persians had just the opposite policy. They encouraged

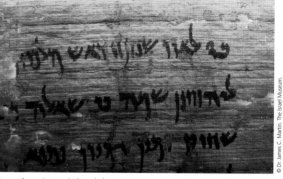

Samaritan Aramaic legal document written on papyrus (ca. 375–335 BC). When Jewish leaders returned from exile to rebuild the Temple, their rejection of help from the Samaritans led to centuries of tension between the two groups.

displaced peoples to return to their homeland and re-establish worship there.[15]

Although the coast of the Promised Land was exploding with new wealth and the promise of prosperity, many returning from captivity settled in Jerusalem to rebuild the Lord's Temple on the site of its predecessor for a reason.[16] These Jews returning from captivity to the Promised Land represented those whose hearts had been stirred by God for this assignment to rebuild the Temple (Ezra 1:5), and they wanted to get things right this

The Cyrus Cylinder. Cyrus issued a decree that allowed the Jews in exile to return to Jerusalem to rebuild the Temple.

time. That made the decision about where to live and where to rebuild the Temple one that was given careful thought. There were at least three advantages to rebuilding the Temple on its old site.

First, it allowed the returning Jewish community to reclaim the historical and religious high ground that this location represented. David had taken Jerusalem as his capital city, and the hope for a messianic deliverer became intertwined with its buildings and streets (2 Sam. 7:5–16). Also, the first Temple that Solomon had built there made it the focal point of Israelite identity and expectations. This was the city and Temple location God had chosen. The Babylonians had destroyed Jerusalem and the Temple; restoration of the Temple in Jerusalem would now be a visual aid of God's faithfulness, foresight, and capability to keep his part of his covenant with the descendants of Abraham.

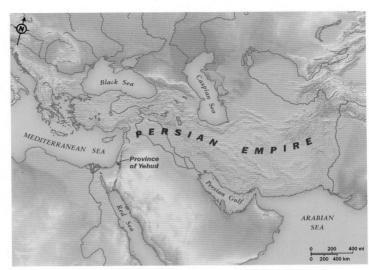

Persian Empire and the province of Yehud (Judah)

Second, the reconstruction of the Temple on its original site was likely to recall the pain of idolatry in the nation's previous history. Some of the very same stones that had been knocked down by Babylonian soldiers would be reclaimed and used in the new Temple. Building somewhere else would put these bad memories out of sight, but these stones that heard the warnings related through Jeremiah and felt the blows of Babylonian soldiers were visual reminders of what it meant to abandon exclusive worship of the Lord—painful yet worthwhile reminders.

Third, the rebuilding of the Temple on this location would bring vindication for the Lord. The Babylonians had removed worship items from the Temple sanctuaries and sent them back to Babylon in humiliation before the victors (cf. 1 Samuel 5). Then in 586 BC Persian King Cyrus directed that those items be returned (Ezra 1:7–8).

The return of its contents and rebuilding of the Temple at its original location happened for a reason. The returning Jewish community could reclaim its historical

The base of this tower excavated in Jerusalem dates to the days of Ezra and Nehemiah.

and religious heritage, be reminded of past idolatry and its consequences, and proclaim the Lord's faithfulness in the fulfilled promise of a return after seventy years (Jer. 25:12–14; 29:10–14).

SOME JEWISH EXILES REMAIN IN PERSIA

ESTHER, DANIEL

The exiles from Judah had spent seventy years as captives of the Babylonians. After Babylon's defeat, the victorious Persian King Cyrus set those captives free (2 Chron. 36:23). Many, though not all (Ezra 2; Nehemiah 7), took advantage of this right of return. Others remained in Persia for a reason.

The routine of daily living was very different for Jews in Persia when compared to the Persian district of Yehud.[17] The glorious days of a wealthy Judah, with its sophisticated architecture and art, had been replaced by a more austere lifestyle.[18] In contrast, the Persian monarchs had built magnificent cities in their land, such as Ecbatana, Persepolis, and Susa. Each was filled with its own beautiful art and stunning architecture.[19] Reaching its zenith during the days of Darius I, the culture of Persia was known as the most advanced of its time. Among other strengths, Persian citizens could justifiably be proud of their enhanced legal system, the freshly minted coins in circulation, and the postal system that used couriers on horseback traversing the length of the Royal Road from Susa (in modern Iran) to Sardis (in modern western Turkey).[20]

The fact that they had already adjusted to living in a healthy economy may have played a role in the decision of some Judean captives to remain in Persia. The cultural expansion described above was powered by increasing wealth within the nation. The architecture from this period in Persepolis still looks opulent by today's standards as does the royal feast with all its embellishments described in the first chapter of Esther. While not everyone

Achaemenid palace at Persepolis, used during the periods of Darius I (522–486 BC), Xerxes (486–465 BC), Artaxerxes I (465–424), and Artaxerxes III (359–338).

benefited from the wealth of this expanding empire in the same way, the Jewish historian Josephus notes that many Jews elected not to return to their homeland. Those who remained in the foreign lands had been accumulating wealth,[21] evident in the gifts sent back to Jerusalem by those who did not return (Ezra 1:6). Thus, many Jews, though free to leave Persia, decided to stay.

Yet wealth was not the only thing that motivated Jews to remain abroad. Some who remained in Persia, such as Daniel and Esther, became powerful witnesses of the one true God. The Lord placed Daniel (ca. 605–536 BC) in

Inscription of Xerxes I (486–465 BC), son of Darius I, describing his building projects.

© Dr. James C. Martin. Mus'ee du Louvre; Autorisation de photographer et de filmer—LOUVRE.

the highest governmental positions in Babylon and later in Persia. He stayed true to the Lord even when facing the depths of the lion's den (Daniel 6), thus providing a witness to those governments and their captives alike. Esther, in the events described in the book bearing her name (ca. 484–474 BC), shaped public policy in ways that provided security and success for Jews throughout Persia. As this young Jewish woman found herself rising to the status of the favored queen of Xerxes, she kept her national heritage secret until the day she could keep the secret no longer. Haman, an enemy of her people, manipulated Esther's husband into issuing a decree that would annihilate Jews across his grand empire (Esther 3:8–14). At the right moment Esther's elder cousin, Mordecai, came to her with the encourage-

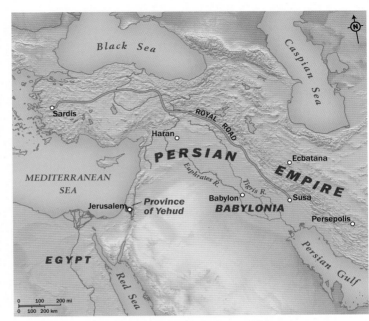

Central and western Persia, ca. 500 BC

ment to reveal her national identity. He prodded her to action with the telling question, "And who knows but that you have come to royal position for such a time as this?" (Esther 4:14). And there it was. Esther had not returned to the Promised Land, yet she had great influence where she was, reversing the plot against her people and providing them with a more secure standing than they had before (Esther 9–14).

There was great excitement in hearing of the edict of Cyrus that allowed exiled Israelites to return to the Promised Land. Some, however, like Daniel and Esther, chose to remain in Persia for a reason. Their presence not only offered encouragement to Jews living in the Persian Diaspora but in some cases was responsible for the sparing of thousands of lives.

Frieze with relief of Persepolis guards.

THE ABOMINATION THAT CAUSES DESOLATION AT THE TEMPLE

DANIEL 7–12

Although Daniel lived during Babylonian and Medo-Persian periods, the Lord gave him a glimpse of the coming Greek and Roman Empires. Of particular interest is the prophecy regarding a future enemy of God's Kingdom: "His armed forces will rise up to desecrate the temple fortress and will abolish the daily sacrifice. Then they will set up the abomination that causes desolation" (Dan. 11:31). This occurred in Jerusalem's Temple in 168 BC under the Greek ruler Antiochus IV Epiphanes (175–164 BC), and it happened where it did for a reason.

Following the desires of his father, Alexander the Great led the Greek army in a bid to overcome the Persian Empire. Combining superior military tactics with winning leadership, Alexander marched across the Dardanelles in 334 BC and did not stop his conquest until the Greek army had reached the Indus River. During this conquest, the Promised Land came under the control of the Greeks.[22]

At the death of Alexander the Great, the time of the Ptolemies and Seleucids began. His "successors" (*diadochoi*) fought for the right to govern what Alexander's conquests had won. Two of those successors come into the spotlight of history—Ptolemy and Seleucus. Each formed a dynasty ruling in separate portions of Alexander's empire. The Ptolemies ruled Egypt while the Seleucids ruled Syria and Mesopotamia. Because both these ruling dynasties wanted to dominate the

King Antiochus III of Syria (223–187 BC).

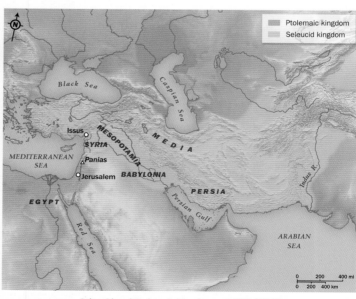

Seleucid and Ptolemaic kingdoms, ca. 323–198 BC

The so-called "Alexander Sarcophagus" (fourth century BC) portrays Alexander the Great fighting against the Persians at the Battle of Issus.

other and because the Promised Land resided between them, Israel became a battleground on which these two kingdoms fought for decades. At first the Ptolemies enjoyed control over the land of Israel. They were interested in building a united Greek state, but they allowed those living in the Promised Land relative independence in exchange for nominal loyalty and the payment of taxes.[23] But following a seventy-five-year war between the Ptolemies and Seleucids (the Syrian Wars), the latter won a defining victory at Panias (later known as Caesarea Philippi), located on Israel's northern border at the base of Mount Hermon—a victory that established Seleucid rule in the Promised Land.[24] While the Seleucids were fighting the Ptolemies, they were also fighting with Rome and losing. The Peace of Apamea treaty (189 BC) ended the Greek war with Rome and in turn ended the Seleucid control of Asia Minor. The Romans imposed a serious war tribute on the Seleucids that weighed heavily on Antiochus IV (175–164 BC).

In a bid to unite his kingdom and improve revenue, Antiochus IV began a program of oppression. The plan of Antiochus IV was to Hellenize Jerusalem and Judea, a process that would take place over a number of years. As those years unfolded, we find an increasing imposition of Greek culture in the Promised Land. This king's need for power and influence quickly turned to the high priesthood. He deposed the legitimate priestly family of the Zadokites, who had led God's people since the time of Solomon. In their place he appointed priests who promised to provide him with the most income and who were willing to support his efforts to Hellenize the Jewish regions.[25] When he needed even more money than the corrupt high priest

Silver tetradrachm of Antiochus IV Epiphanes (215–164 BC) wearing the royal diadem.
© Dr. James C. Martin. The Eretz Israel Museum.

could offer, Antiochus himself entered the Temple and looted its precincts and treasury.[26] But not even this was enough for Antiochus. He demanded resolute loyalty from Jerusalem, which in his eyes meant that the people there had to adopt all the ways of Greek culture. Torah scrolls were burned, the Sabbath was not observed, the distinctive Jewish diet was outlawed, and those who circumcised their children were executed.[27]

The "abomination that causes desolation" happened at the Temple in Jerusalem for a reason. In a culminating act meant to deal a deathblow to Jewish identity and strengthen the Seleucid Empire, Antiochus IV renamed the Lord's Temple in honor of Olympian Zeus and ordered that a pig be sacrificed in the sanctuary.[28] Thus the prophecy of Daniel was fulfilled: "the abomination that causes desolation" came to Jerusalem's Temple (Dan. 11:31).

Bronze statuette of a sacrificial boar. Antiochus IV desecrated Jerusalem's Temple by sacrificing a pig on the Temple altar. © Dr. James C. Martin. The British Museum.

PART 7

THE BIRTH
AND EARLY YEARS
OF JESUS

Sheep and goats outside Bethlehem.

MATTHEW 1–4; LUKE 1–4; JOHN 1

Among those who honored the proclamation of Moses and the prophets were those who eagerly awaited the arrival of the anointed Rescuer, also known as the Son of Man, the Prophet, and the Son of David. While this longing persisted through the time between the return of the exiles and the opening pages of the Gospels, geopolitical and social changes had created a very new environment in the land of Canaan. The regional map of the Promised Land during the Greek and Roman periods took on a new appearance. These empires seized the Promised Land and subdivided it according to their own plans. Galilee, Samaria, Judea, the Decapolis, and Perea all found places on the new map. The Romans also brought in new and more complex politics. At the time of Jesus's birth, Herod the Great, the official king of Israel, was not a descendant of David but an Idumean political appointee of the Roman Senate.

Religious life in the country was also in flux. The Temple rituals and services were still in full swing but were marred by a corrupt leadership of a religious party known as the Sadducees. The Pharisees, on the other hand, made their influence felt in the synagogues that dotted the Promised Land. There the Scriptures were read, but the intended meaning was often lost in the interpretation of the rabbis. And sadly, for many the anticipation of the coming Messiah was also corrupted. They longed for a politician descended from David who would overthrow the Romans and restore political independence to Israel.

Part 7 explores the birth and early years of Jesus in order to reveal how these events related to their locations. We will journey from Nazareth to Bethlehem and the manger. We will travel to the shepherds' fields in order to review how Jesus's birth, the angels' visit, the adoration of the Magi (wise men), and Herod's paranoia all have important connections to location. But our stay in Bethlehem will be very short. No sooner had Jesus arrived in the Promised Land than we see him whisked away to Egypt. We will explore why some in Egypt safeguarded the precious promises of God. Following the sojourn in Egypt, it is back to Nazareth and then to the Temple in Jerusalem, when Jesus was twelve years of age.

The next time we meet Jesus, nearly two decades later, he has traveled to the Jordan River where John baptized him in a setting suited to the meaning of this event. The baptism of Jesus was such a threat to Satan that he immediately sought to destroy Jesus's mission through three temptations. We will explore how setting played a role in each of the temptations. And finally, we will see that Nazareth was Jesus's hometown—a fact that often shaped the initial response to Jesus's messianic authority and fulfilled the words of the prophets. Many things had changed since the return of the exiles, but this one thing remained the same: the events of Jesus's birth and early years happened where they did for a reason.

The palace-fortress of Herod the Great, called the Herodium, was built about three miles southeast of Bethlehem (ca. 15 BC).

Seats like this basalt stone seat discovered in the ancient synagogue at Korazin were known as the Seat of Moses (Matt. 23:1–2).

© Dr. James C. Martin. The Israel Museum.

This synagogue at Gamla (located on the hills on the northeast side of the Sea of Galilee) was in use when the disciples were sent by Jesus to various villages in the area.

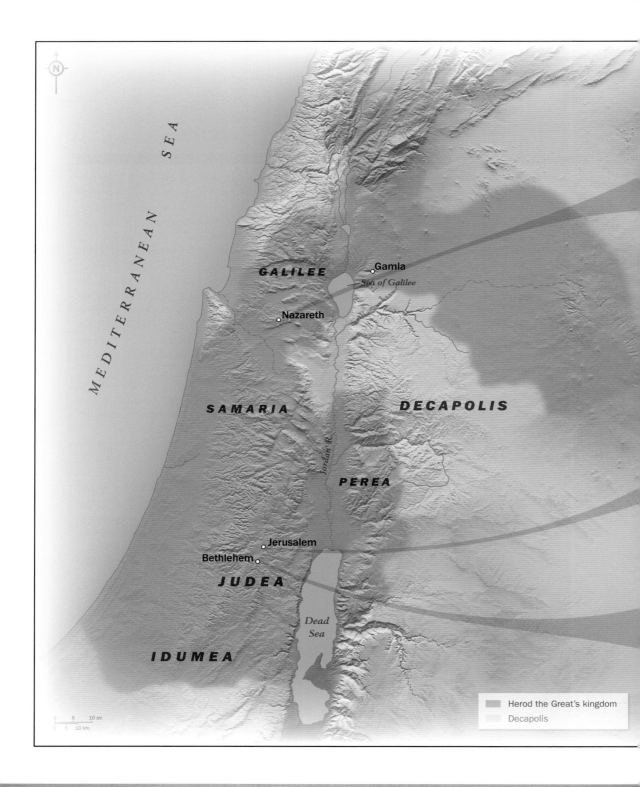

MEDITERRANEAN SEA

GALILEE

Gamla

Sea of Galilee

Nazareth

SAMARIA

DECAPOLIS

Jordan R.

PEREA

Jerusalem

Bethlehem

JUDEA

Dead Sea

IDUMEA

Herod the Great's kingdom

Decapolis

0   5   10 mi
0   5   10 km

The Birth and Early Years of Jesus

The Church of Annunciation in Nazareth. The angel Gabriel visited Mary in Nazareth. The site is now marked by the Church of Annunciation, which is built over much of the ancient village.

Model of the Jerusalem Temple platform (view looking north). The main entrance into the Temple was from the south, where Joseph and Mary brought Jesus to be dedicated as an infant.

Bethlehem. A shepherd near Bethlehem takes his flocks into the grain fields after the harvest is complete.

THE BIRTH OF JESUS
IN BETHLEHEM
LUKE 2:1–7

Mary and Joseph were betrothed and living in Nazareth when the angel Gabriel announced the coming birth of Jesus. But Bethlehem, not Nazareth, provided the environs for Jesus's birth. A Roman census initiated by Caesar Augustus required everyone who owned property to register it in person for taxation purposes. Because Joseph was from Bethlehem, the census set Mary and Joseph on the road to that village (Luke 2:1–4). During their stay, Mary gave birth to her son and placed him in a manger—events that happened where they did for a reason.

The Gospel writers make special effort to be sure we know that Jesus was born in Bethlehem (Matt. 2:5–6; Luke 2:4–7). Matthew goes a step further by telling why this detail is so important. It happened there to fulfill a promise the Lord had made through the prophet Micah:

> But you, Bethlehem Ephrathah,
>   though you are small among the clans of
>   Judah,
> out of you will come for me
> one who will be ruler over Israel,
> whose origins are from of old,
> from ancient times.
>
>   Micah 5:2[1]

Facade of the entrance of a house similar to Jesus's birthplace.

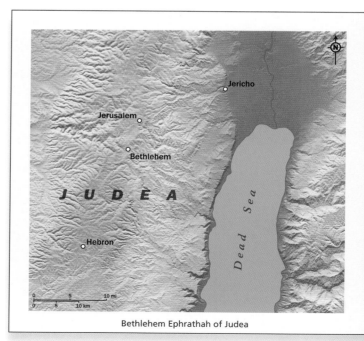

Bethlehem Ephrathah of Judea

The main living area of the style of house where Jesus was born was built over a cave (basement) that held livestock.

breath in carefully cleaned rooms within the palace. Not so with this King. An animal feeding trough, not the guest room (*kataluma*),[2] welcomed this monarch (Luke 2:7). Such mangers are found in animal shelters, and in first-century Bethlehem of Judah, animal shelters were typically associated with caves. In this region, many families built their homes over caves. The cave was used as a basement in which the family's animals were kept.[3] Through several unique turns down the road of Roman history, the identity of the area in which Jesus was born has been preserved by the Church of the Nativity in Bethlehem.[4]

Events surrounding the birth of Jesus happened where they did for a reason. Jesus's identity as the promised Messiah was affirmed by his birth in Bethlehem; he was and is the legitimate King. He continued the throne of David and established the Kingdom of God. Mangers (i.e., feeding troughs) were common in ancient Israel but not common to royal birthing chambers. The lowly circumstances into which he was born, however, sent quite a different message about the character of this monarch, lest anyone think of him as privileged royalty unconnected with his subjects and distant from his people. Jesus could have been born in David's Jerusalem under the shadow of the Temple, but he was born in David's Bethlehem under the shadow of Micah's prophecy. A royal birth in a decidedly ordinary place resets our expectations about this monarch sent from God.

Many babies were born in the Promised Land, but only a child born in Bethlehem qualified for consideration as the promised Messiah.

Why did the Lord pick Bethlehem? This was David's hometown (1 Sam. 16:4), a village that had enjoyed a very long association with David's ancestors (Ruth 1:1; 4:13–22). To think about Bethlehem was to think about David. To think about David meant to think about the powerful promise the Lord had given him. One of David's descendants would rise to sit on Israel's throne and rule an eternal kingdom (2 Sam. 7:12–16). Thus an important link was forged through family history and prophecy. The promise of the royal Rescuer from the line of King David would be fulfilled in his hometown, Bethlehem.

While Jesus's birth in Bethlehem confirmed his identity as the Messiah, the specific place of his birth in Bethlehem suggested there was something different about this King. Other royal descendants of David who had risen to the throne drew their first

Some feeding troughs (i.e., mangers) were made out of mud.

THE ANGELS' ANNOUNCEMENT TO SHEPHERDS IN THE FIELDS

LUKE 2:8–20

Angels had been waiting excitedly to announce the good news that would forever change the world. When the time came, they appeared over the fields of Bethlehem. As the shepherds watched their flocks that evening, angels shattered the night air with shouts and singing that echoed through the hills. Brilliant lights and booming voices sent the fear-filled shepherds scurrying for cover. When they found their feet, the shepherds realized that angels had delivered the message to them in these fields for a reason (Luke 2:8–20).

The village of Bethlehem was well known for its grain fields. In most parts of Judea,[5] the narrow valleys that wind between the mountains provide limited space for field crops. Not so in the areas just east of Bethlehem. Here the valleys open and widen allowing farmers to plant acres of barley and wheat.[6] While that precious grain was growing in the fields, the shepherds with their hungry flocks were required to keep their distance. But following the harvest, the shepherds were invited to bring their animals to the fields to nose through the stubble in search of kernels that had fallen through the hands of the harvesters. In return, the flocks left behind a deposit of manure that fertilized the soil in advance of the next planting season. Shepherds tending flocks

Caves in the Bethlehem area were used as sheepfolds.

in these fields received the remarkable announcement of the Messiah's birth.

Why did the angels bring this announcement of the new King's birth to shepherds, and why to shepherds in the fields of Bethlehem? On the one hand, shepherds might be regarded as representatives of those who needed the message more than most. On the social scale of first-century Judea, shepherds ranked very near the bottom. Traditional Jewish teaching discouraged children from becoming shepherds because "their trade is the trade of thieves."[7] For that reason, no family was to purchase wool, milk, or young goats directly from a shepherd since these products were most likely stolen from their rightful owner.[8] From the first-century perspective, shepherds needed more forgiveness and acceptance than most, so it is fitting that the announcement came to those who might value it the most.

On the other hand, these shepherds also connect to

Sarcophagus frieze (300–330 AD) of the adoration of the shepherds.

another set of shepherds we met earlier in Scripture: Abraham, Jacob, Moses, and David (Gen. 13:7; 46:32; Exod. 3:1; 1 Sam. 16:11). In each case, these previous shepherds received key components of God's plan to rescue the world and anxiously awaited the day of Jesus's birth. They died without realizing that dream, but the shepherds of Bethlehem who heard the angels' message saw the fulfillment of all the promises the Lord had made to those shepherds of an earlier time.

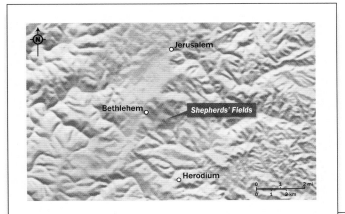

The angels could have appeared to shepherds who lived anywhere in the Promised Land. Why did they come to the shepherds watching their flocks in these fields around Bethlehem? There was something special about the fields east of Bethlehem for they were used to raise a unique set of animals. Historically, these were the fields where the Temple shepherds cared for the animals that were used for sacrifices in Jerusalem.[9] If that is the case, we find the announcement of the angels taking on new meaning, for the lambs over which the announcement of Jesus's birth was trumpeted—the lambs destined for sacrifice at the Temple—were about to find their true purpose as symbols of the Lamb of God, who would take away the sins of the world. No wonder these shepherds returned from the manger praising and glorifying God. They realized that the angels had come to announce the birth of Jesus to them in these fields for a reason.

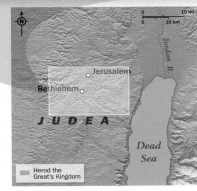

Grain fields around Bethlehem

"Shepherds' Fields" is a generic term for the agricultural grain fields east of Bethlehem.

THE MAGI AND HEROD'S SOLDIERS DESCEND ON BETHLEHEM

MATTHEW 2:1–12

Following the birth of Jesus, Joseph and Mary remained in Bethlehem for many months. Apart from the shepherds who visited this family, the Bible tells us about two other groups who went to find Jesus in Bethlehem: the Magi (wise men) and Herod's soldiers. One group traveled a very long distance while another traveled a very short distance. One group was armed with gifts while the other was armed with swords. One group came to honor the Christ child and the other came to eliminate him. Treasure and terror descended upon the village of Bethlehem for a reason (Matt. 2:1–12).

We know little about the Magi who journeyed from the east to find Jesus. It is possible they were descendants of Jews who had been sent east during the Babylonian captivity in the time of Daniel and who now returned to their homeland seeking the Messiah.[10] What is striking is that the sophistication of their inquiry

and the expensive gifts they carried suggest they were official representatives sent as emissaries to honor the new King of this ancient land. They began their trip in the "east" (Matt. 2:1). The most compelling evidence suggests that these visitors came to the Promised Land from Parthia and so had traveled the International Highway for months.[11]

They had come to Bethlehem because they believed that the legitimate King of the Jews had been born. A star had appeared that suggested that the promise of the Lord made in Numbers 24:17 had come to pass: "A star will come out of Jacob; a scepter will rise out of Israel." This expectation of a royal Messiah had continued to live among those who had been exiled to the east by the Babylonians. And in the footsteps of faithful Israelites like Daniel, they too anticipated the coming of the Messiah. Consequently, they followed the star that was leading them across hundreds of miles in order to honor the newborn King with their treasures.

But Herod the Great had quite a different reception in mind for Jesus and a very different reason for sending visitors to Bethlehem. Herod was an Idumean whose family was trusted by the leadership in Rome. Several decades before Jesus was born, Jewish loyalists had enlisted the aid of Parthians (Persians) to drive Herod and his family from power in Jerusalem. Herod fled to Rome, where the Roman Senate honored him with the title "King of the Jews." But when Herod returned to Israel in 37 BC, he had to fight long and hard for the right to bear that title. Since that

This sandstone stela from 100 BC–AD 100 represents Parthian dress. © Dr. James C. Martin. The Istanbul Archaeological Museum.

Herod the Great had his name inscribed on certain coins minted during his reign.

Sarcophagus scene (fourth century AD) of the adoration of the Magi.

time, he had ruthlessly defended it against all those whom he saw as a threat, even killing his own sons and wives when he felt they were conspiring to remove him from the throne.[12]

The Magi entered Jerusalem with Herod's royal paranoia still intact. Given the expensive gifts these Parthian wise men were bearing, they would have entered the city of Jerusalem with an armed escort. We can only imagine the panic that must have occurred in Herod and his court when they heard that men from the east were in Jerusalem looking for the legitimate "King of the Jews." Such news got Herod's attention in a big way. Some thirty years had passed since Herod's last encounter with Parthians. Since he was in no position to begin a war, he began to gather from the Magi all the information he could under the guise of longing to worship this Jewish king. When he learned that his rival was a child living in Bethlehem, Herod dispatched his soldiers to kill every male two years of age and under in the village. Apart from the shepherds, two other very different groups had come seeking the child Messiah in Bethlehem. And so it was that treasure and terror descended upon Bethlehem for two very different reasons.

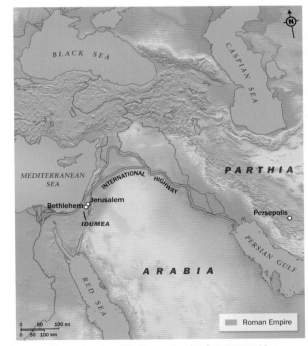

Eastern border of the Roman Empire, first century AD

THE FLIGHT TO EGYPT

MATTHEW 2:13–20

Brimming with paranoia over the newborn King of the Jews, Herod the Great dispatched soldiers to Bethlehem on a heinous quest. They were to find and kill all boys in Bethlehem two years of age and under. This made it necessary for the vulnerable infant Messiah to be rescued so that later he could rescue the world. Therefore the Lord sent an angel to Joseph in a dream with this urgent message: "Take the child and his mother and escape to Egypt" (Matt. 2:13). The pressing command rings with irony. In Moses's time, the pharaoh of Egypt ordered the execution of Israelite male infants just before the Israelite exodus from Egypt to the safer reaches of the Promised Land (Exod. 1). Now the slaughter of Israelite children in the Promised Land brought about a flight to the safer reaches of Egypt. Though we are not always aware of God's greater plan, we can see purposeful reasons in Joseph being led by the Lord to Egypt (Matt. 2:13–18; Hosea 11:1).

While Matthew tells us about the start of this journey, exact routes and destination in Egypt are unknown. It is likely that Joseph and his family fled by the quickest route to Gaza, where they could join the International Highway. From Gaza, the family would travel as far as Pelusium, the portal of entry for greater Egypt. That is where things become less certain, so we must admit that locations visited by Jesus and his family during their stay in Egypt remain as much a mystery to us as they did to those who pursued them.

We can be a bit more certain about why they were sent to Egypt. It lay well outside Herod's influence and had numerous, thriving Jewish centers. It was no accident that the influence of Herod the Great stopped at the border of Egypt. During the contentious days following the death of Julius

Scuola Nuova tapestry (Brussels, AD 1524–31) with the scene of the massacre of the innocents.

Caesar, Mark Antony achieved mastery over Syria while investing romantic energy in Cleopatra VII. Her passion to possess key portions of the Promised Land was indulged by Antony at the expense of Herod. Large and significant tracts of Herod's holdings were transferred into the hands of Cleopatra in 35 BC. But just five years later, Antony and Cleopatra took their own lives, allowing Herod to regain control of land he had lost to her. From that time on, Herod's word was law in the Promised Land. Nevertheless, the legacy of Antony and Cleopatra meant that Herod's control never reached

Tetradrachm of Cleopatra VII.

deeply into Egypt, so it was the closest region that lay beyond his control.[13]

Another reason Egypt was such a desirable haven is that it held thriving Jewish communities. During earlier assaults on the Promised Land, Jews fled to various places throughout Upper and Lower Egypt (Isa. 11:11). Descendants of those Jewish refugees remained and formed the largest and most affluent Jewish population in the Diaspora.[14] This included the descendants of the true Zadokite priesthood functioning at the temple of Onias in Leontopolis.[15]

Perhaps the reason the Lord instructed Joseph to take the family to Egypt was not only to escape from Herod but also to go toward faithful members of their extended Jewish family who might welcome them and provide support during their time of exile. It is strikingly ironic that Jesus left the Promised Land for Egypt ahead of the killing in Bethlehem. Just as God had instigated Jacob's move to Egypt centuries earlier, now the Lord instructed Joseph to take Mary and Jesus. It made perfect sense in terms of what Egypt had to offer: a harbor of safety from Herod's soldiers and a community of Jewish families who wished to separate themselves from the corrupt leadership of the Jerusalem Temple.

Eastern border of the Roman Empire, first century AD

Leontopolis—Tell el-Yahudiya, twenty miles north of Cairo.

AT THE AGE OF TWELVE JESUS TRAVELS TO THE TEMPLE

LUKE 2:41–52

etween his return from Egypt to Nazareth and his baptism, the Gospels relate a significant journey of Jesus that reveals that he is already set on the course of his Father's will. At age twelve he traveled with his parents to the Temple in Jerusalem (Luke 2:41–52). We will see that he made this trip to this place at this time in his life for a reason.

The fact that this family was traveling to Jerusalem is not surprising. The Lord had directed the Israelites to travel to the Temple three times a year for the high festivals (Luke 2:41). These trips served many purposes, one of which was associated with the education of Israelite children. Jesus was raised in Nazareth, where he "grew in wisdom and stature, and in favor with God and men" (Luke 2:52). Since Mary and Joseph are consistently portrayed as faithful Jews, their home must have surrounded Jesus with the in-depth teachings of Scripture (Deut. 6:4–9).[16]

The route from Nazareth to Jerusalem was a reflective experience in itself. Each time Jesus and his family traveled in the caravan along the Ridge Route,[17] they were reliving Israel's history. When they passed Shechem, they could recall God's covenant with Abram (Gen. 12:1–3).

Celebrating the Feast of Tabernacles at the western wall of the Temple Mount.

Perhaps they would have pointed to the spot on Mount Ebal where Joshua built an altar of rededication after entering the Promised Land (Josh. 8:30). While traveling through Bethel, families had the opportunity to recall the words and promises of God spoken there to Jacob (Gen. 28:10–21). As he walked the historic road to Jerusalem, Jesus could review the history of his people and their purpose.

Once Jesus reached Jerusalem a whole array of experiences presented themselves. The remarkable buildings that were part of the Temple complex, the smoke rising from the sacrifices, the intoned rituals, and the readings were also part of his history and purpose. He even participated in the question-and-answer sessions within the Temple, astounding religious scholars with his understanding of Scriptures (Luke 2:46).[18]

What makes this particular trip to Jerusalem so special is what Jesus's presence in Jerusalem teaches about his identity. The lesson has to do with his age. Jesus was twelve years old when he made this recorded visit to Jerusalem (Luke 2:42). This was the age when a young man would practice the skills needed for his Bar Mitzvah, which would occur the following year. More than that, Jesus's twelfth year of life incarnate corresponded to a Jewish expectation about the coming of the Rescuer. The number seventy had become an important number in Judaism. The Babylonians destroyed the Temple in 586 BC, and it was rebuilt by the returning exiles in 517 BC—seventy years later. Thus the number seventy became connected to great acts of divine rescue (Jer. 25:11–12). At age twelve when Jesus remained behind in Jerusalem to be in his Father's house, approximately seventy years had passed since the Romans had seized control of Israel (63 BC). So at the very time when faithful Jews had counted to seventy again and were looking for a deliverer to arise, Jesus was making his unique presence felt in the Temple courts.[19]

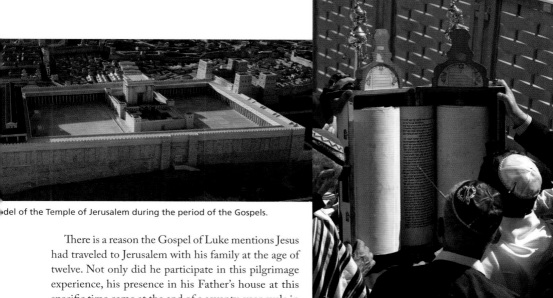

del of the Temple of Jerusalem during the period of the Gospels.

There is a reason the Gospel of Luke mentions Jesus had traveled to Jerusalem with his family at the age of twelve. Not only did he participate in this pilgrimage experience, his presence in his Father's house at this specific time came at the end of a seventy-year cycle in which the doors of messianic hope had begun to open. Shepherds, wise men, Simeon, and the prophetess Anna had already recognized the Promised One (Micah 5:2; Matt. 2:2, 9–12; Luke 2:15, 20, 26, 36–38). The Gospel record of this particular journey had an objective: to help us understand that Jesus was well aware of his purpose and true identity as Messiah from a young age.

Bar Mitzvah celebration at the western wall of the Temple.

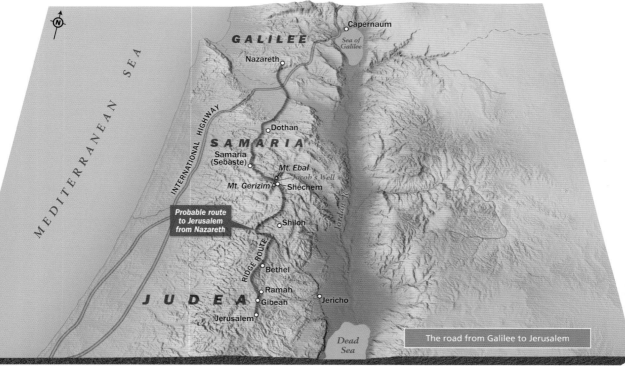

The road from Galilee to Jerusalem

JESUS IS BAPTIZED AT BETHANY ON THE OTHER SIDE OF THE JORDAN

MATTHEW 3:13–17; MARK 1:9–11; LUKE 3:21–22; JOHN 1:29–34

The birth of Jesus brings life-changing news to a sin-ruined world. For that reason the anniversary of his birth deserves all the attention it gets. The day of Jesus's baptism is no less important, for it is the day Jesus emerges from the water with the proclamation that the Kingdom of God has come. Jesus's baptism was the day of his consecration into his rabbinic authority. This meant that his interpretation of the Scriptures would be both welcomed in the conversation and considered authoritative.[20] In many respects Jesus's baptism could have occurred anywhere that an appropriate supply of water existed. But it happened at Bethany on the other side of the Jordan for a reason.[21]

Bethany on the other side of the Jordan, 0.9 miles east of the Jordan River and adjacent to the spring at the head of Wadi Gharrar. On the hill known as Elijah's Hill is the remains of a Byzantine monastery from the fifth or sixth century.

The Jordan River near the village of Bethany on the other side of the Jordan.

An accumulation of the most persuasive evidence places the baptism of Jesus in a location northeast of the Dead Sea in the Jordan Valley. John's Gospel says that this event happened "at Bethany on the other side of the Jordan" (John 1:28).[22] Matthew tells us that John the Baptist was preaching in the Desert of Judea where he addressed crowds that had come from Jerusalem and the region of Judea (Matt. 3:1). All of this suggests that we can seek this Bethany somewhere in the southern reaches of the Jordan Valley on the east side of the river. As early as the fourth century, Christian pilgrims have provided us with reports of a church and monastery dedicated to John the Baptist located opposite Jericho, on the east side of the Jordan River, about four and one-half miles north of the Dead Sea.[23]

Three earlier events that occurred in this area combine to make this spot a powerful setting for Jesus's baptism. The first preceded Israel's entrance into the Promised Land when the multitude of Israelites was encamped on the plains of Moab northeast of the Dead Sea (Num. 22:1). Their presence made the Moabites so nervous that they hired Balaam, who practiced divination, to put a curse on the Israelites. Time after time,

Neo-Assyrian Black Obelisk of Shalmaneser III (858–824 BC), portraying an Israelite robe from the time of Elijah. Elijah transferred authority to Elisha through the passing of the robe (i.e., mantle).

© Dr. James C. Martin. The British Museum.

Balaam's curses became blessings. On his fourth attempt as he looked over Jacob's children, he spoke of one special son of Jacob yet to come:

> I see him, but not now;
> I behold him, but not near.
> A star will come out of Jacob;
> a scepter will rise out of Israel.
>
> Numbers 24:17

What Balaam could see in the distant future as he overlooked the southern Jordan Valley was now emerging from the water in the very region this prophecy was made.

This is also the location where Joshua assumed his role as leader of the Israelites. Moses had led the Israelites for decades, but God made it clear that Joshua, not Moses, was to take the people into the Promised Land (Num. 20:12). The Lord commissioned Joshua through Moses as the new leader of the people of Israel—a consecration that occurred near the future location of Jesus's baptism (Deut. 31:14; 34:9).[24]

Years later a third significant event occurred near the location of Jesus's baptism. Following years of faithful service in the school of the prophets, Elijah left Jericho and crossed the Jordan River, where Elisha saw a chariot and horses of fire carry Elijah away in a whirlwind (2 Kings 2:11). A memorial site where Elisha received Elijah's cloak of authority and saw Elijah's dramatic departure is at a small hill that lies just east of where Jesus was baptized.[25] God had promised the world that before the Messiah's birth a new Elijah would be born and prepare the way (Mal. 4:5). John was this new Elijah (Matt. 11:14; 17:12). By baptizing Jesus near the hill from which Elijah ascended, John was carrying out his assignment that became part of the message—another reason this event happened where it did.

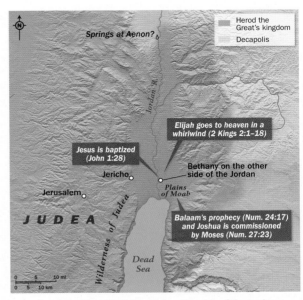

Jesus's baptism at Bethany on the other side of the Jordan

THREE TEMPTATIONS
IN THREE LOCATIONS

MATTHEW 4:1–11

The baptism of Jesus signaled that the Kingdom of God had come. This news set fallen angels scheming for ways to ruin Jesus's rescue mission. After leaving John the Baptist, Jesus was tempted by Satan in three different ways that connect with three different locations. Three temptations, in three locations; each happened where it did for a reason.

Following his baptism, the Spirit led Jesus into the wilderness (Matt. 4:1). The mention of *wilderness* anywhere in the Gospels recalls the forty-year stay of the Israelites in the wilderness at the time of Moses. Although the location of these two events is different, the rugged terrain and lack of natural resources is common to both. In fact, conditions were so harsh for the Israelites in the wilderness of the exodus that the Lord miraculously provided a supply of daily bread. The Lord tested Israel to see if they would follow his instructions regarding this manna from heaven (Exod. 16:4). Now, conversely, the adversary challenged the Son of God to do a similar miracle. Jesus could easily have turned stones into bread, and after forty days of fasting, he was hungry. But he refused and stayed true to the Lord by using a quotation from Deuteronomy that speaks of the manna test in the wilderness (Deut. 8:2–3). Where Israel had failed in the wilderness, Jesus overcame.

For the second temptation, Jesus was taken to the highest point of the Temple at Jerusalem (Matt. 4:5). Herod the Great had invested considerable effort in expanding the confines of the Temple complex.[26] Consequently, it is not clear exactly where on the Temple grounds this temptation occurred. The key point is that it occurred at the Temple.

The Lord had promised that the son of David who would be the Messiah was a man who would take control of the Temple (2 Sam. 7:13). Satan offered Jesus the chance to claim his authority over the Temple prematurely. He invited Jesus to prove his heritage and claim his prize by stepping into thin air, assured that the angels would safeguard his descent to the ground below (Matt. 4:6). This was an entrance those looking for personal gain could only dream about, but Jesus would not participate in such antics. Jesus again rebuked

The Monastery of Temptation on the cliffs above Jericho.

Model of Jerusalem's Temple depicting the pinnacle of the Temple (perhaps the southwest corner of the Temple Mount or one of the corners of the Temple).

the tempter with Scripture that rejected this misuse of God's promises and recalled Deuteronomy 6:16. He would assume leadership of the Temple according to his Father's plan, not Satan's.

Finally the devil took Jesus to a very high mountain (Matt. 4:8). Mountains of varying height are found throughout the Promised Land. The mountain most distinctive because it is the highest in the region is Mount Hermon. At an elevation of 9,232 feet, the snowcapped heights of Mount Hermon can be seen from many places in the Promised Land, and it is so massive that it blocks and funnels traffic moving along its flanks on the International Highway. Consequently, the armies of the ancient world desired control of the Mount Hermon region in order to dominate the commercial, political, and military jurisdiction over the trade routes and resources connecting Asia, Africa, and Europe.

Jesus had come to overthrow the kingdoms of the world and the works of Satan (Psalm 2; 1 John 3:8). He would retake his rightful ownership of God's creation by his death and resurrection. But the adversary promised an easier way—a shortcut that would have resulted in the Lord losing his objective—but Jesus saw through this deception. Thus he replied, "Away from me, Satan! For it is written: 'Worship the Lord your God, and serve him only'" (Matt. 4:10).

Three temptations associated with three locations: bread in the wilderness, worship at the Temple, and political power at Israel's northern border. All offered immediate results without Jesus having to go to the cross. All happened where they did for a reason.

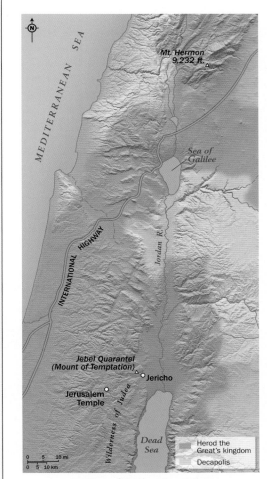

Locations of the three temptations

◀ Saint George's Monastery lies on the northern edge of Wadi Qelt in the Judean Wilderness.

JESUS IS BROUGHT UP IN NAZARETH

JOHN 1:35–51

When we are introduced to someone, we often ask, "Where are you from?" because our hometown says something about who we are. Whether we are from a large city or rural township, the mountain west or the eastern seaboard, our hometown creates flattering and sometimes not so flattering expectations. So where is Jesus from? Within the first two chapters, each of the four Gospel writers answer that question: Jesus is from Nazareth (Matt. 2:23; Mark 1:9; Luke 1:26; 4:16; John 1:45). That news immediately begins to shape expectations, which will show us that Jesus grew up in Nazareth for a reason.

The location and character of Nazareth are noteworthy in that both are so little worthy of note. Nazareth is located in the northern portion of the Promised Land within a region known as Lower Galilee. This small village was nestled into a sheltered ridge that overlooks the Jezreel Valley, far from the religious hustle and bustle of Jerusalem. Archaeological investigation of this site shows that Nazareth was occupied as early as the time of Abraham, yet it never became a large city like others in the region.[27] Generally, little is known about this small village, apparently because there is little to know. It is most distinguished by the fact that it is remote and

The Church of Annunciation in the center of Nazareth.

rather insignificant, unmentioned in any scriptural reference prior to the Gospels and absent from the writings of Josephus or the Mishnah (i.e., Jewish oral law).[28] In the Gospels we hear Nathanael's delivery of the local, first-century reputation of this village: "Nazareth! Can anything good come from there?" (John 1:46).[29]

Matthew answers his question with a profound *yes*. "So was fulfilled what was said through the prophets: 'He will be called a Nazarene'" (Matt. 2:23). But which prophecy does Matthew have in mind? Two options present themselves. Matthew may be linking the name of the village with the prophecy in Isaiah 11:1. Using picture-filled language, Isaiah promises that the Messiah will grow like a shoot (Hebrew, *ntsr*) from the stump of David's dynasty. Perhaps Matthew knew that his Hebrew-savvy audience would hear the similarity in sound between *Nazareth* and *ntsr,* thus making the connection that Jesus of Nazareth is the *ntsr,* growing from the stump of Jesse promised by Isaiah. Certainly Bartimaeus made this connection: "When he heard that it was Jesus of Nazareth, he began to shout, 'Jesus, Son of David, have mercy on me!'" (Mark 10:47).

Another explanation is also appealing; it draws on the character of Nazareth that, by association, is extended

Grotto of the Annunciation at Nazareth.

to Jesus. Nathanael makes it plain that people from Nazareth were considered insignificant; therefore Jesus was insignificant by association. And this fulfills another prophecy of Isaiah, which tells the world to expect a Messiah who is despised and not esteemed (Isa. 53:3). Ironically, the Messiah drew attention to himself by the very fact that he drew so little attention to himself, just like Nazareth. No one from Nazareth was ever expected to amount to anything, and so someone from Nazareth fits the prophecy of Isaiah. This low expectation is paraded at the time of Jesus's execution as the Romans mocked the Jews and Jesus's kingly aspirations by posting a notice on the cross that read, "Jesus of Nazareth, the King of the Jews" (John 19:19).

So where was Jesus from? All four Gospel writers answer in union: he is from Nazareth. While this lowers the expectation of the world, those who take Isaiah's promises seriously lean in for a closer look, for someone from Nazareth might well be the Messiah. It was Jesus's hometown for a reason.

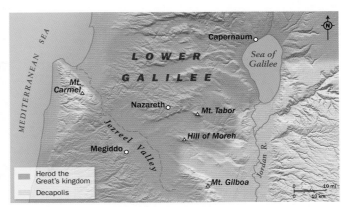

Nazareth of the Lower Galilee

The ancient village of Nazareth is centrally located in the Nazareth Ridge.

PART 8

JESUS'S MESSIANIC MISSION IN SAMARIA, GALILEE, AND PHOENICIA

Fishermen using a dragnet at the Sea of Galilee.
© Direct Design

MATTHEW 4–18; LUKE 4–18; JOHN 1–4

Although each of the Gospel writers recounts the life of Jesus in his own way, they all follow a general geographic pattern. First they report on Jesus's activity in the region of Galilee where he takes his message and miracles to the lost sheep of the house of Israel. After the death of John the Baptist and with increasing criticism from the Pharisees of Judea, we see Jesus withdrawing into regions more heavily populated with Gentiles—places like Phoenicia and the Decapolis. After this withdrawal, Luke offers us a unique report on Jesus's messianic mission in and around Perea. All the Gospel writers end their narratives with accounts of his activities in Judea and Jerusalem. Although there are exceptions, this pattern provides us with a geographic course traveled by the Messiah. Toward that end, part 8 will focus on the first segments of Jesus's messianic endeavors in the north—his time in Galilee, Samaria, and Phoenicia.

Jesus frequently used visual aids and references to hint (Hebrew, *remez*) at the significance of events in their geographical setting when shaping the learning experiences of his disciples. For example, we might ask why Jesus did his very first miracle in Cana of Galilee. A closer look reveals that Jesus had a potential identity problem with the disciples. Galileans, in general, regarded people from Nazareth as lacking in importance and value (John 1:46). Consequently, the very first miracle was performed in Cana of Galilee in order for Jesus to establish a baseline of confidence with his Galilean disciples. Jesus acknowledged the title of Messiah at Caesarea Philippi and at Jacob's well outside Sychar (Matt. 16:13–20; John 4:1–42). One location was a Greco-Roman worship center associated with political control; the other was steeped in biblical history that anticipated the coming of the Messiah. In both cases, the geographic settings for each of these messianic proclamations had a distinct historic significance.

On two separate occasions we find Jesus providing a miraculous meal for thousands of people (Matt. 14:13–21; 15:29–39). The feeding of the five thousand and the feeding of the four thousand are similar in many ways. But the different geographic setting of each, as well as the ethnic distinctions between the people who participated, allows these two multiplication miracles to teach very different lessons.

Jesus clearly showed his connection to the prophets of Scripture. As we will see in the raising of the widow's son at Nain and in the healing of the ten lepers on the Samaria-Galilee border, Jesus demonstrated that connection by performing miracles in proximity to locations where prophets had also performed miracles (2 Kings 4:8–37; Luke 7:11–17). And Jesus healed ten lepers on the road to Dothan (Luke 17:11–19), near the location where Elisha encountered Naaman the leper.

In these ways and others, Jesus not only taught in the Promised Land, he used the Promised Land to remind and teach. Consequently, the more we know about these locations, the more we will gain from the Gospels' report about them.

Sea of Galilee (view looking north).

Babylonian clay demon mask (1800–1600 BC). Observant Jews of Galilee had long been aware of demons associated with Gentiles.

Restored Galilee boat (first century BC) discovered near the ancient harbor of Gennesaret.

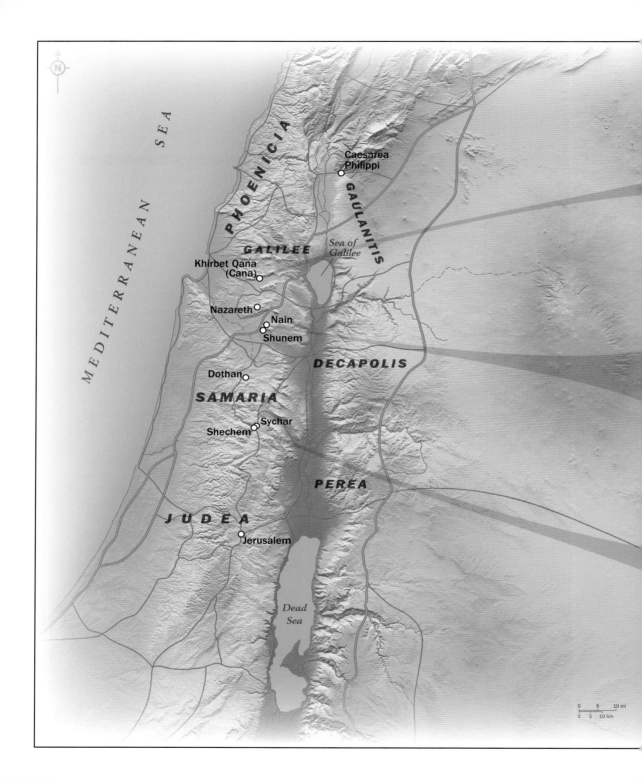

Jesus's Messianic Mission in Samaria, Galilee, and Phoenicia

Cana of Galilee. The rocky hill of Kh Qana (center) is thought to be the site of ancient Cana, where Jesus changed water into wine.

Nain (view looking south). The modern village of Nain, located on the northern base of Mount Moreh, marks the memory of the ancient village where Jesus raised a widow's son.

Jacob's well. Jesus spoke with a Samaritan woman at Jacob's well, which is now covered by a Greek Orthodox church.

JESUS'S FIRST MIRACLE OCCURS AT CANA OF GALILEE

JOHN 2:1–11

nyone who has taught, no matter what the setting, knows how important it is for students to have confidence in their teacher. This is doubly true when the learning experience will take the students into more difficult and threatening circumstances. Day after day Jesus asked his disciples to do just that. Step one way and you touch off the anger of the Roman authorities. Step another and the religious leaders in Jerusalem are calling for your death. In this atmosphere, Jesus needed the disciples' uncompromised trust. His first miracle occurred at Cana, happening where it did for a reason.

Although Jesus had by then become a rabbi with an increasing public presence, he continued to participate in social events with his family. So we find him attending a wedding in Cana of Galilee (John 2:1–11). It was traditional for Jewish families to wash regularly as part of the process of ritual purification. Since a wedding celebration lasted for several days, gallons of water were kept in stone water jars for that purpose.[1]

The water was intended for ritual cleansing, not bathing or drinking. But when the supply of wine at this wedding gave out, Jesus's mother urged him to do something that only he could do. The water in the six stone jars was turned into choice wine.

When we go to put Jesus's first miracle on the map, three possible

The site of Cana of Galilee (Khirbet Qana) located on the southern edge of the Bet Netofa Ridge.

Large limestone vessels, which could be used for storing ritually pure water, did not transmit ritual impurity.

© Dr. James C. Martin.
The Israel Museum.

locations present themselves as options. The first is Kanah (Cana), located within the tribal territory of Asher near Greater Sidon (Josh. 19:28). While it receives the support of Eusebius, this Cana seems too far from Nazareth to fit the narrative.[2] The second choice is Kefr Kana. Since the sixth century, Christian pilgrims have traveled to this village just four miles northeast of modern Nazareth to visit churches commemorating this miracle. But archaeological discoveries thus far do not reveal a first-century existence for this village of Cana as does a third site—Khirbet Qana, located eight miles north of Nazareth.[3] This village, which sits atop a perpendicular outcrop of the Bet Netofa Ridge, is the most likely site of Jesus's first miracle.

How does this location connect with strengthening the confidence of Jesus's disciples? First, we note that some of the initial disciples Jesus called included Andrew, Simon, Philip, and Nathanael (John 1:40–49). Andrew, Simon, and Philip were from Bethsaida (John 1:44). Nathanael was from Cana (John 21:2). Since these four students were all from Galilee, they were going to encounter the negative Galilean perspective about people from Nazareth—a perspective noted just a few verses earlier in John's Gospel. When Philip found

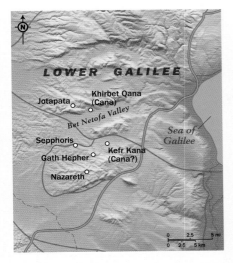

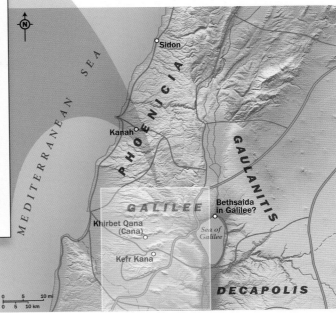

Cana (Khirbet Qana) of Galilee

Nathanael and told him they had found the promised Messiah in Jesus of Nazareth, Nathanael replied, "Nazareth! Can anything good come from there?" (John 1:46). Initially, as Jesus moved about in Galilee, these low expectations followed him and created an obstacle to his authority.[4] And though Nathanael quickly believed Jesus was the Messiah upon meeting him (John 1:47–49), these same low expectations threatened to undermine the confidence of the disciples whom he had called from Galilean cities to become his students.

Consequently, there was a reason Jesus did the first miracle in their Galilean backyard and right in Nathanael's hometown on an east/west roadway that connected Galilee with the Mediterranean Sea. Certainly this miracle helped out the troubled wedding host by removing the embarrassment of running out of wine. More importantly, it sent an early message throughout Galilee in general and to the Galilean disciples in particular. Encouraged to see Jesus as special, they could confidently trust his identity as Messiah. John goes on to tell us that this first miracle in Cana had exactly the intended results: "He thus revealed his glory, and his disciples put their faith in him" (John 2:11).

Sarcophagus scene (fourth century AD) of Jesus's first miracle—changing the water into wine at Cana.

JESUS MOVES TO CAPERNAUM

MATTHEW 4:12–17

esus left Nazareth and made Capernaum "his own town" (Matt. 9:1). This move to Capernaum was not random but in direct fulfillment of a prophecy given by Isaiah (Matt. 4:13–16). Further investigation reveals two additional benefits of moving to Capernaum: providing a symbol of hope to a region long under Gentile oppression and exposing the Kingdom of God to an international audience.

Seven centuries earlier Isaiah spoke to the Israelites about the current state of their affairs in the Promised Land as well as what they might expect in the future. He announced that while the tribal territories of Zebulun and Naphtali felt the deep pain of the Assyrian invasion, those same territories would personally experience the coming of the Kingdom of God—when Messiah himself, Jesus, would come to Galilee (Isa. 9:1–7). A light would shine into this region so darkened by gloom and distress of Assyrian invasion and Gentile occupation (Luke 2:32; John 8:12).[5]

Jesus's move to Capernaum brought hope to a portion of the Promised Land that desperately needed it. The dark soils and darker stones[6] of Naphtali pale when compared to the darkness that hung over this region like a thick blanket, for it regularly had felt the pain of invasion and oppression. That dark oppression began

Capernaum (view looking southwest).

when the Assyrians devastated the land during the life of Isaiah (2 Kings 15:29). The darkness continued during the days of Hasmonean rule when, according to 1 Maccabees 5:15, the Jews of this region faced annihilation. Later, when Jewish loyalists were holding out against Herod the Great in the caves near Arbela (above the Valley of the Pigeons, also known as the Arbel Cliffs), west of Capernaum, this region witnessed a daring raid by Herod the Great's soldiers, who violently wiped out entire families.[7]

Jesus's home at Capernaum also exposed his message to an international audience. The International Highway that connected the continents of Asia, Africa, and Europe passed just outside the city limits of Capernaum. Merchants from throughout the world used this highway to transport their goods from one end of the known world to the other. Along with the olive oil, aromatic spices, and wool, they also delivered the news of the day. Although less speedy than the bytes cascading through the wire and space of today, these merchants constantly broadcasted the salient news of their day. Jesus's earthly activities were very localized and his teaching and miracles were often witnessed by smaller groups of people. Yet what he did and said was desperately needed for all. His move from Nazareth to Capernaum is nothing less than a move from the shadows into the spotlight. Nazareth was isolated from the world, a place where one's words were likely destined for anonymity. Capernaum was engaged with the world via the International Highway.[8] By living there, Jesus could be assured that what he did and said would be carried far and wide to the larger audience for whom those deeds and words were intended.

Jesus left Nazareth in the tribal territory of Zebulun and moved to Capernaum for a reason. The distance between these locations is small, but the implications of that move are nothing less than phenomenal. Capernaum is located in the tribal territory of Naphtali, in the Galilee of the Gentiles, and by the way of the sea.[9] Matthew directly links this move to the fulfillment of Isaiah's prophecy (Matt. 4:13–16). Thus Jesus moved from Nazareth to Capernaum in order to fulfill Isaiah 9:1–7. The Promised Land had witnessed many dark and violent days, and out of this darkness the Morning Star (Rev. 22:16) was bringing a new day (2 Pet. 1:16–21). As Isaiah had promised, "The people living in darkness have seen a great light; on those living in the land of the shadow of death, a light has dawned" (Matt. 4:16). Jesus's move to Capernaum was a fulfillment that, as Messiah, he would "reign on David's throne and over his kingdom ... with justice and righteousness from that time on and forever" (Isa. 9:7).

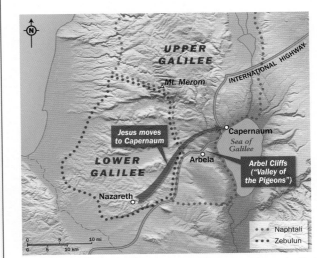

Jesus moves from Nazareth (in Zebulun) to Capernaum (in Naphtali)

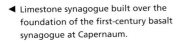

◄ Limestone synagogue built over the foundation of the first-century basalt synagogue at Capernaum.

Capernaum "Via Maris" mile marker of Hadrianus (second century AD).

JESUS SPEAKS TO A WOMAN AT JACOB'S WELL

JOHN 4:1–42

Jesus regularly demonstrated that he was the long-awaited Messiah not only by what he said and did but by where he said and did things. Particularly relevant was his conversation with the Samaritan woman at Jacob's well. At the frontier of her own understanding, she proclaimed, "'I know that Messiah' (called Christ) 'is coming. When he comes, he will explain everything to us.' Then Jesus declared, 'I who speak to you am he'" (John 4:25–26). We will see that it was not the fact that Jesus spoke to a Samaritan or that he spoke to a woman that offers the most insight into this declaration but that he said it where he did for a reason.

The Gospel of John tells us that Jesus had been in Judea and was returning to Galilee. The shortest and most efficient route led through the region of Samaria, which brought Jesus to a well outside the village of Sychar (John 4:4–6). Although Sychar is not mentioned in Scripture prior to John's Gospel, it resides a short walk from ancient Shechem, which was in ruins centuries before Jesus made his way to the well. This was an area of considerable Bible history.[10]

Once the Northern Kingdom was conquered, the Assyrians deported the Jewish residents of higher standing while importing new citizens from a variety of other conquered nations. From that time on, the territories of Manasseh (the part that lay west of the Jordan River) and Ephraim remained mixed both ethnically and religiously (2 Kings 17:24–41). After the Babylonian captivity was over and exiles were allowed to return, these two tribal regions became known as Samaria. Since then, persistent tension had existed between Hebrews and people living in this region, who were called Samaritans (John 4:9).[11]

When we go back in time, long before the period of the Divided Kingdom, we find that the location of Sychar had deep and vital connections to the promise of the Messiah, which made it a powerful location for Jesus's messianic declaration. When God called Abram, he brought him to the Promised Land in general and to

Remains of a Byzantine church that now lay atop Mount Gerizim, where the Samaritan temple once stood.

Shechem in particular. The Lord appeared to Abram at Shechem and made him three powerful promises: that he would have descendants, possess land, and be a blessing to the nations (Gen. 12:1–3). Abram built a memorial altar at Shechem to commemorate these promises. Jacob purchased land there, built his own memorial altar, and dug a well, apparently to serve those coming to use the worship site (Gen. 33:18–19). The well was still in use at the time of Jesus and became the setting for the conversation with the Samaritan woman (John 4:6).

After the time of Jacob when Joshua brought the Israelites back to the Promised Land, he led the nation of Israel to this location for a service of rededication (Deuteronomy 27–28; Josh. 8:30–35). The laws given to Israel at Mount Sinai were written on large stones, and a memorial altar was built on Mount Ebal. At this place the law of God was read to the people. At the time of Joshua the location of Shechem (a short distance from Sychar) became Israel's first national sacred gathering place.

Jesus spoke to a Samaritan woman at Jacob's well for a reason. It was at that well, outside the village of Sychar and near the ancient ruins of Shechem, that

Mount Gerizim (view looking southwest).

Jesus pronounced his messianic identity. Given all the historical events associated with this spot, it is no coincidence that Jesus came to Jacob's well to make the powerful announcement: "I who speak to you am he" (John 4:26). With the words of the covenant given to Abram (Gen. 12:7) and the covenant messages given to Moses (Deut. 18:15; Acts 3:22; 7:37) echoing in the air, Jesus proclaimed that he was the Prophet and the Messiah, the fulfillment of all messianic expectation.

Greek Orthodox priest drawing water from Jacob's well at Sychar (Askar).

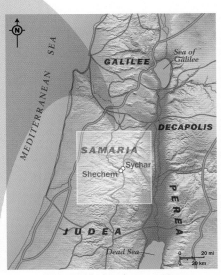

Sychar and Shechem between Mounts Ebal and Gerizim in Samaria

JESUS GOES TO THE *OTHER SIDE*

MARK 4:35–5:20

Given Jesus's attention to the lost sheep of the house of Israel (Matt. 10:6; 15:24), first-century Jews might well presume that God's Kingdom would be composed of Jewish citizens living within the old borders of David's kingdom. But that was not to be the case. Jesus was bringing a much different Kingdom—a Kingdom that would encompass God's entire creation and put an end to Satan's fraudulent rule (1 John 3:8; Rev. 21:24, 26). We get a look at the power of the Kingdom of God as Jesus goes to overthrow Satan's control of the *other side* of the Sea of Galilee (Mark 5:1–20).

With evening approaching and a full day of teaching behind him, Jesus said to his disciples, "Let us go over to the other side" (Mark 4:35). The *other side* was local jargon for the east side of the Sea of Galilee. But there was more to it than that, for the *other side* was not only on a different side of the lake, it literally was the *other side* both spiritually and culturally.[12]

The *other side* was thoroughly invested in the idolatry of Hellenism that permeated the cities of the Decapolis.

Eastern shoreline of the Sea of Galilee near Gergesa.

These cities, located mostly east of the Sea of Galilee and Jordan River, were showplaces for Greek and Roman architecture and culture. Their populations were largely composed of Gentiles who were part of the Greco-Roman culture of the day.[13] It was not just in the cities but also in the agricultural fields around those cities where the influence of Gentile culture was felt. Here one could raise herds of pigs numbering in the thousands (Mark 5:13), because the Jewish prohibition on pork was not observed on the *other side*. Moreover, the Gospel writers tell of a man possessed by multiple demons living among the tombs, terrorizing all who came near. In contrast to Jewish communities on the northwest shore of the Sea of Galilee, the *other side* was intimately linked to Satan and his kingdom.

When Jesus and the disciples traveled to the *other side*, they were going to the side of the lake where Satan's grasp was firm. As Jesus's boat traveled east across the lake, a furious squall (associated with the eastern wind known in Arabic as a *sharkia*)[14] arose, threatening to drive Jesus away from the east side of the lake

Mosaic discovered at Magdala (first century AD), illustrating a boat used for sailing into the deep water of the Sea of Galilee.

(Mark 4:37–41). The windstorm filled the boat with water and Jesus's disciples with fear. In a panic, they awakened Jesus, who seemed to have surrendered all control of the boat to the squall even though he was near the rudder. Jesus knew exactly what he was doing and calmed the wind, quieted the sea, and let Satan know that the Kingdom of God had come to the *other side*.

Roman coin with the image of a running boar, which was the symbol of the Tenth Roman Legion (LXF). © Dr. James C. Martin. The Rockefeller Museum, Jerusalem.

Jesus went to the *other side* of the Sea of Galilee for a reason. When he arrived on the *other side*, a man possessed by a legion of demons approached him. The demons pleaded with Jesus to be allowed to enter a nearby herd of pigs. Jesus agreed, and those pigs ran down the steep slope of the hillside and drowned in the Sea of Galilee. Two important pieces of information throw light on the significance of this event: in general pigs are buoyant and therefore good swimmers; and at the time, the "running boar" was a symbol of the Roman tenth legion that controlled the *other side*.

Thus the demons' request was a ruse. If the adversary could not prevent the King from coming to the *other side* to proclaim God's Kingdom, at least the demons could attempt to discredit the King by entering the mascot of the Roman legion (i.e., the running boar) and destroying the financial base of the local population. Initially, the enemy appeared successful as people in the surrounding areas came to Jesus and asked him to leave. But this was not the case, for Jesus had demonstrated the rescuing power of God and his authority over the adversary, Roman military conquerors, and the ritually defiled economy of those who lived on the *other side*.

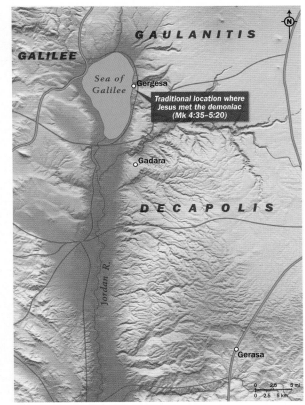

Gadara, Gerasa, and Gergesa

JESUS'S MIRACLES IN THE EVANGELICAL TRIANGLE

MATTHEW 11:20–24

In reading the Gospel accounts, we may get the impression that Jesus's miracles were dispensed in an arbitrary way across the countryside at random locations, but Matthew 11:20–24 suggests otherwise. In this judgment speech Jesus pronounces *woes* on Korazin, Bethsaida, and Capernaum. Although these cities had seen more of Jesus's miracles than any other location in the Promised Land, they had not received Jesus as the Messiah. When we put those cities on a map, they form a triangle sometimes referred to as the "Evangelical Triangle." Capernaum (Kefar Nahum) was located along the northern shoreline of the Sea of Galilee. Korazin was situated about an hour and a half walk (approximately two and a half miles) up the hillside above Capernaum. And Bethsaida was near the Jordan River inlet. When we consider the nature of the population in this area and the relationship of this triangle to the International Highway, we will see that Jesus performed the bulk of his miracles in this region for a reason.

We note that Jesus had primarily dedicated his teaching and miracles to those who belonged to the "lost sheep of Israel" (Matt. 10:6; 15:24). While a variety of cultures made their presence felt around the Sea of Galilee in the Gospels, the area defined by the Evangelical Triangle hosted a significant population of observant Jews.[15] By doing more miracles in this area than in any other, Jesus was clearly fulfilling his great passion to rescue and heal the "lost sheep of Israel."

But the Kingdom of God was not restricted to those "lost sheep." His focus on teaching along the northern shore of the Sea of Galilee reveals a larger strategy behind the sites of the majority of his miracles. To see that strategy at work, we need to draw a line between each of the three cities mentioned in these verses in order to form a triangle.[16] When we add the International Highway to that drawing, we find that this roadway passes adjacent to our triangle. For travelers of the ancient world, Israel was a land bridge that allowed passage between

Plain of Magdala (view looking northeast).

the trackless desert to the east and the forbidding waves of the Mediterranean Sea to the west. The International Highway that connected the people of Asia, Africa, and Europe passed directly through the Promised Land and near Korazin, Bethsaida, and Capernaum. People from countless nations and families passed through this region. As they did, news about God's Kingdom through Jesus's teachings and miracles traveled with them. Those exposed to the Good News in the Evangelical Triangle would then return via that road system to the far-flung nations of the world so that those who never set foot in the Promised Land might learn about God's Anointed and his plan of rescue and restoration.

The site of Bethsaida Julias in Gaulanitis (view looking southeast).

Jesus's miracles occurred in the Evangelical Triangle for a reason. A casual reading of the Gospels might suggest that Jesus's miracles were randomly scattered across the countryside. But Jesus performed more miracles in the Evangelical Triangle than in any other place both to reach out to the lost sheep of the house of Israel and to reach beyond the bounds of Israel to the Gentiles of the world with the life-giving message that the Rescuer had arrived.

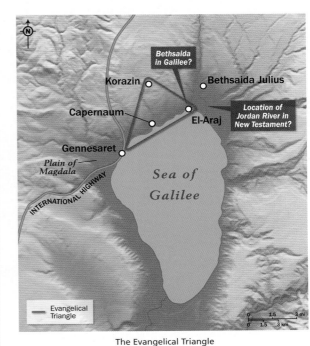

The Evangelical Triangle

Reconstructed village of second-century Korazin (view looking northwest).

JESUS RAISES THE WIDOW'S SON AT NAIN

LUKE 7:11–17

We know of three separate instances in which Jesus raised a person who had died. Around Capernaum when the daughter of Jairus died, Jesus restored life to this young girl (Luke 8:40–56). At Bethany, Jesus called his dear friend Lazarus from the tomb (John 11:38–44). The first recorded time Jesus showed his authority over death (John 6:44; 11:25) was at Nain. The circumstances were particularly tragic: a woman who was already widowed had now lost her only son. A large crowd of people accompanied her, offering her support as her son was carried to the cemetery. Another large crowd was following Jesus, who had just healed the centurion's son at Capernaum. These two crowds joined forces at the gate of Nain (Luke 7:11–12). Based on the event that followed, "They were all filled with awe and praised God. 'A great prophet has appeared among us,' they said. 'God has come to help his people'" (Luke 7:16). We will see that this miracle happened at Nain for a reason.

The modern village of Nain, located on the northern slope of Mount Moreh and built over the ancient site of Nain (view looking south).

Over the centuries we have learned to delay the arrival of death and to soften the pain of the process. But no amount of human might or power can bring back life to those who have truly died. That fact alone explains the awe and excitement that filled the crowds that day.

But there was more to it than that. When the people began to shout that a "great prophet" had appeared among them, they were recalling a previous event when Elisha had performed a similar miracle. At Shunem a family offered Elisha a room and meals while he was working in the area. In time and in response to Elisha's prayer, the wife of this family was able to conceive and give birth to a son. Later, tragedy struck and this young boy died. But as Elisha prayed, the Lord returned life to the young man (2 Kings 4:8–37). Because the raising of the widow's son at Nain closely resembled the Lord's miracle at Shunem, the crowd correctly realized that a great prophet was among them.

The most powerful component in this event is the one most easily missed: it happened at Nain.[17] The Lord used Elisha in restoring life to the young man

Sarcophagus frieze (ca. 330 AD) illustrating the raising of the widow's son at Nain.

The modern village of Shunem, located on the southern side of Mount Moreh.

at Shunem, located on the southern base of Mount Moreh.[18] Nain, where Jesus raised the widow's son, lies just a short distance away on the north base of Mount Moreh.[19] Certainly death had made its presence felt in many families and in many communities throughout the Promised Land. But of all the places where Jesus could have raised a widow's son, he did so at Nain. The people there could make the geographic connection. Jesus was doing a miracle similar to the one that had occurred on the opposite side of the same hill when the Lord answered Elisha's prayer!

Jesus raised the widow's son at Nain for a reason. The townspeople not only celebrated the presence of a "great prophet" among them, they also linked the event to Elisha. Elisha's name is composed of two Hebrew words that mean "God rescues." By proclaiming, "God has come to help his people" (Luke 7:16), the people of Nain made the connection that the Lord had come to help them just as the Lord had answered Elisha's prayer at Shunem.

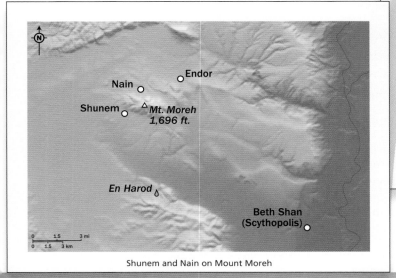

Shunem and Nain on Mount Moreh

JESUS FEEDS THE FIVE THOUSAND IN A REMOTE PLACE

MATTHEW 14:13–21

Jesus's work in Galilee was drawing ever larger crowds. On most occasions his time with them hummed to a regular rhythm. Jesus met with, taught, and healed the crowds who came to him during the daylight hours. But when evening approached, he sent the thronging crowds home or away to the local villages where they could secure an evening meal and overnight accommodations. But that standard operating procedure did not hold on the day of the feeding of the five thousand. As the customary time came for sending the people away, Jesus instead directed the crowd to be seated and eat a meal that he would provide. The unique rhythm of this day and the miraculous provision of food were designed to teach a truth about Jesus—a truth that gains power and depth when we realize that it happened where it did for a reason.

All four Gospel writers include this event (Matt. 14:13–21; Mark 6:30–44; Luke 9:10–17; John 6:1–15). And when we assemble evidence from each of these inspired writers, we get some sense for the location of the miracle.[20] Luke says that Jesus took the disciples and

Sarcophagus scene (fourth century AD) of the miracle of the multiplication of loaves.

withdrew to a place near Bethsaida (Luke 9:10), and more precisely to the side of a mountain near Bethsaida, according to John (John 6:3).[21] But what really catches the attention of Matthew, Mark, and Luke is the character of this place. They each describe it as a remote and solitary location (Matt. 14:13, 15; Mark 6:31–32, 35; Luke 9:12). Although the English translators have used a variety of words like *solitary*, *remote*, and *quiet* in these verses, these words are all used to translate a

single Greek word, *erēmos*, which means "a place that is noteworthy for its lack of people." So when we assemble the information from all four Gospels, we can place this miracle on a mountainside near Bethsaida in a region that is basically *deserted*.

In order to fully appreciate the selection of this location, it is necessary to recognize the connection between this miracle and the celebration of the Jewish Passover. Note that in contrast to what we will see in the feeding of the four thousand, this was a Jewish audience on their way to celebrate the Passover in Jerusalem (John 6:4). Passover was designed to remind people of the Lord's delivering Israel out of Egypt and providing for them during their time in the *deserted* Sinai Wilderness through the miraculous provision of food and water. Now Jesus was about to do the same thing. He had the people sit down in groups of hundreds and fifties (Mark 6:40), recalling the way Moses divided the people during their stay in the wilderness (Exod. 18:21). Using five loaves of bread and two fish, he more than satisfied the hunger of thousands.

Jesus fed the five thousand in a remote place for a reason. The location Jesus selected to perform this miracle helped these people make the connection between this miracle and the Lord's provision at the time of Moses. The Greek word *erēmos*, which the Gospel writers repeatedly use to characterize the setting of Jesus's miracle, is the same word the Septuagint (Greek edition of the Old Testament) uses to describe the remote and uninhabited regions of the Sinai Wilderness.

Geographical references in the Gospels suggest the feeding of the five thousand may have occurred on the hillside west (left) of the Jordan River inlet to the Sea of Galilee.

Mosaic of the Loaves and Fish from the Church of Tabgha (ancient Heptapegon).

Plain of Bethsaida (view looking west).

They are making the geographic link for us. Jesus had led the crowd into this remote setting just as the Lord had led the Israelites with Moses into a remote setting. Once there, Jesus led them to a mountain as the Lord had led Israel to Mount Sinai. Jesus had miraculously provided food for the crowd to eat as the Lord had miraculously provided manna for the Israelites in the wilderness. There is no mistaking the connection. For this Jewish audience with Passover on their minds, Jesus was clearly identifying himself with the great acts of the Lord (John 6:32–33, 35).[22]

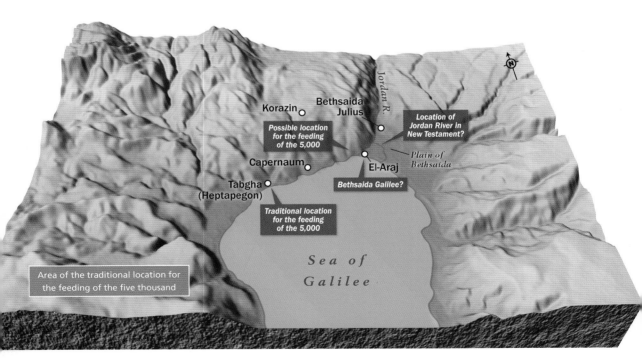

JESUS HEALS A CANAANITE WOMAN'S DAUGHTER NEAR TYRE

MATTHEW 15:21–28

Following the feeding of the five thousand, Matthew and Luke both describe an extended trip north during which Jesus withdrew from the Promised Land for a time. During that trip he entered the region of Tyre and Sidon, where he healed the daughter of a Canaanite woman and celebrated her faith (Matt. 15:21–28; Mark 7:24–30). When we view this unique trip of Jesus in light of Scripture, we see that he made this trip to ancient Phoenicia for a reason.

Following the miraculous feeding of the five thousand, the news about Jesus reached deeply into the heart of Judea. Upon hearing about this Galilean rabbi, the Pharisees of Jerusalem were so disturbed that they traveled to the shores of the Sea of Galilee. Their goal was not to learn from Jesus but to put a stop to his assumed heretical teaching (Matt. 15:1–20; Mark 7:1–23). In particular, these rabbis from Jerusalem thought the rabbi from Galilee had it all wrong when it came to understanding what was ritually clean and unclean in God's eyes. It was in this context that Jesus took his disciples on a trip into the region of Tyre and Sidon.

As Jesus left the Promised Land and entered the region of Tyre, he was stepping into the geographic domain of ancient Phoenicia that the Romans had since wrapped into the larger province of Syria. There is no escaping the fact that this region and its people would evoke very negative feelings for the disciples, who were aware of the previous interaction between Israelites and Phoenicians. There were a few early positive moments during the days of King Hiram of Tyre, who supplied David and Solomon with the raw materials, technicians, and expertise needed for the major renovation of Jerusalem (2 Sam. 5:11; 1 Kings 5:10–18). Hiram also helped Israel develop a well-built trading fleet (1 Kings 9:26–28).[23] But in subsequent years the relationship between Israel and Phoenicia deteriorated considerably. During the days of King Ahab it was his Phoenician wife, Jezebel, who aggressively sought to install Baal as the national idol of Israel (1 Kings 16:31–33). And when such idolatry became so rampant among the Israelites that the Lord allowed them to be defeated and exiled by the Babylonians, the citizens of Tyre cheered their defeat and even sold the remaining unprotected Jews that remained as slaves. Such cruelty motivated the Lord to target Tyre with a variety of harsh prophecies (Jer. 25:22; Ezek. 26:1–28:19; Amos 1:9–10). Thus the Jews of later years had little affection for the residents of Tyre and Sidon.

Jesus brought his disciples to Tyre to heal the Canaanite woman's daughter for a reason. There were many Gentile regions into which Jesus could have led his disciples for a lesson in what was truly clean and unclean, but the region of Tyre was his choice. Here a Canaanite woman[24] that religious Judaism considered "unclean" begged Jesus for assistance because her daughter was possessed by a demon. This woman was a descendant of those who had brought much pain to ancient Israelites. Her initial pleas were met by Jesus's silence. When she

Relief of a Phoenician woman.

© Dr. James C. Martin. Mus'ee du Louvre; Autorisation de photographer et de filmer—LOUVRE.

persisted his language was unbending: "I was sent only to the lost sheep of Israel. . . . It is not right to take the children's bread and toss it to their dogs" (Matt. 15:24, 26). When the woman continued through all these obstacles, Jesus gave her faith the acknowledgment it warranted: "Woman, you have great faith! Your request is granted" (Matt. 15:28).[25] This encounter would leave an enduring impression on his disciples. Even there in Baal's backyard among all that was unclean, the Rescuer could make "clean" the daughter of this Gentile woman. That is the lesson in ritual cleanness that the Pharisees in Jerusalem had missed.

Tyre and Sidon in Phoenicia

Palaestra at Tyre (Al Mina excavation).

◀ Phoenician stela relief expressing adoration.

© Dr. James C. Martin. Mus'ee du Louvre; Autorisation de photographer et de filmer—LOUVRE.

JESUS FEEDS THE FOUR THOUSAND IN THE DECAPOLIS

MATTHEW 15:29–39

I f there is one place where reading the Gospels is likely to give us the feeling of déjà vu, it is when reading the multiplication miracles—the feeding of the five thousand and the feeding of the four thousand. In both Matthew and Mark the feeding of the four thousand comes second (Matt. 15:29–39; Mark 8:1–10). When we come to those verses in either Gospel, we get the feeling that we have been there before. Jesus encouraged thousands of people to sit down on a mountainside in a remote place where he miraculously turned a small amount of food into an abundant feast with leftovers to spare. These details are common to both multiplication accounts. But while both share such similarities, it is in their differences that we find the emerging message. As we shall see, Jesus feeds over four thousand people in the Decapolis for a reason.[26]

Mark reports that after Jesus had left the vicinity of Tyre and Sidon, he traveled down the east shore of the Sea of Galilee into the Decapolis (Mark 7:31). The Decapolis cities and their region lay largely east of the Sea of Galilee and Jordan River. These were Greco-Roman cities either founded or reestablished with a

The cardo (main street) of the Decapolis city of Gadara (view looking west).

dual mission: to guard the important transportation routes near them and to display all that Greek culture had to offer. Although the region these cities controlled had been part of the land that Joshua had assigned the eastern tribes of Israel (Josh. 13:8), the Decapolis was dominated by Gentiles during the time of the events recorded in the Gospels.[27] While the exact spot where this miracle occurred is unknown, the Gospels firmly place the feeding of the four thousand east of the Sea of Galilee in the Decapolis.

Once we have the correct location for the miracle, we can put the right participants on the hillside. As Jesus sat down along the eastern side of the Sea of Galilee, great crowds of people encircled him. They brought those who were physically disabled to Jesus, and hundreds were healed by his touch. But these were not observant Jews like those who had been with Jesus when he fed the five thousand; these were Gentiles,[28] and not just any Gentiles at that! These were Gentiles who had come to Jesus because of a powerful witness given by a man formerly possessed by hundreds of demons (Mark 5:9; see also Matt. 8:28–34; Mark 5:1–17). After Jesus had sent the

Excavations of the Decapolis city of Scythopolis (view looking northeast).

demons into a herd of pigs, this man begged Jesus to let him go along with him. But Jesus refused his request, instead telling him to circulate the news about his experience in his homeland. And that is what he did throughout the Decapolis (Mark 5:18–20). In contrast to the last time Jesus had been in this region and the residents had asked him to leave after their pigs ran headlong into the Sea of Galilee, this time we find these Gentiles flocking to Jesus and praising "the God of Israel" (Matt. 15:31).

Jesus fed the four thousand in the Decapolis for a reason.[29] His entire journey away from the Jewish side of the northwestern shore of the Sea of Galilee had begun when certain Pharisees from Jerusalem challenged Jesus for failing to observe practices that would maintain their views of ritual purity (Matt. 15:1–20; Mark 7:1–23). In response, Jesus went to the region of Tyre and Sidon, where he affirmed the faith of what these Pharisees considered an unclean Canaanite woman (Matt. 15:21–28; Mark 7:24–30). From there, Jesus traveled to the *other side*, the Decapolis, where he healed hundreds and fed thousands of non-Jews with a miraculous bounty of food, just as he had healed and fed observant Jews during the feeding of the five thousand. The Jerusalem Pharisees believed that all Gentiles were unclean, but through this miracle Jesus made it clear that the Kingdom of God had come to all people.

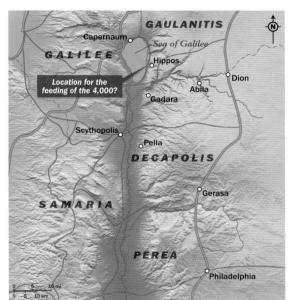

The Decapolis and feeding of the four thousand

The Decapolis city of Hippos (Susita), located on the east side of the Sea of Galilee (view looking west).

JESUS TAKES HIS DISCIPLES TO CAESAREA PHILIPPI

MATTHEW 16:13–28

Some biblical events amaze us because of their uniqueness. Jesus's time with the disciples in the region of Caesarea Philippi[30] is just such a moment (Matt. 16:13–20; Mark 8:27–30). Here Jesus further defined his messianic mission to overthrow the works of the adversary. All of this occurred in the region of Caesarea Philippi for a reason.

The trip to the region of Caesarea Philippi was a continuation of the extended experience that had taken Jesus and the disciples north into the region of Tyre and Sidon (Matt. 15:21) and east to the region of the Decapolis (Mark 7:31). Jesus took his followers to the area of Caesarea Philippi and asked two questions: "Who do people say the Son of Man is?" and "Who do you say I am?" (Matt. 16:13, 15). From the collage of popular options, Jesus identified Peter's answer as the accurate one and then proceeded to use the setting of the exchange to show why.

Three qualities of this location seem particularly meaningful with regard to Jesus's proclamation. Caesarea Philippi was a place of idolatry, the entrance into Hades, and a region associated with political control. Since Mount Hermon (9,232 feet) rises as the dramatic backdrop for Caesarea Philippi, we might expect this spot to sprout worship centers associated with idols. So it was with Caesarea Philippi, which boasted a worship area dedicated to the Greek idol Pan that shared ground with a marble temple dedicated to the worship of Augustus.[31] It was also here that a large, yawning cave was popularly perceived to be the gateway into Hades.[32] In addition to being a place of idolatry, the region of Caesarea Philippi was also a hub from which to exercise political control into Asia, Africa, and Europe. The extraordinary mass of Mount Hermon blocks and channels international traffic along its lower flanks. Wherever geography limits travel options, political control may be exercised. That was clearly the case with Caesarea Philippi.[33]

When Jesus asked who people thought he was, Peter responded with what has often been called the great confession: "You are the Christ, the Son of the living God" (Matt. 16:16). Note the visual surroundings of the setting. In contrast to all other claimants, mortal or mythical, Jesus could stand in the shadow of ostentatious idolatry and acknowledge that he alone was the Christ, God's Anointed and King of Kings. He affirmed Peter's confession. Also on that rocky facade on which the temple of Pan and entrance into Hades were located, Jesus declared that the community of his disciples would overthrow the present idolatry and the gates of Hades would not prevail against it (Matt. 16:18).

Jesus took his disciples to Caesarea Philippi for a reason. As Jesus revealed more about his true identity, he spoke of the overthrow of political control associated with Caesarea Philippi. Many Jews of Jesus's day were awaiting a Davidic king who would lead Israel in battle and throw off the oppressive Roman occupation of the Promised Land.[34] They viewed the Roman occupation

Niche carved into the bedrock facade of Caesarea Philippi to house an image of the idol Pan.

The Romans considered this cave at the base of the bedrock escarpment to be an entrance into Hades.

The region of Caesarea Philippi (view looking north).

as synonymous with the kingdom of evil. Jesus, however, had come to overthrow not just the symptom of evil (that is, the Roman occupation) but its cause, the adversary (Satan). So Jesus went to Caesarea Philippi to announce that the Kingdom of God would overthrow the adversary and all his mortal allies. There was not a question about the outcome of the war, for not even the gates of Hades would withstand the victory in the making.

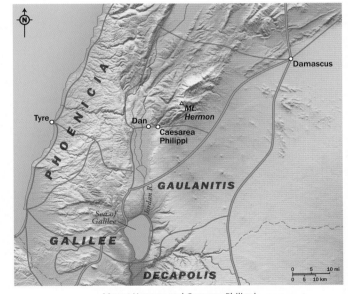

Mount Hermon and Caesarea Philippi

JESUS IS TRANSFIGURED ON AN ANONYMOUS HIGH MOUNTAIN

MATTHEW 17:1–13

On most days Jesus's outward appearance set him apart as a rabbi but not as the Son of God. That all changed on the day of his transfiguration.[35] Two of the Gospel writers tell us that this stunning change in Jesus's appearance occurred on a "high mountain" (Matt. 17:1; Mark 9:2). The geographically curious wish these writers had provided more specific information. But it appears the anonymity of this location plays a role in delivering the message. As we shall see, Jesus's appearance was transfigured before Peter, James, and John on an anonymous "high mountain" for a reason.

Within a week of Peter's great confession at Caesarea Philippi (Matt. 16:16), Jesus asked three of his disciples to join him on a private excursion. Secluded on the side of a nearby mountain, Jesus's face glowed like the sun and his clothing was illuminated. Moses and Elijah suddenly appeared with Jesus, talking with him about all the events that would occur in the last week of Jesus's life in Jerusalem. And as if that were not enough, the disciples fell face down on the ground when a bright cloud enveloped them and a voice declared, "This is my Son, whom I love; with him I am well pleased. Listen to him!" (Matt. 17:5).

This was an atypical day even in the life of Jesus's disciples, who had grown accustomed to atypical days.

Mount Hermon (view looking northwest).

The transfiguration was designed to affirm the plan Jesus had recently laid out before the disciples and to demonstrate that it had an intimate link with expectations recorded in the Scriptures. At Caesarea Philippi Peter voiced a wonderful confession, naming Jesus as the Messiah, the Son of the living God. Shortly after, Jesus began to lay out the details of the days ahead. He would go to Jerusalem where he would suffer many things and be executed (Matt. 16:21). Peter, among others, found this plan to be outrageous. "Never, Lord! This shall never happen to you!" (v. 22). Peter, James, and John needed assurance that this was the right plan and that it conformed to divine expectation. Toward that end, Moses and Elijah appeared and discussed the plan with Jesus as the heavenly Father signaled his approval (Luke 9:30–31, 34–35).

Although there is no shortage of opinions about where this event took place, the Gospel writers are united in keeping the specific name of the mountain out of their record. As early as the fourth century, Christians were pointing their fingers in three different directions when marking the setting for Jesus's transfiguration: Mount Tabor, the Mount of Olives, and Mount Hermon.[36] Although the contemporary Church of the Transfiguration was built on the top of Mount Tabor,

Mosaic of the transfiguration from the apse of the Church of the Transfiguration (Mount Tabor).

commemorating the event, Mount Hermon and its proximity to Caesarea Philippi is more likely because it is the last known position of Jesus before the transfiguration.[37]

It seems likely the Gospel writers did not name the "high mountain" for a reason. In the accounts of the transfiguration, the unnamed mountain represents Mount Horeb (i.e., Mount Sinai). The bright light, the cloud, and the voice of God remind us of the encounters both Moses and Elijah had with the Lord on Mount Horeb (Exod. 19:16–19; 1 Kings 19:8).[38] And although we do not know on which high mountain the transfiguration occurred, the nameless high mountain is a significant reminder that Jesus came to fulfill the law given to Moses on Mount Horeb (Matt. 5:17).

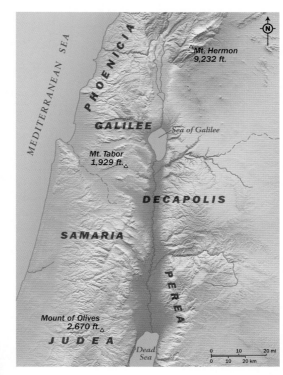

Mount Hermon, Mount Tabor, and Mount of Olives as possible locations for the transfiguration

Mountains of Sinai with Elijah's Spring.

JESUS HEALS TEN LEPERS ON THE ROAD TO DOTHAN

LUKE 17:11–19

As Jesus drew his activities in the north to a close, he turned his thoughts toward Jerusalem (Luke 18:31–33). It was during this time that Jesus met and healed ten men whose lives had been claimed and defined by their disease: leprosy. Jesus's heartfelt compassion provided a healing miracle. But the parallels between this miracle (Luke 17:11–19) and the healing of Naaman mentioned in 2 Kings 5 suggest that this was much more than a random act of compassion. That is particularly so when we note the geographic symmetry of the message. Jesus healed ten men afflicted with leprosy on the road to Dothan for a reason.

Given the physical pain and the social stigma that attended their disease, these ten outcasts had banded together outside the village between Samaria and Galilee in support of one another. The reputation of Jesus's curative ability had long since reached their displaced neighborhood. So when they heard he was nearby, these beleaguered men lifted their voices in unison: "Jesus, Master, have pity on us!" (Luke 17:13). The words reached Jesus's ears and touched his heart. Nevertheless he did not heal them on the spot but rather sent them to Jerusalem's Temple. Their healing came as they journeyed to the chamber of lepers in the Temple, where their healing could be acknowledged by the religious leaders, who doubled as public health inspectors (Lev.

Aramaean (Syrian) funerary inscription (seventh century BC).

Model of the chamber of lepers, the building located to the right of the semicircular steps adjacent to the bronze gate of Nicanor.

13:2–3; 14:2–32). But only one man, a Samaritan, returned to Jesus, overflowing with words of praise and thanks.[39]

This miracle has much to say standing on its own, but it becomes even more powerful when we observe the links between it and the healing of Naaman (2 Kings 5). Naaman, like the man who returned to Jesus, was a foreigner afflicted with leprosy. He was the commander of the Syrian (i.e., Aramaean) army and a man who had led many successful raids against Israel. One of those raids brought a young Jewish girl into his home as a slave. She knew of the Lord's healing power through Elisha, so she encouraged her master to seek his aid. Naaman went to Elisha, but he, like the lepers mentioned in Luke's Gospel, was sent away to be healed at a distance. Elisha directed Naaman to go and wash seven times in the Jordan River and he would be healed. Although he hesitated at first, Naaman did go, washed, and was healed. Following the miracle he rushed back to Elisha declaring, "Now I know that there is no God in all the world except in Israel" (2 Kings 5:15).

There are a number of parallels with the healing of the ten lepers. In each case a foreigner had contracted leprosy. They engaged a prophet whom they believed could help them. The prophet then sent each man away to be healed at a distant location. Both the Syrian and the Samaritan went away, were healed, and came to believe in the living God. Now if we add location to the list of comparisons, we will find yet another parallel, for the meeting of Elisha and Naaman occurred in nearly the same place that Jesus met with the ten lepers.[40] Elisha resided in Dothan, a city near the border of Galilee and Samaria (2 Kings 6:13).[41] Although Dothan is not mentioned, Luke tells us that Jesus entered a village located on that same border.[42] While the precise location of both events remains unknown, there is no doubt that the meeting of Elisha and Naaman and the restoration of the ten lepers occurred within a few miles of one another.

Jesus healed ten lepers on the road to Dothan for a reason. Once again Jesus linked himself to an earlier prophet of God not only through association of similar events but by events that occurred in the same location. The Kingdom of God not only came for the restoration of all nations, it came to restore the outcasts of those nations.

Jesus encountered ten lepers near this city of Dothan (view looking southeast), the same area where Elisha encountered Naaman the leper.

Jesus encountered ten lepers;
Elisha encountered Naaman

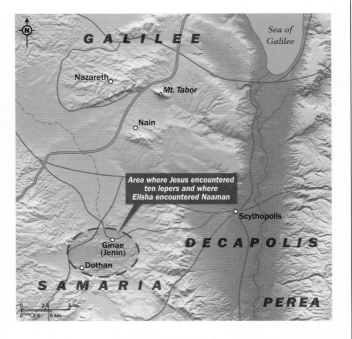

PART 9

JESUS'S LAST DAYS IN AND AROUND JERUSALEM

Model of the first-century Jerusalem Temple.

MATTHEW 19–28; MARK 10–16; LUKE 18–24; JOHN 11–21

Jesus moved from the quieter and more peaceful moments in Galilee to the turbulent days in Jerusalem as he faced his crucifixion and resurrection. The busy city corresponded with a faster pace and sharp exchanges between Jesus and Jerusalem's corrupt Temple leaders, sometimes translated into English as "the Jews." It was in this city, where the Temple had witnessed hundreds of thousands of sacrifices, that the Lamb of God who takes away the sin of the world surrendered his life. All the events of Jesus's last days occurred in and around Jerusalem for a reason.

One event after the other during these final weeks in the Gospels finds new depth of meaning in its relationship to this city. A major catalyst to the events leading to the cross was the raising of a dead man, Lazarus, about forty days earlier in Bethany, a suburb of Jerusalem (John 11:1–44). The blessing and backlash of this miracle quickly followed. When Jesus made this strategic ride into Jerusalem during his "triumphal entry" (also referred to as "Palm Sunday"), his mode of transportation and the scene it overlooked confirmed prophecies, and the crowds corroborated that by shouting: "Hosanna to the Son of David!" The celebration further disturbed those who saw Jesus as a threat. They advanced their plan to have him executed. Jesus returned to Bethany, and when he went back to Jerusalem on Monday, he provided his disciples with a lesson on authentic faith, illustrated by visual aids along the way: a fig tree, the Herodium, and the Dead Sea.

As we come to the momentous conclusion of the final days up through his crucifixion, resurrection, and ascension, we find the events of Jesus's life taking on new meaning and power in their settings. We will explore his celebration of Passover in Jerusalem, in the upper room, and around a special table. We will walk with Jesus to Gethsemane and see how this familiar and comforting place takes on a darker hue as it adds to his struggle and provides an opportunity for his arrest. We will probe the setting of Jesus's interrogations before Caiaphas and Pilate, the location of his crucifixion, and the place of his burial in order to gain fresh insights into the familiar events that revolutionize our life. And finally, we will return to Galilee, where Jesus began his proclamation of God's Kingdom and his first recorded miracles. We will see that he made postresurrection appearances to commission and reassure the apostles in Galilee after he had shown himself to them following his resurrection in Jerusalem (Luke 24:1–3, 13–15, 33–36). From Bethany to the Mount of Olives to the cross, the tomb, the resurrection, and the ascension, we will see that the events of Jesus's last days on earth happened where they did for a reason.

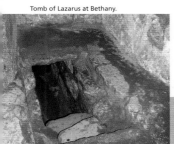

Tomb of Lazarus at Bethany.

Greek Orthodox painting of Peter cutting off the ear of the servant of the high priest (Church of the Holy Sepulcher).

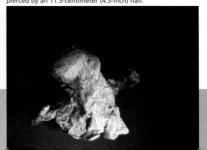

Heel bone of a crucified man, which was horizontally pierced by an 11.5-centimeter (4.5-inch) nail.

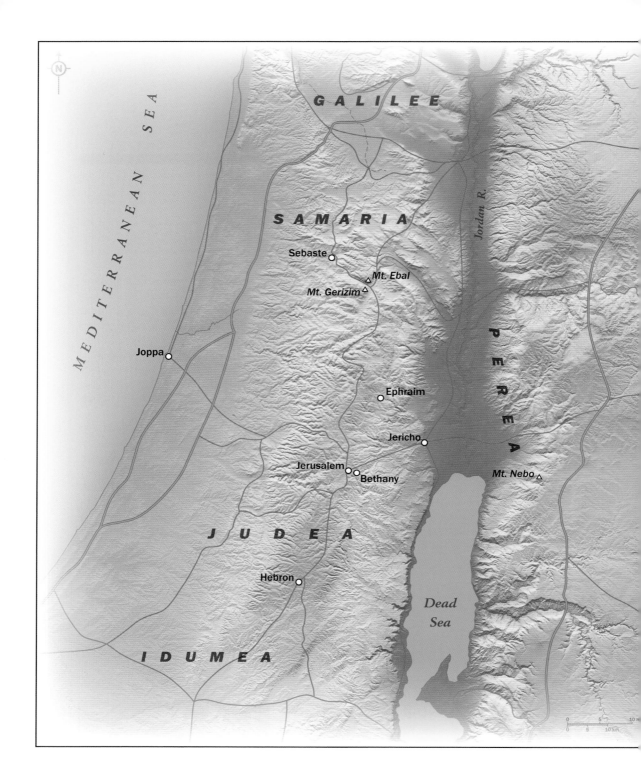

N

MEDITERRANEAN SEA

GALILEE

SAMARIA

Sebaste

Mt. Ebal
Mt. Gerizim

PEREA

Jordan R.

Joppa

Ephraim

Jericho

Jerusalem
Bethany

Mt. Nebo

JUDEA

Hebron

Dead
Sea

IDUMEA

0   5   10 mi
0   5   10 km

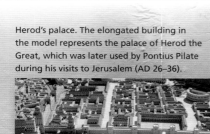

Herod's palace. The elongated building in the model represents the palace of Herod the Great, which was later used by Pontius Pilate during his visits to Jerusalem (AD 26–36).

Model representing the location of the Bethesda pools (foreground) where Jesus healed a crippled man (John 5:1–15).

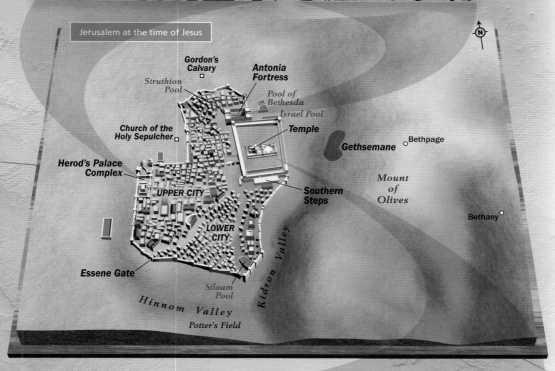

Jerusalem at the time of Jesus

Gordon's Calvary

Antonia Fortress

Struthion Pool

Pool of Bethesda

Israel Pool

Church of the Holy Sepulcher

Temple

Gethsemane

Bethpage

Herod's Palace Complex

UPPER CITY

Southern Steps

Mount of Olives

Bethany

LOWER CITY

Essene Gate

Kidron Valley

Siloam Pool

Hinnom Valley

Potter's Field

Model of the Jerusalem Temple (view looking west). The Sadducees controlled the business activities related to the Temple.

JESUS RAISES LAZARUS IN BETHANY

JOHN 11

During Jesus's earlier trips to Jerusalem, he had frequently stayed in the home of Mary, Martha, and Lazarus (Luke 10:38–42). Since the Judean village of Bethany where they lived was only a short distance away from Jerusalem, Jesus welcomed the open invitation to lodge with this family and enjoyed a deepening friendship with them. That made it all the more difficult when he was away in the region of Perea at Bethany, across the Jordan where John had been baptizing (John 10:40), and news reached him that Lazarus was gravely ill. Jesus had already demonstrated his capacity to heal (e.g., John 4:43–54). But instead of hurrying to Lazarus, Jesus responded by saying, "This sickness will not end in death. No, it is for God's glory so that God's son may be glorified through it" (John 11:4). Not long after, Lazarus died and was buried in a tomb near Bethany (in Judea).[1]

Four days after the death of Lazarus, Martha went out to meet Jesus and his disciples, who were en route from Jericho to Bethany (in Judea). When they met, Jesus told Martha that her brother would rise again (John 11:23–25). Jesus then asked Martha if she believed this to be true. She affirmed her confidence in Jesus's ability and observed that the person who is able to raise the dead can be none other than the Christ, the promised Messiah (John 11:25–27).

First-century Jewish perspectives held that on the fourth day after death the soul left the body and the process of decomposition began.[2] Thus when Jesus proceeded to the tomb on the fourth day after Lazarus's death, Lazarus was considered dead by every definition. In defiance of all mortal limits, the Son of God called for the lifeless, decomposing body of Lazarus to rise and exit the tomb—and it did just that. As the pulse returned to his lifeless arms and legs, Lazarus fought against the tight wrappings that had bound his dead body. He emerged from the tomb as alive as anyone who witnessed the event. There now could be no doubt; this miracle proved Jesus to be the Messiah!

Jesus raised Lazarus in Bethany for a reason. He had done miracles like this before. He had raised the daughter of Jairus in Capernaum (Luke 8:40–56), and he had raised the widow's son at Nain (Luke 7:11–17). But those miracles had occurred in Galilee, far from the Temple, and on the person's day of death—not four days later. The raising of Lazarus occurred in Bethany of Judea after Lazarus's body was decomposing. This fact is so important to John that he makes special note of it (John 11:18). Because the home of Mary, Martha, and Lazarus was less than two miles from Jerusalem, the news of the miracle ran wildly through the streets of that city (John 12:17–18). A miracle

After Lazarus's death, Jesus and his disciples would have traveled from Jericho to Bethany in Judea along the southern (right) ridge adjacent to the ravine (Wadi Qelt) in the center of the photo.

Jesus would have stopped at this spring, En Shemesh, prior to continuing his journey up the hill to Bethany.

Greek Orthodox Church at Bethany.

so close to Jerusalem, so easy to confirm, some forty days before the high festival of Passover when crowds would flood the city (John 12:12) meant Jesus was guaranteed an audience at every stop in the coming days. It also guaranteed that those already concerned about him were ready to act. That is particularly so since some of the leaders of the Pharisees in Jerusalem had witnessed the miracle and were now putting their faith in Jesus (John 12:9–11).[3] This was too much for the high priest, Caiaphas, to bear, and he could no longer tolerate the risk that this miracle brought against his own hold on power. Consequently, he called certain members of the Sanhedrin (i.e., the Jewish supreme court) together who not only voiced concerns about this rabbi from Galilee but also advanced their planning of

his execution (John 11:45–53).[4] The raising of Lazarus happening in Bethany, so close to Jerusalem, became a vital catalyst for the events that surrounded the last days before Jesus's crucifixion.

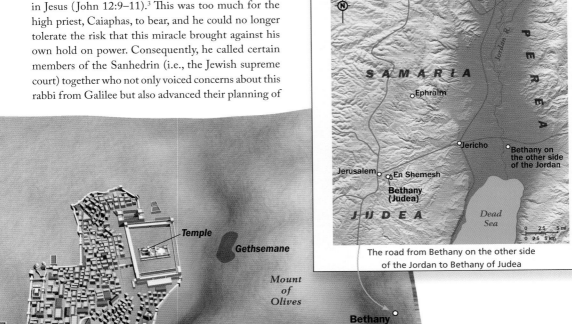

The road from Bethany on the other side of the Jordan to Bethany of Judea

193

JESUS GETS ON A DONKEY AT BETHPAGE

MATTHEW 21:1–11; JOHN 12:12–19

After raising Lazarus, Jesus went with his disciples to the village of Ephraim for a few days before continuing on to the Jordan Valley (John 11:54–57). He did not return to the Jerusalem area again until six days before Passover, when he had dinner in Bethany at the home of Mary, Martha, and Lazarus (John 12:1–2). The next morning generated a tremendously popular response as he rode into the city on his triumphal entry.[5] Throngs of people went out to meet Jesus—so many that it appeared the "whole world" had gone after him (John 12:19). Some in the large crowd spread their cloaks on the ground before him, as one would before a king (2 Kings 9:13). Still others spread palm branches before him, symbolic of the freedom this king might bring to them.[6] And they joined in singing the words of Psalm 118, revealing their hope that this son of David was the long-awaited Messiah.[7] All this happened because Jesus got on a donkey's colt at Bethpage for a reason.

Jesus had left the home of Mary, Martha, and Lazarus in Bethany and begun the ascent along the eastern road of the Mount of Olives en route to Jerusalem. Before he arrived at the village of Bethpage, Jesus sent two of his disciples ahead to secure a colt of a donkey.

Jesus had just walked for twenty minutes up the steep path from Bethany toward Bethpage. If he intended to make this trip to Jerusalem easier on himself, he would have secured the donkey at Bethany. But he walked from Bethany nearly to the top of the Mount of Olives to get on an animal at Bethpage so he could ride downhill into Jerusalem. The village of Bethpage, just one-half mile east of the summit of the Mount of Olives, was recognized as the city limits of Jerusalem.[8]

Jesus continued his ride down the western saddle of the Mount of Olives on a road that overlooked the

Jerusalem with the Mount of Olives (top right).

Kidron Valley and the City of David.[9] As the crowd saw Jesus's silhouette superimposed on the City of David and the Gihon Spring, they made a powerful connection. It was in the City of David that the Lord had promised King David that one of his descendants would sit on his throne forever (2 Sam. 7:1, 11–16). When David's immediate heir, Solomon, took his father's throne, he did so by riding a mule to the Gihon Spring in the Kidron Valley, where he was anointed king (1 Kings 1:32–35). In a scene filled with meaning in light of past events, Jesus rode down the Mount of Olives that overlooked the setting in which David received the promise and Solomon received his crown. The crowd understood this and celebrated the coming of the one who would sit on the throne of David forever as they cried out: "Hosanna to the Son of David!" (Matt. 21:9).

▲ The crowds waved palm branches during the triumphal entry as a symbol of Jewish nationalism. The "Judea Captive" coin, depicting a Jewish captive under a palm tree, was minted by the Romans to commemorate the destruction of Jewish nationalism and the Temple in AD 70. © Dr. James C. Martin. The Eretz Israel Museum.

Jesus had gotten on the donkey colt at Bethpage not to make his travel easier but for a more important reason. By doing this he announced the beginning of his triumphal entry into Jerusalem. The welcoming masses understood exactly what Jesus was doing. He was presenting himself to the holy city of Jerusalem as the Messiah prophesied by Zechariah (Zech. 9:9; Matt. 21:4–5). But Jesus cautiously used a form of communication that would not arouse the anger and suspicions of the Roman authorities. As he fulfilled scriptural promises about the Messiah, he used symbolic actions that were linked to his entry. In doing so, his Jewish audience received the message while bypassing the Roman authorities who kept a close watch on all the affairs of the city from the Antonia Fortress that overlooked the Temple Mount. Clearly the throng of people came out to meet Jesus on his triumphal entry (i.e., Palm Sunday) because he got on a donkey's colt at Bethpage.

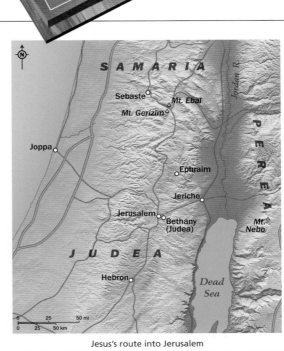

Antonia Fortress

Temple

Jesus gets on the donkey's colt at Bethpage and rides down the Mount of Olives to Jerusalem

City of David

Kidron Valley

Gihon Spring

Bethpage

Mount of Olives

Jesus walks from Bethany to Bethpage

Bethany

Triumphal entry

Jesus rode a young donkey into Jerusalem during his triumphal entry.

SAMARIA

Jordan R.

Sebaste

Mt. Ebal

Mt. Gerizim

Joppa

PEREA

Ephraim

Jericho

Jerusalem

Bethany (Judea)

Mt. Nebo

JUDEA

Hebron

Dead Sea

0   25   50 mi
0   25   50 km

Jesus's route into Jerusalem

JESUS CURSES A FIG TREE NEAR BETHPAGE ON THE ROAD TO JERUSALEM

MATTHEW 21:18–22; MARK 11:20–26

The triumphal entry (Palm Sunday) brought Jesus toe-to-toe with the religious and political leadership in Jerusalem. In advance of upcoming confrontations with the corrupt Temple leadership and a scandal-laden Roman governor, Jesus took time to speak with his disciples about authentic faith[10] and what the authority of the Kingdom of God really meant. So following their Sunday night stay in Bethany, he and his disciples retraced their steps to Jerusalem, and along the way Jesus presented a lesson on the nature of God's Kingdom in the context of true faith (Matt. 21:18–22). He did it near Bethpage (Hebrew for "house of the preseason fig") on the road from Bethany to Jerusalem for a reason.

Preseason figs were known as *pagés*.

The first lesson involved a fig tree. From a distance, the tree looked healthy, boasting the appropriate small green leaves of spring. Because fig trees were one of the signature trees of the Promised Land (Num. 13:23; 1 Kings 4:25), locals were familiar with its annual cycle. Following the winter season when the branches look like old gray bones, small leaves and the early season fig (called *pagé*) make their appearance simultaneously in the springtime.[11] So when Jesus saw this fig tree in leaf, he expected to find preseason figs among those leaves. But Jesus found the tree to be hypocritical. It

had leaves (the signs of fruit) but no fruit. "Then he said to it, 'May you never bear fruit again!' Immediately the tree withered" (Matt. 21:19).

What was Jesus teaching? The Temple aristocracy portrayed their religiosity by wearing priestly garments. But like the fig tree, they were hypocritical. They had the symbols of faith (religious garments as required by Exod. 28:1–4) but failed to produce the fruit of faith. As often portrayed in the Scriptures, the fig tree was enlisted as a symbol of judgment against those whose faith is fraudulent (Isa. 34:4; Jer. 5:17; 8:13; Hosea 2:12). Jesus's message to the disciples is clear: don't be afraid of the corrupt Temple leaders, for they will end up like this withered fig tree.

It was not just the religious leaders the disciples would have to deal with but also with the political power of Rome. Jesus then said, "I tell you the truth, if you have faith and do not doubt, not only can you do what was done to the fig tree, but also you can say to this mountain, 'Go, throw yourself into the sea,' and it will be done" (Matt. 21:21). To know the implications of this statement, it helps to understand the locale where Jesus made this pronouncement.

Dead Sea (view looking east). Jewish law instructed that objects of idolatry be thrown into the Dead Sea.

Jesus cursed the fig tree near Bethpage where one can see two landmarks: the Herodium and the Dead Sea. The Herodium was a manmade landmark no one could miss. Herod the Great had directed his builders to move a mountain in order to construct a palace-fortress on the edge of the Judean Wilderness southeast of Bethlehem.[12] Herod created this palace-fortress named after himself to command the attention of everyone in the region.[13] From the location of the fig tree looking east beyond the Herodium, the disciples could make out traces of the Dead Sea. According to Jewish oral law (i.e., Mishnah, circa 200 BC–AD 200), this body of water has a special role in ridding the land of idolatrous influence. The Mishnah directs that any items contaminated by idolatry, whether symbols or associated idolatrous practices, must be thrown into the Dead Sea.[14] Herod represented Roman interests in the Promised Land and had moved a mountain a short distance in order to advance his own security needs and perhaps to feed his own hungry ego. With the power of Rome, Herod could move a mountain. But in the power of the Kingdom of God, faith can throw Herod's mountain (representing Rome) into the Dead Sea!

Herod the Great "moved a mountain" by having the hill to the left shaved off and placed on the hill to the right in order to build his palace-fortress called the Herodium.

Jesus cursed a fig tree near Bethpage on the road to Jerusalem for a reason. It was from Bethpage that the cursing of the fig tree encouraged the disciples not to fear the corrupt Temple leaders. It was from this same location that the disciples could see the Herodium and the Dead Sea. Jesus taught his disciples not to fear Rome, for every time they acted in accordance to God's truth, the power of the Kingdom of God would overthrow all the idolatrous powers the Herodium represented and cast them into the place appropriate for idolatry. So as disciples of Jesus, we can learn the meaning and power of faith from the fig tree, the mountain, and the Dead Sea, all seen near Bethpage on the road that leads to Jerusalem.

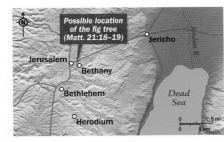

Jesus curses a fig tree

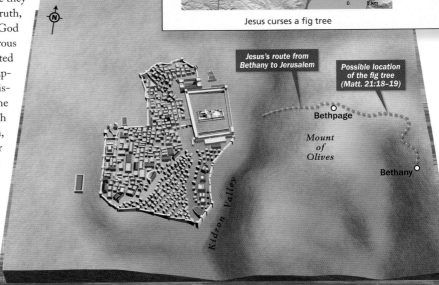

JESUS CELEBRATES THE PASSOVER IN THE UPPER ROOM

MATTHEW 26:17–35; MARK 14:12–31; LUKE 22:7–38; JOHN 13–17

Following his reception into Jerusalem, Jesus spent the first few days of the week teaching in and around the Temple complex. Because the week would culminate in the celebration of Passover, Jesus's disciples asked him where he would like to eat the special meal.[15] Two disciples were instructed to follow a man carrying water to a home with an upper room (Mark 14:13–15; Luke 22:10–12). Although the particulars of that meal and Jesus's words have long been the center of conversation, here we focus on its setting within Jerusalem—in a "guest room" and around a triclinium table for a reason.

As Jesus directed his disciples in their quest to find a suitable place for the Passover meal, he sent them into the city of Jerusalem (Mark 14:13; Luke 22:10). On the other days of this week, it appears that Jesus had been teaching in Jerusalem during the day and then returning to Bethany for the evening meal and overnight stay (Matt. 21:17–18; 26:6–7; Mark 14:1–3). But that routine was going to be broken because Deuteronomy 16:5–8 required the Passover meal be eaten within the city of Jerusalem.

The location for this meal was an upper room that is also called a "guest room."[16] As Luke describes this room, he uses a special term, calling it the "guest room" of

Jerusalem model representing the area of the upper room.

the home (*kataluma*). Within his entire book, Luke only uses this Greek word two times (Luke 2:7; 22:11). The first occurs in connection with Jesus's birth. Mary and Joseph were denied the opportunity to use the "guest room" for Jesus's birth. The second time Luke mentions a "guest room" is here as Jesus's earthly purpose was nearing its completion. With this subtle but powerful choice in words, Luke signals that Jesus's earthly life had now come full circle and was reaching its final moment: the guest room that was denied at the time of his birth was offered to him in the hours before his death.

Finally we note that this room is fully "furnished" (Mark 14:15; Luke 22:12) so that those eating could recline (Matt. 26:20; Luke 22:14). This suggests that Jesus and his disciples were dining around a *triclinium* table, which provided a U-shaped, three-sided eating surface. The table was set low to the ground so that those eating on the outer three sides of the table could recline on the left elbow while eating with the right hand.

Relief of a banquet scene at a reclining table.

Passover / Last Supper seating arrangement
(after Edersheim). © Dr. James C. Martin. Illustration by Timothy Ladwig.

John Jesus Judas
 X   X   X   X   X
                        X
                        X
                        X
 X   X   X   X   X
Peter

Guests took a seat around the table according to a prescribed social norm, where seating position carried the connotation of either greater or lesser honor. The need to determine who sat where apparently prompted discussion among the disciples about who was greatest, perhaps to clarify their seating position for the future (Luke 22:24–30). The seating arrangement around this table also permits us to better understand how certain conversations were public and others more private. Jesus was likely sitting in the second position at the table—the host's position. John reclined to the right of Jesus, allowing his head to rest on Jesus's chest, with Judas to the left of Jesus. This meant Jesus could have private conversations with either Judas or John while Peter, who perhaps was sitting at the servant's position, signaled to John across the table to learn more about the content of those conversations (John 13:21–27).[17]

So the setting of the Passover meal in all its facets was carefully selected by Jesus for a reason. Israelites interpreted Deuteronomy 16:5–8 to mean that the Passover was to be celebrated in Jerusalem. The "guest room" was a reminder that the incarnate life of Jesus had come full circle. And the seating arrangements around the table help us better understand several of the conversations that occurred that evening.

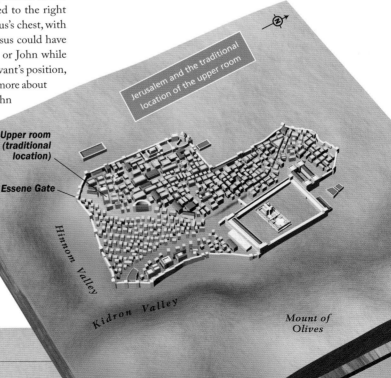

Jerusalem and the traditional location of the upper room

Upper room (traditional location)

Essene Gate

Hinnom Valley

Kidron Valley

Mount of Olives

JESUS PRAYS IN GETHSEMANE
MATTHEW 26:36–56; MARK 14:32–52; LUKE 22:39–53; JOHN 18:1–11

With the Passover meal in the upper room concluded, Jesus led his disciples across the Kidron Valley and along the lower slopes of the Mount of Olives. Retracing familiar footsteps, they made their way to a location they had frequented during less difficult days. Gethsemane was an industrial olive orchard at the western base of the Mount of Olives where Jesus and the disciples could have a quiet place to talk and pray (John 18:2). But this night Jesus's struggle would be defined and intensified by its location.

On this evening when Jesus fell to his knees in prayer, we see him hard-pressed. He turned to those closest to him and said, "My soul is overwhelmed with sorrow to the point of death" (Matt. 26:38). Yet, as events unfolded, even the most trusted of his disciples failed him. He had no one to whom he could turn for help and support but his Father who sent him on this rescue mission. As he poured out his heart in prayer, we see his soul and his struggle laid bare: "My Father, if it is possible, may this cup be taken from me. Yet not as I will, but as you will" (Matt. 26:39). Jesus had brought his disciples to the Mount of Olives earlier in the week and had warned them of the Temple's destruction (Matt.

Wood "screw" olive press (first century AD).

Segment of bedrock in the Basilica of the Agony (Church of All Nations) that preserves the memory of Jesus's final prayers before his arrest in Gethsemane.

24:1–2, 15–19), as he would later warn the women weeping for him on the way to his crucifixion (Luke 23:28–31). Now on the Mount of Olives he had come face to face with the crucifixion awaiting him.

The traditional location of this event is marked by the Church of All Nations, built in 1924.[18] It is the most recent of several churches that have graced this spot since the fourth century. At least since that time, Christians have pointed to bedrock that lies near the church altar as the rock on which Jesus was so powerfully pressed.[19] Here Jesus experienced the rare phenomenon known as *hemohidrosis*. This physiological response occurs when intense emotional pressure causes capillaries in the hands and forehead to rupture, causing a bloody sweat.[20] Note the connection between this phenomenon and its location. *Gethsemane* (from the Hebrew, *gat shemen*) means "oil press." Jesus had come to Gethsemane, the place of the oil press, where he was powerfully pressed to the point that "his sweat was like drops of blood" (Luke 22:44) as he experienced hemohidrosis.

Jesus's struggle in Gethsemane was intensified by this location's proximity to the Judean Wilderness. Jerusalem was built on the fringes of this wilderness—a rugged and forbidding landscape largely unfit for human habitation.

Yet throughout time it had continued to function in one important way: it was the place a person could go to get away from everyone else. Jesus knew all too well that a forty-five minute walk over the top of the Mount of Olives and into the Judean Wilderness promised him geographic isolation and protection against those who wanted him dead. In the Judean Wilderness he would be well beyond the reach of the chief priests and the Roman authorities, and he could be in a place far away from the brutality and pain that marked the hours ahead. But the victory over the immediate temptation to escape into the Judean Wilderness had already been won in Jesus's response to the adversary who had earlier tempted him in the wilderness soon after his baptism by John. He had withstood that temptation, and now Jesus stood firm in this situation.[21]

Jesus had come to Gethsemane to pray for a reason. It was a familiar place that he had used with his disciples before. Moreover, Gethsemane (i.e., the place of the oil press) was the place where Jesus was pressed as he surrendered himself to the cross rather than escaping into the Judean Wilderness. On this night Gethsemane became a place that both defined and intensified his struggle in his choice to lay down his life as the sacrificed Lamb.

Upper room (traditional location)

Kidron Valley

Gethsemane (traditional location)

Possible location of Gethsemane

To Judean Wilderness

New Testament Jerusalem and the Garden of Gethsemane

Mount of Olives, Church of All Nations, and Gethsemane (view looking east).

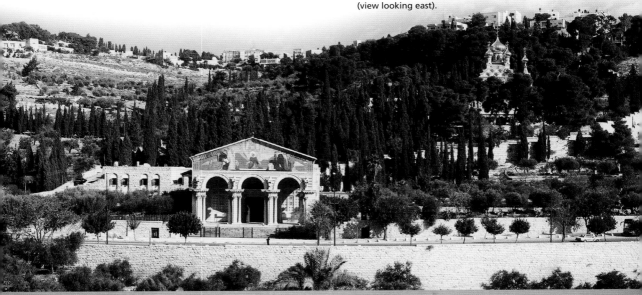

CAIAPHAS ACCUSES JESUS OF BLASPHEMY IN A WHOLE COURT OF THE SANHEDRIN

MATTHEW 26:57–68; MARK 14:53–65; LUKE 22:47–53; JOHN 18:12–24

Soon after the arrest of Jesus by the Temple guard, he was taken before the high priest, Caiaphas, who was president of the Sanhedrin court, and other select members of the court. Before Jesus left their presence, the high priest tore his robe and announced that Jesus was guilty of blasphemy.

We know something of the composition and role of the Sanhedrin court from the Gospels as well as the Mishnah (a record of Jewish oral law). The Great Sanhedrin was composed of seventy-one individuals and drew its members from the priestly aristocracy, the Pharisees, and heads of the most influential nonclergy families.[22] Although the Pharisees and Sadducees differed in many ways, they did have one thing in common: both placed a high value on the institution of the Temple, though for very different reasons. For the Sadducees, the institution of the Temple was a business that promised to net them a hefty annual income.[23] For the Pharisees, this institution was important because it defined Judaism, unified Judaism, and got one right with God. Given the importance of the Temple institution to both Sadducees and Pharisees, it is not surprising to find that the Great Sanhedrin of seventy-one members met within this complex. The Great Sanhedrin was divided into three whole courts, each consisting of twenty-three members. While noncapital offenses were tried by fewer members, cases involving the death penalty required a whole court of twenty-three members.[24]

When certain Sanhedrin members perceived Jesus had been speaking against the Temple, it got their attention (John 5:18). When Jesus raised Lazarus from the dead, Caiaphas concluded, "If we let him go on like this, everyone will believe in him, and then the Romans will come and take away both our place and our nation" (John 11:48; see also vv. 45–54). As the Sanhedrin members saw their position and authority being challenged, it was with some urgency that Caiaphas[25] searched for charges in order to bring Jesus before a

Caiaphas ossuary with the Aramaic inscription "Yehosef bar Kayafa" (Joseph, son of Caiaphas).

whole court (Matt. 26:59) of twenty-three Sanhedrin members, where he could be sentenced to death.[26]

They intended to make the case that Jesus was threatening the institution of the Temple, a charge that would not only sully the popularity of Jesus but would also bring the Romans into the picture because the Romans were obligated to assure the safety and sanctity of the Temple.[27] Of course Jesus had spoken of his death and resurrection metaphorically as the destruction and rebuilding of the Temple in three days. Although the corrupt Sanhedrin leaders did their best to turn this into an actionable threat against the Temple, problems with witnesses caused this effort to fail (Mark 14:58–59).

Caiaphas accused Jesus of blasphemy in a whole court of the Sanhedrin for a reason. The Temple leadership was looking for a way to rid themselves of the threat of Jesus. In short order Jesus offered a statement before the court that the high priest branded as blasphemy. During the questioning, Jesus claimed the title "Son of

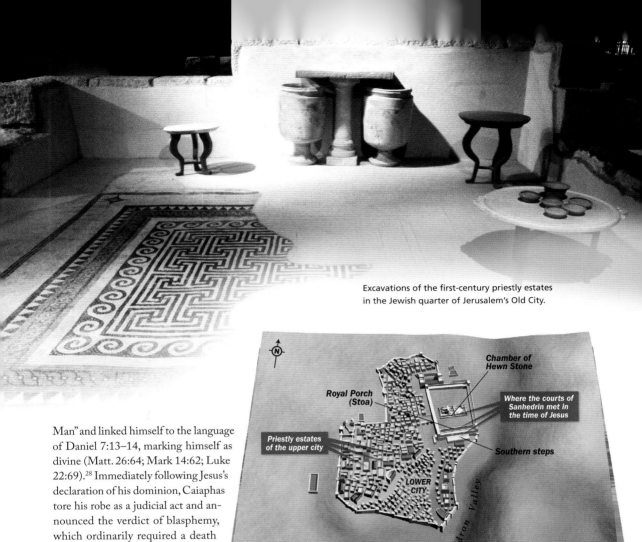

Excavations of the first-century priestly estates in the Jewish quarter of Jerusalem's Old City.

Man" and linked himself to the language of Daniel 7:13–14, marking himself as divine (Matt. 26:64; Mark 14:62; Luke 22:69).[28] Immediately following Jesus's declaration of his dominion, Caiaphas tore his robe as a judicial act and announced the verdict of blasphemy, which ordinarily required a death sentence (John 19:7).

Chamber of Hewn Stone

Royal Porch (Stoa)

Where the courts of Sanhedrin met in the time of Jesus

Priestly estates of the upper city

Southern steps

LOWER CITY

Kidron Valley

Hinnom Valley

Location of Sanhedrin courts

Inside passage through the Huldah Gates, where one court of the Sanhedrin is believed to have convened.

© Garo Nalbandian.

CAIAPHAS BLASPHEMES BEFORE PILATE

MATTHEW 27:11–26; MARK 15:1–15; LUKE 23:1–25; JOHN 18:29–19:16

Following the verdict of Caiaphas, the next move was to secure Jesus's execution. Determining to avoid potential religious and political problems that would result from executing Jesus themselves (cf. John 18:28), the whole court of twenty-three Sanhedrin members delivered Jesus into the hands of the Roman authorities. This group of corrupt Temple leaders told Pilate, the Roman military governor, that Jesus had incited uprisings, discouraged payment of taxes to Caesar, and boldly spoken of himself as a king (Luke 23:2, 5). The last of the charges was the most serious because sedition against the emperor of Rome was a capital crime.

Pilate had assumed his role as military governor and civil judge (procurator) of Judea in AD 26 and held it until he was banished in AD 36. During most of his days in office, Pilate lived in Caesarea Maritima.[29] But he moved to Jerusalem during the winter months, from Hanukkah through the high holiday of Passover—festivals that inspired Jewish independence. While in Jerusalem, it is most likely that he lived in the palace Herod the Great had built on the western ridge of Jerusalem. The courtyard of that palace may well be the Stone Pavement that became the setting for Jesus's trial (John 19:13).[30]

As Jesus stood on that pavement, he could see Rome because wherever Pilate went, the authority and power of Rome went with him. As an imperial procurator, Pilate was empowered to hear evidence and render verdicts that could only be overturned by the emperor himself.[31] Pilate knew the power of his position as he upbraided Jesus for not responding to him. "Don't you realize I have power either to free you or to crucify you?" (John 19:10).

Although it was true Pilate had the power of Rome, on numerous previous occasions his cultural insensitivity and heartless cruelty had brought him perilously close to removal from office.[32] As a result of certain actions of Pilate, the Jerusalem leadership had even threatened to send an embassy to Emperor Tiberius to protest. According to Philo,

It was this final point that particularly exasperated Pilate, for he feared that if they actually sent an embassy,

Model of the Herodian palace, where Jesus was taken to Pilate.

Honorary inscription from Pontius Pilate, dedicated to the emperor Tiberius.

© Dr. James C. Martin. The Israel Museum.

Model of the Antonia Fortress (possibly the place of Rome's scourging of Jesus) with the Temple in the background.

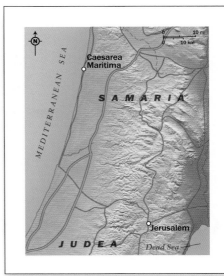

they would also expose the rest of his conduct as governor by stating in full the briberies, insults, robberies, outrages and wanton injuries, executions without trial, and ceaseless and supremely grievous cruelty. So with all his vindictiveness and furious temper, he was in a difficult position.[33]

Caiaphas subsequently blasphemed before Pilate for a reason. Given Pilate's weak standing with his superior, Pilate wanted to make sure he had sufficient justification to appease Tiberius if a riot occurred as a result of Jesus's execution. He first attempted to dodge the trial by freeing Jesus according to his custom of releasing a prisoner during the feast (Matt. 27:15–18) and then by shuffling the Galilean off to the tetrarch who controlled Galilee, Herod Antipas (Luke 23:5–12). When Pilate appeared to be on the brink of releasing Jesus, he was threatened that his actions would be reported to Rome (John 19:12). So what was Pilate waiting for? Perhaps he was waiting for Caiaphas and the Temple leadership to offer him something with which he could justify himself if the death of Jesus caused a riot. The moment came when Caiaphas and the chief priests, in order to influence Pilate to do the deed, blasphemed by

claiming, "We have no king but Caesar" (John 19:15). With such a proclamation, the Temple leadership had repudiated the God of Israel. Now if there was a riot, Pilate could explain to the emperor that the riot was worth it, for the corrupt priestly families of Sadducees agreed to reject the Creator of the universe as God and King and go to direct imperial worship in exchange for Pilate doing the deed.

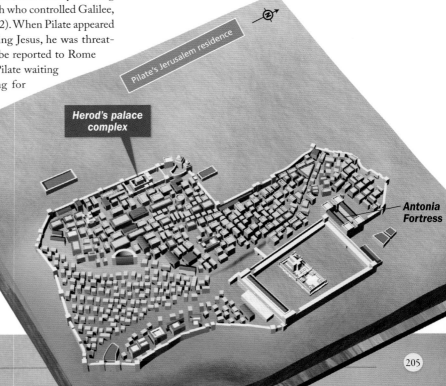

Pilate's Jerusalem residence

Herod's palace complex

Antonia Fortress

ROMAN SOLDIERS CRUCIFY JESUS AT CALVARY

MATTHEW 27:27–56; MARK 15:16–41; LUKE 23:33–49; JOHN 19:17–37

Jesus was severely scourged by the Roman soldiers in preparation for his crucifixion. The Romans did this by using a *flagellum*—a crude whip made from a wooden handle and leather straps. Metal balls and pieces of bone were affixed to the straps so the lashes would tear deeply into the flesh.[34] The scourging was part of the torture associated with the execution and was designed to diminish the resistance of the one being crucified.[35] When Pilate's soldiers finished mocking Jesus, they led him away to be crucified. Initially, Jesus carried his cross (John 19:17), but later Roman soldiers forced Simon, a man passing by, to carry it (Mark 15:21). When they finally arrived at the place of execution, the soldiers nailed Jesus to the cross with the written charge fixed above his head: "JESUS OF NAZARETH, THE KING OF THE JEWS" (John 19:19). These are the events that brought Jesus to the place of the Skull or Golgotha,[36] where he died as the sacrificed Lamb of God.

Two locations in Jerusalem, the Church of the Holy Sepulcher and Gordon's Calvary, are recognized as possible locations of the crucifixion and burial site of Jesus.[37] A visit to either spot helps us understand that Jesus was crucified in a cemetery, along a public roadway, and on a cross for a reason.

First we note that Jesus was executed in a cemetery (John 19:41). Contact with the deceased and with a cemetery made one ritually unclean by Jewish reckoning. The Romans knew this, and they executed Jews in a cemetery because it added another layer of indignity to an already undignified

Model of Golgotha (in the location of the Church of the Holy Sepulcher), outside the city wall of Jerusalem during the Gospel period.

death. Thus it was no accident that Jesus was crucified in a cemetery to further humiliate him and desecrate the Jewish tombs in the area.

Second, we note that this humiliation took place in a very public setting because Jesus was crucified alongside a public roadway. The Romans chose such public thoroughfares rather than remote locations because they wanted crucifixion, in all its horror, to act as a deterrent to future crime. So they crucified Jesus where an audience might gather. This meant his enemies had easy access to taunt and mock him. "Those who passed by hurled insults at him, shaking their heads and saying, 'You who are going to destroy the temple and build it in three days, save yourself! Come down from the cross, if you are the Son of God'" (Matt. 27:39–40). This verbal abuse was a fulfillment of the prophecy of Psalm 22, where the Lord said that the Messiah would face exactly the kind of treatment and hear exactly the language that Matthew reports (cf. Ps. 22:7–8; Matt. 27:39–43). Ironically, those who had wished to demean Jesus were actually validating his claim to be Messiah by fulfilling

Illustration of crucifixion on an olive tree.
© Dr. James C. Martin. Illustration by Timothy Ladwig.

Mosaic floor representing the Temple veil.

the prophecy of Psalm 22. All of this happened as Jesus was crucified alongside a public roadway.

Finally we note that Jesus died on a cross.[38] This form of capital punishment was particularly reserved for those found guilty of treason against the Roman Empire, designed to shame and humiliate them.[39] What is more, it carried a negative connotation within the Jewish culture: to be executed in this way was to be under God's curse (Deut. 21:22–23). In many ways it appears to be a contradiction of the first order that the Messiah, God's Son, should die in this way. But Paul helps us see that even Jesus's death on the cross was part of the purpose of the Messiah: "Christ redeemed us from the curse of the law by becoming a curse for us, for it is written: 'Cursed is everyone who is hung on a tree'" (Gal. 3:13).

The Roman soldiers crucified Jesus at Calvary for a reason. There the Roman government could kill him in a cemetery in order to desecrate Jewish tombs, alongside a public roadway for a warning to others, and on a cross to undermine his claim to be the King of the Jews.

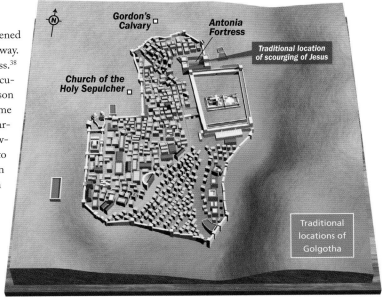

Gordon's Calvary

Antonia Fortress

Traditional location of scourging of Jesus

Church of the Holy Sepulcher

Traditional locations of Golgotha

JESUS IS PREPARED FOR BURIAL AND PLACED IN A TOMB

MATTHEW 27:57–61; MARK 15:42–47; LUKE 23:50–56; JOHN 19:38–42

After Jesus surrendered his life on the cross, Joseph of Arimathea requested that the body of Jesus be released into his custody so he could bury Jesus in his own tomb—a new tomb that lay in the cemetery where Jesus had been executed (Mark 15:43; John 19:41). Joseph and his associate in this task, Nicodemus, were both members of the Sanhedrin who had objected to the day's events (Luke 23:50–51; John 19:38–39). They had failed to prevent the corrupt Sadducees, Caiaphas, and Pilate from doing their worst, yet they longed to do one last thing for Jesus by providing him with a dignified burial. Both the way in which Jesus's body was prepared and his burial in the tomb revealed they were done for a reason.

The religious party of the Pharisees believed in the physical resurrection of the dead. Jewish customs of Jesus's day did not embalm the deceased but instead wrapped the body in linen cloth and used burial spices to prevent poisonous gases from forming in the sealed tomb—gases that were produced as the body began to decompose. By preparing the body in this way, the family could safely return in order to deal with the remains of their loved one and make room for additional bodies in advance of the resurrection.[40]

Since the Jewish tombs in first-century Judea were constructed according to a typical pattern, archaeological tomb remains provide us with a probable depiction of Jesus's tomb.[41] Such a tomb was typically hewn out of rock, often enlarging and modifying an existing cave. A low, U-shaped bench lined the inside walls of the chamber and provided a station for preparing the body. Once preparations were complete, the deceased was placed into a niche (*kokh*) cut perpendicular to the bench, where it would reside for a year or more while the softer tissue decomposed. Once the decomposition of the flesh was complete, select family members returned to the tomb and placed the bones into an ossuary—a small stone box that became the permanent resting place for the skeletal remains. Each step of this burial process, from preparation of the body to the second burial in the ossuary, reflected the hope that one day the body placed in the tomb would rise from the dead.[42]

Joseph and Nicodemus placed Jesus's body on the bench in the tomb (John 19:40–42).[43] But there were rumblings of discontent even after that. The chief priests and other Temple leaders returned to Pilate concerned that someone might steal the body and claim that Jesus's promise to rise from the dead had been fulfilled. So

Limestone burial boxes known as ossuaries.

Pilate instructed Caiaphas to secure the large stone that closed the tomb with an official seal, and a Temple guard was stationed to prevent tampering (Matt. 27:62–66).

Jesus was prepared for burial and placed in a tomb for a reason. The followers of Jesus were looking forward to the future resurrection of the dead. Although, for many, hope of the messianic Kingdom had been dashed with the crucifixion of Jesus, he too would be raised, and so his body had to be prepared accordingly. When the women came to the tomb on the first day of the week in order to complete the process of preparing Jesus's body, they were amazed to find things different from when they had left two days earlier. The guard was gone, the seal on the tomb was broken, and the stone had been removed from the entrance. When they looked inside, the body was gone,[44] and the linens that had been wrapped so lovingly around the body of Jesus were lying neatly on the bench (Matt. 28:1–10; Mark 16:1–8; John 20:1–9). It was clear Jesus had gone, but what had happened? The absence of a body on the bench begged for an explanation. God gave it through an angel: "He is not here; he has risen, just as he said" (Matt. 28:6).

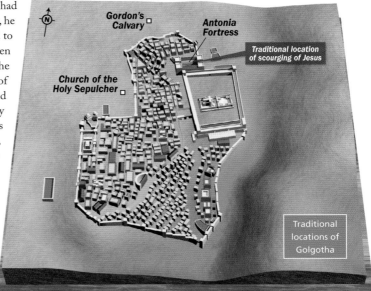

◀ Burial shroud.   © Dr. James C. Martin. The Cairo Museum.
◀ (left inset) Rolling-stone tomb door (first century AD).
◀ (right inset) Kochim tomb.

THE RESURRECTED JESUS MEETS THE DISCIPLES IN GALILEE

JOHN 21

In the hours and days following his resurrection, Jesus spent considerable time in and around Jerusalem confirming that he had risen. He appeared to a number of his followers at the tomb (John 20:1–18). He conversed with two disciples on their way to Emmaus (Luke 24:13–35). And he appeared to some disciples in the upper room on at least two occasions, where they were overjoyed to see Jesus and even received the Holy Spirit from Jesus himself (Luke 24:36–49; John 20:19–31). These appearances continued for forty days (Acts 1:3),[45] but not all of them took place in Judea. In fact, Jesus directed the apostles to leave Jerusalem and meet him in Galilee for a reason (Matt. 28:10).

It was in Galilee that Jesus commissioned his disciples as the ones who would teach the nations about him (Matt. 28:16–20). The fact that Jesus's rescue efforts included all people was already made clear with the Lord's promise to Abram that through him all nations would be blessed (Gen. 12:1–3). This promise was fulfilled with the overthrow of the adversary by the teaching, miracles, cross, and resurrection of Jesus the Messiah (the Son of Man, the Prophet, and the Son of David). With his purpose on earth now accomplished, Jesus said to the apostles, "Therefore go and make disciples of all nations" (Matt. 28:19). This commissioning did not occur just anywhere but in the very region of the Promised Land known as the "Galilee of the Gentiles" (Isa. 9:1). This setting illustrates the future purpose of the disciples. In Galilee Jesus not only commissioned his disciples but reaffirmed their relationship with him as well. The disciples traveled to Galilee as Jesus directed. Once there, Peter told Thomas, Nathanael, the sons of Zebedee, and two others that he was "going out to fish," and they replied, "We'll go with you" (John 21:1–3).

A few years earlier, Jesus had informed these men that he would make them "fishers of men" (Mark 1:17). Now they returned to the Sea of Galilee to fish for fish. To reaffirm their purpose and relationship with the

Scuola Nuova tapestry (AD 1524–31) depicting the supper at Emmaus.

resurrected Lord, Jesus came to the apostles alongside the Sea of Galilee in a scene that will sound increasingly familiar to us. Peter and his colleagues pushed off into the Sea of Galilee from its northwestern shore.[46] They fished in boats all night but caught no fish. As they returned early in the morning, a man on the shore redirected their efforts. As a result, and even at the time of day when the hope for a successful catch had expired, their nets filled with an unmanageable number of fish. These events occurred on the shore of the Sea of Galilee

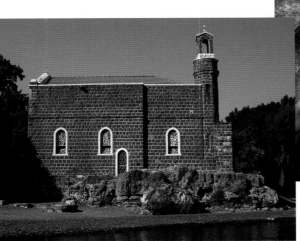

Saint Peter's fish—*Tilapia galilea* in Latin (also known as *amnun*, "nurse fish," in Hebrew).

The Franciscan chapel known as the Primacy of St. Peter was built on the northern shore of the Sea of Galilee in 1933, on the site of a fourth-century church thought to be the place where Jesus met with Peter in John 21.

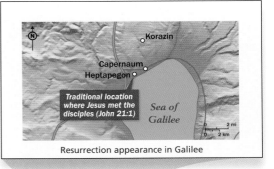

Resurrection appearance in Galilee

after Jesus's resurrection and are nearly an exact parallel to those on the day when Jesus first called the men to be his disciples (cf. Luke 5:1–11; John 21:1–6). A few years earlier it was on this spot that Jesus said to Peter, "Don't be afraid; from now on you will catch men" (Luke 5:10). He did not have to say those words again; the place joined with the event to say it all.

Was it really possible for these men to still be Jesus's disciples after they had deserted him? And what of Peter, who had denied Jesus three times on that difficult day in Jerusalem? Very soon after his resurrection Jesus had eaten with his disciples (Luke 24:40–43). He had already forgiven them, and now he was saying, "Come and have breakfast" (John 21:12). This was no ordinary meal but one that represented an ancient custom that uses a meal to assure those who are invited of forgiveness and acceptance.[47]

The resurrected Jesus met his disciples in Galilee for a reason. They had denied the Lord and run away. Not only had full reconciliation been acknowledged with meals, but the disciples were also reminded of their purpose as Abraham's descendants and as God's messengers. Thus Jesus came to them in Galilee of the Nations (Isa. 9:1; i.e., the district of the nations) where he first called them to be fishers of men. There he reaffirmed a message of forgiveness by means of the meal covenant and called them to proclaim him as Messiah and make disciples from people of all nations.

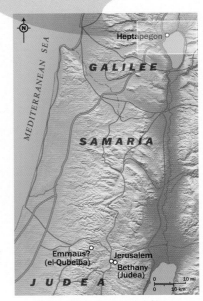

Resurrection appearances of Jesus

PART 10

THE GOOD NEWS TRAVELS FROM JERUSALEM TO THE WORLD

This inscription warned against bringing any Gentiles beyond the dividing wall surrounding the Temple sanctuary.

© Dr. James C. Martin. The Israel Museum.

ACTS

Although they would witness his ascension from the earth, Jesus promised his disciples that he would be with them always. They were to go and make disciples of all nations (Matt. 28:18–20). The disciples got the message, and the book of Acts tells of their experiences and journeys to take this Good News from Jerusalem into Judea, Samaria, and throughout the world (Acts 1:8).

The goal of part 10 is to see how the church[1] moved from inside the walls of observant Judaism into a world of nations, cultures, races, and languages and illustrates the important relationship between event and place. We will begin in Jerusalem in order to see that the outpouring of the Holy Spirit during the Jewish holiday of Pentecost (*Shevuot*) happened there for a reason. While those Pentecost visitors returned to their homes, Peter and John made their home in Jerusalem. We will see how the apostles repeatedly returned to the Temple complex to assert Jesus's legitimate authority in that place, proclaiming the news of Jesus in Solomon's Colonnade and witnessing the healing of a crippled man at the Gate Beautiful.

The narrative of Acts then moves from Jerusalem to follow the travels of Philip. We will pay attention to two locations where he traveled: the region of Samaria and the desert road on the way to Gaza. We will see why a thriving community of followers of Jesus developed in Samaria and how the roadside visit with an Ethiopian eunuch transported the church into Africa in a way that the events of Pentecost did not.

Two leaders of the early church, Paul and Peter, both underwent significant changes in the days after the Holy Spirit's outpouring at Pentecost. We will see why Jesus appeared to Paul on the road to Damascus and how Peter's worldview was changed as he traveled from Joppa to the home of a Roman centurion in Caesarea Maritima. But not everyone changed at the same time or so easily. One issue in particular demanded the attention of the apostles in Jerusalem: was it necessary for Gentiles who submitted to the Messiah Jesus to undergo ritual circumcision? We will learn why this became a matter of grave importance at Antioch of Syria and why all eyes turned to Jerusalem for the answer.

The bulk of the book of Acts provides an account of Paul's three journeys. Each journey deserves special attention, so we will summarize them, focusing on the importance of one place visited on each journey: Antioch of Syria, Athens, and Troas.

Through the power of the Holy Spirit, the church grew in ever-widening circles. No matter how people come to hear about the Messiah Jesus, their experience links at some point with the book of Acts. That is more than enough reason for us to turn through the pages of Acts. And as we do, we will see that one event after the other happened where it did for a reason.

Crusader capital showing the beheading of the apostle James, the brother of John.

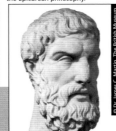

Epikouros (ca. 342–270 BC) founded the Epicurean philosophy.

© Dr. James C. Martin. The British Museum.

The mound of Lystra (view looking west).

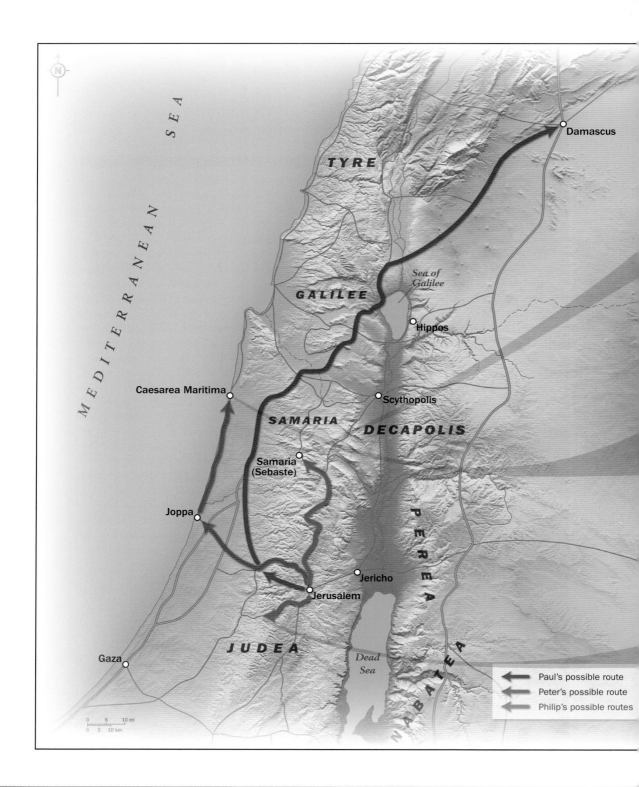

N

MEDITERRANEAN SEA

SEA

TYRE

Sea of
Galilee

GALILEE

Hippos

Damascus

Caesarea Maritima

SAMARIA

Scythopolis

DECAPOLIS

Samaria
(Sebaste)

P
E
R
E
A

Joppa

Jericho

Jerusalem

Gaza

JUDEA

Dead
Sea

N
A
B
A
T
E
A

Paul's possible route
Peter's possible route
Philip's possible routes

0   5   10 mi
0 5 10 km

The forum of the city of Samaria. The apostles Peter and John traveled to the city of Samaria (also called Sebaste) to pray for the new Samaritan converts (Acts 8:14).

The Caesarea Maritima palace (bottom left), stadium (center), and harbor (top). The Roman centurion Cornelius and his family lived in the city of Caesarea Maritima (Acts 10).

Roman road. The foundation of this road, located between Jerusalem and Gaza, was once overlaid with pounded chalk to make a smoother journey for travelers like the Ethiopian eunuch (Acts 8:26–39).

THE HOLY SPIRIT'S OUTPOURING AT PENTECOST IN JERUSALEM

ACTS 2

The Good News of God's rescue was intended for everyone, and the Lord had a plan for getting it to them. After Jesus's resurrection, the Lord sent the Holy Spirit on Pentecost (the Jewish festival of *Shevuot*) and filled many of the Jewish pilgrims in Jerusalem with an inspired faith that they could take home with them. Those who were present at that Pentecost took the Good News of the overthrow of the adversary by the Messiah Jesus to the world—a miracle that started in Jerusalem for a reason.

This outpouring of the Holy Spirit was something that Jesus had promised and that the disciples definitely needed. Although they had been with Jesus, walking and talking with him on a daily basis, their understanding frequently proved fallible (see, e.g., Acts 1:6). So Jesus promised these men that the Holy Spirit would come upon them and "guide [them] into all truth" (John 16:12–13). Little did they suspect how this would occur.

The Festival of Pentecost is a Jewish high holiday, so the apostles had special plans for this day, which included time at the Temple. But those plans and that trip to the Temple took an extraordinary turn. The place in which they sat was filled by the sound of a rushing wind, and what looked like tongues of fire appeared and rested upon them (Acts 2:1–3).[2]

Jerusalem model (view looking northeast from the Lower City toward the Temple complex).

The southern steps of the Temple Mount, sometimes referred to as the "rabbis' teaching staircase."

Such strange phenomena brought people rushing to see what was going on. Soon the pressing crowd grew so large that the apostles had to move to an outdoor setting, most likely the southern steps that served as the public entry into the Temple complex and functioned as the rabbis' teaching steps.[3] There a miracle allowed thousands to hear the message of God's rescue in their own language. All eyes turned to Peter as he stepped to the foreground in order to deliver a powerful address that connected this event and the life of Jesus to promises made throughout Scripture. He called for those listening to turn from mutiny, submit to Jesus, and be baptized in Jesus's name. They responded, with about three thousand listeners accepting his message that day (Acts 2:14–41).

For centuries, the Lord had required his people to come to Jerusalem fifty days after Passover to give thanks for the grain harvests and to recall the presentation of the law on Mount Sinai (Num. 28:26–31; Deut. 16:9–12). This gathering was called the Feast of Weeks (i.e., Pentecost, *Shevuot*).[4] Consequently, hundreds of thousands of people filled the streets of Jerusalem during that time.[5] Since this call went out to all Jews no matter

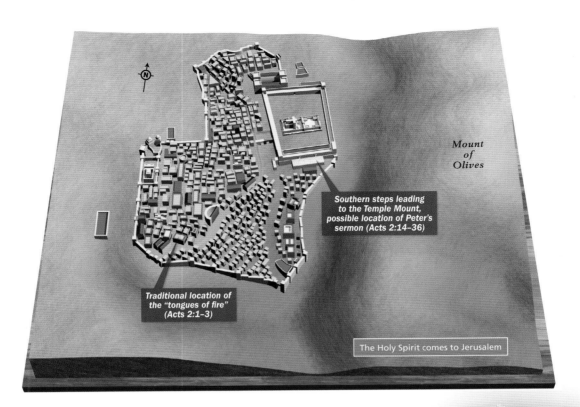

Southern steps leading to the Temple Mount, possible location of Peter's sermon (Acts 2:14–36)

Traditional location of the "tongues of fire" (Acts 2:1–3)

Mount of Olives

The Holy Spirit comes to Jerusalem

where they lived, the apostles were guaranteed that this large audience focused on God would also be an international group. Acts reports that the people gathered around the apostles were from at least fifteen different international regions (Acts 2:9–11). They would return to their own regions with the Good News of Jesus and the empowerment of the Holy Spirit.

The outpouring of God's Holy Spirit at Pentecost happened in Jerusalem for a reason. Jesus had directed the apostles to remain in Jerusalem because all the events summarized above would happen in that city (Acts 1:4) where, at that time, the apostles were guaranteed just the right audience. It would be huge, dedicated, widely international, and capable of assessing the evidence to support what was being proclaimed.

The Tower of Ascension, located on the Mount of Olives.

TEACHING AND HEALING IN THE TEMPLE COMPLEX

ACTS 3:1–4:22

Following the outpouring of the Holy Spirit on Pentecost, the new Jewish believers in Jesus dispersed to their homes, ready to tell others what they had learned. Meanwhile the apostles remained in Jerusalem using the Temple complex as the primary location for their teaching. Despite the risk that found them frequently arrested by corrupt members of the Sanhedrin, the apostles returned again and again to the Temple for a reason.

One day Peter and John went to teach in the Temple complex according to their custom. As they approached the Gate Beautiful, they met a beggar who had been crippled from birth. Peter had something better than money to offer this man—restoration of his legs through the authority of Jesus. As the healed man jumped about praising God, a crowd began to gather. They moved to Solomon's Colonnade, where Peter spoke about Jesus and called for those listening to believe that Jesus was the Messiah spoken of by the prophets. The priests, the captain of the Temple guard, and the Sadducees quickly arrested Peter and John, holding them overnight for trial the next day (Acts 3:1–4:22). At this trial Peter laid out the key issue of legitimate authority: "Judge for yourselves whether it

According to the Mishnah (Jewish oral law), "Gate Beautiful" is to be identified in this model of the Temple with the door at the bottom center of the photo.

is right in God's sight to obey you rather than God" (Acts 4:19).

Why did the apostles continue to preach and heal in the Temple complex despite the risk and opposition? The Temple complex provided the apostles with an audience attuned to their message. For centuries Jews had come to the Temple to worship, anticipating the coming of the Messiah. Therefore the apostles made it a practice to teach in Solomon's Colonnade, located across from the Gate Beautiful, both of which were within the Temple complex.[6] In doing so, the message of Jesus made increasing inroads among their Jewish brothers and sisters. Thousands came to believe, including more of the priests (Acts 4:4; 6:7).

By teaching in Solomon's Colonnade, and through the healing of the man at the Gate Beautiful, the apostles asserted that Jesus, not the Sadducees, was the

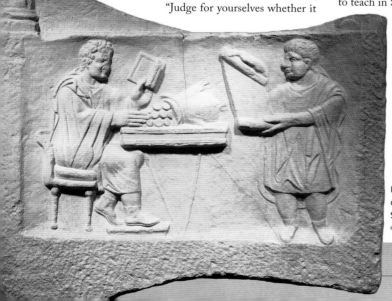

Relief depicting money changers. Money changing was a major industry for the Sadducees, who controlled the Temple.
© Dr. James C. Martin. The Eretz Israel Museum.

true authority of the Temple. In doing so, they went to places in the Temple complex where the message of Jesus was destined to get the attention of the Temple leadership. The disabled man whom the Lord healed was begging near the Gate Beautiful in the vicinity of the Temple treasury, where people came to deposit their contributions. For the Sadducees, who had turned the Temple into a commercial business, this treasury was an important symbol of their authority. By proclaiming the legitimate authority of Jesus at the Gate Beautiful, Peter revoked the Sadducees' claim to Temple authority.

The apostles also taught at Solomon's Colonnade, which was located on the east side of the Temple complex. Since one court of the Sanhedrin met in the Royal Porch that crossed the southern side of the Temple complex,[7] the members of that court of the Sanhedrin could easily see the young church growing just a short distance away.

Teaching and healing in the Temple complex happened where it did for a reason. By proclaiming the authority of Jesus as Messiah at Solomon's Colonnade and through the healing of a man at the Gate Beautiful, the apostles confronted and exposed the illegitimate Temple leadership.

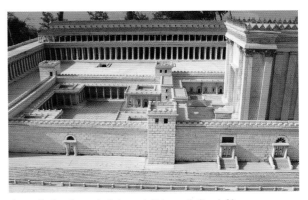

The early church met in Solomon's Colonnade (top left), while the Temple aristocracy did business at the Royal Porch, or Stoa (far back colonnade).

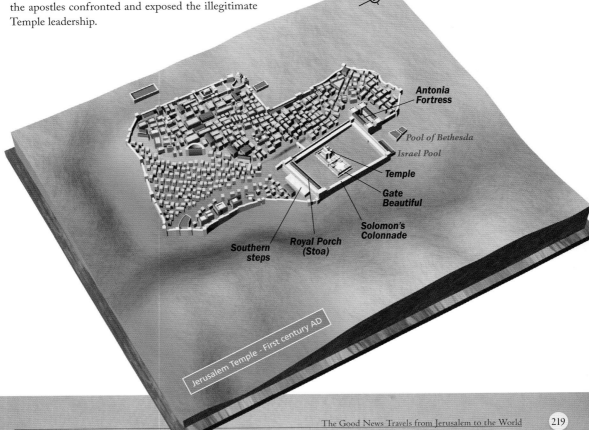

Jerusalem Temple - First century AD

Antonia Fortress
Pool of Bethesda
Israel Pool
Temple
Gate Beautiful
Solomon's Colonnade
Royal Porch (Stoa)
Southern steps

PHILIP TRAVELS TO SAMARIA

ACTS 8:4–25

When Peter challenged the illegitimate authority of the Temple leadership (Acts 4:19–20) and Stephen spoke to the Sanhedrin on the same topic noting their rejection of the Lord's Messiah—the one who held legitimate authority of the Temple (Acts 7:1–53)—"a great persecution broke out against the church at Jerusalem" (Acts 8:1). The Nazarenes (i.e., Jewish believers in Jesus the Messiah, see Acts 24:5) now scattered before Saul, who, with others, was going from house to house dragging believers off to jail (Acts 8:1–3). With this new persecution of Jesus's disciples, the news of Jesus soon spread from Jerusalem to Samaria. There were reasons Philip took the Good News to Samaria and good reasons to expect that the gospel would be received there.[8]

Philip, like Stephen, was one of the men chosen to aid and support the apostles in their work in Jerusalem (Acts 6:5).[9] As a leader in the Jerusalem church, he too was affected by the harassing hunt for believers in Jesus following the death of Stephen. So he went to Samaria, where he spoke about the Messiah and through the power of the risen Lord exorcised demons and restored the health of those who had been paralyzed or crippled. These miracles had the same kind of impact that they did in Jerusalem; crowds of people pressed in for a closer look at this man and to learn the source of his power. When word reached Jerusalem that Samaritans had submitted to Jesus, Peter and John were sent to nurture the church in Samaria (Acts 8:5–25).

There are several reasons why some of the Jewish believers went to Samaria and why the message of Jesus found reception there. First, the Samaritans, like those scattering from Jerusalem, did not recognize Jerusalem's Temple leaders as their authority (Luke 9:52–53). Thus a Greek-speaking Jew like Philip found Samaria a safe haven, particularly since the corrupt leaders in the Temple at Jerusalem looked down on the Samaritans as much as they looked down on the followers of Jesus (John 4:9).

Second, Philip and others who traveled to Samaria found relief from the persecution in Jerusalem among those who were already believers in Jesus. When Jesus visited Sychar, we know that his words found welcoming hearts there. The woman at Jacob's well was so taken by Jesus's conversation with her that she invited her village to come and meet this man who somehow knew all about her, though they had never met before. Many Samaritans followed her lead and received the Messiah (John 4:39–41).

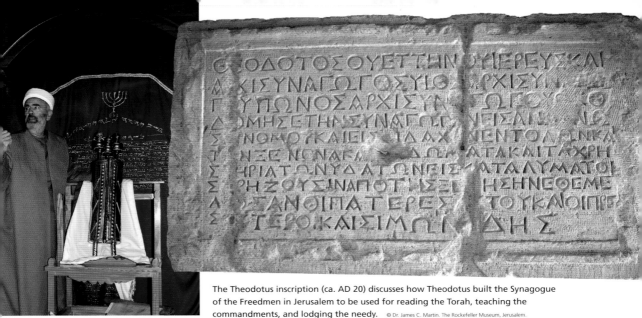

The Theodotus inscription (ca. AD 20) discusses how Theodotus built the Synagogue of the Freedmen in Jerusalem to be used for reading the Torah, teaching the commandments, and lodging the needy. © Dr. James C. Martin. The Rockefeller Museum, Jerusalem.

Samaritan priest.

Finally, we note that those who submitted to Jesus were more welcome here because the Samaritans were a community seeking the Messiah. At one time this region was part of the Northern Kingdom of Israel, a kingdom that immersed itself in idolatry. As a result, the Lord permitted the Assyrians to conquer that kingdom and deport its leading citizens. The population the Assyrians planted became racially and religiously mixed (2 Kings 17). Despite this history and the differences in their theology, Samaritans looked for a time when the Messiah would answer all their questions (John 4:25).

There were reasons Philip traveled to Samaria. Persecution in Jerusalem against followers of Jesus resulted in their scattering to various regions. In many ways the differences that separated Jewish believers in Jesus from Samaritans were considerably less than the differences that separated Jesus's followers from Gentile cultures.[10] Therefore, the proclamation that Jesus was the Messiah and those who celebrated his coming found a welcoming, informed, and ready audience in Samaria.

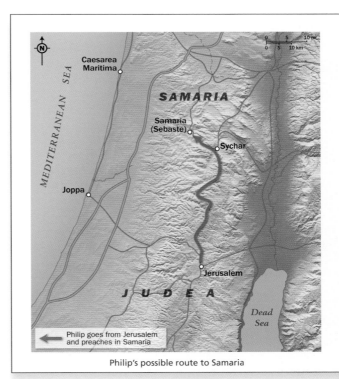

Philip goes from Jerusalem and preaches in Samaria

Philip's possible route to Samaria

◀ The cardo of the town of Samaria, also known as Sebaste.

PHILIP SPEAKS TO THE ETHIOPIAN EUNUCH ON THE ROAD TO GAZA

ACTS 8:26–40

With persecution raging in Jerusalem, followers of Jesus "were scattered throughout Judea and Samaria" (Acts 8:1). The Lord led Philip to speak first with Samaritans and then with a eunuch, whom many Jews considered unfit for the Kingdom of God. After being with the Samaritans, Philip was given new instructions that sent him not to a city nor to a region but to a roadway. "Now an angel of the Lord said to Philip, 'Go south to the road—the desert road—that goes down from Jerusalem to Gaza'" (Acts 8:26). Philip was sent to this roadway for a very specific reason.

The book of Acts refers to this roadway as "the desert road" not necessarily because it traveled through the wilderness but because it led to the wilderness that began at Gaza. Gaza was the portal city at which one could obtain supplies for the trip across the Sinai Wilderness en route to points south, including Africa.[11] That is why the eunuch, a high-ranking official in the Ethiopian royal court, was on this road. It led him homeward after his pilgrimage to Jerusalem's Temple, which he could only see from a distance because eunuchs were not allowed to enter. Along the way he was reading aloud the words of Isaiah 53, which speaks of the coming Messiah. As Philip met the chariot, he asked the Ethiopian if he

Ethiopian Bible manuscript (eighteenth century AD).

© Dr. James C. Martin. Sola Scriptura. The Van Kampen Collection.

understood what he was reading. That question opened a conversation between the two men. Philip started with the very passage the Ethiopian was reading, Isaiah 53:7–8, in order to explain that Jesus had come because the Kingdom of God was open to all nations. Reading forward, Philip would have arrived at the words of Isaiah 56:3–7, which note that even foreigners and eunuchs were welcome in God's Kingdom.[12] Before long the Spirit led the Ethiopian to faith in Jesus and baptism (Acts 8:26–39).

The Ethiopian was using the road as a way to get home, but the Spirit of God used the roadway to proclaim the Good News of Jesus in Ethiopia through this man. In earlier Scriptures we find evidence of a growing Jewish community associated with Ethiopia.[13] Some were Ethiopians who lived in the Promised Land while others were Jews who lived in Ethiopia. For example, Ebed-Melech was an Ethiopian eunuch who served as an official in Jerusalem's royal court. He advocated for Jeremiah and secured his release when Jeremiah was taken captive and thrown into a cistern (Jer. 38:7–13). Jeremiah notes that this African man was a fellow believer in the Lord (Jer. 39:15–18). We also know that

Ethiopian monk at the Church of the Holy Sepulcher.
© Direct Design

Section of a Roman road foundation ▶ that connected Jerusalem to Gaza.

some Jews had left the Promised Land and resided in exile within Ethiopia because the Lord spoke words of comfort and encouragement to them, assuring them that they would one day return from their exile (Isa. 11:11; Zeph. 3:10). The Ethiopian eunuch represents a community in Africa, outside the Promised Land, that was connected to the promises of Abraham.

Philip spoke to the Ethiopian eunuch on the road to Gaza for a reason. In Acts 2 Luke tells us that pilgrims from fifteen different international regions experienced the outpouring of the Holy Spirit on Pentecost, came to know Jesus as the promised Messiah, and returned with the news to their family and friends (Acts 2:9–11). But when we inspect that list carefully, we find that no region south of Egypt is mentioned.[14] Perhaps this is why the Holy Spirit led Philip to the desert road that goes down to Gaza for an encounter that would do for Africa what Pentecost did for the other international regions.

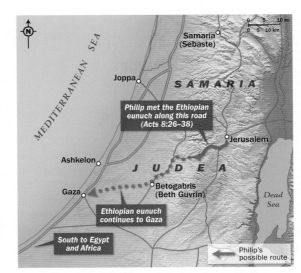

Philip met the Ethiopian eunuch along the road to Gaza

Ethiopian worshipers in the Church of the Holy Sepulcher.

JESUS ENCOUNTERS SAUL OF TARSUS ON THE ROAD TO DAMASCUS

ACTS 9:1–31

Saul of Tarsus had a remarkable encounter on the road to Damascus that completely rocked his worldview. In this experience Saul, the persecutor of Jewish believers in Jesus, was transformed by Jesus and so began the transition that would produce Paul, a celebrated ambassador of the Messiah Jesus (Acts 9:15). Jesus appeared to Saul on the road to Damascus for a reason.

Saul was well-trained in Pharisaic Judaism and was eager to remain loyal to the Temple in Jerusalem. Because he initially viewed Jesus of Nazareth as an opponent of that Temple (John 2:19–22), Saul participated in the passionate persecution of the young church in Jerusalem. Word arrived that this same movement was finding increasing success in Jewish communities in Damascus. So Saul secured a letter from Jerusalem's high priest, Caiaphas, to enlist the aid of the Damascus synagogues in identifying and arresting followers of Jesus so they could be brought to Jerusalem for trial and punishment (Acts 8:1–3; 9:1–2; 22:3–5; 26:4–12).

The large Jewish community in Damascus and its key location explain why Saul felt so compelled to persecute and weaken the church there. He did not want the sizable Jewish population compromised by what he believed was false teaching. In addition, Saul did not want Jews traveling through Damascus on the way to Jerusalem to hear this new message that explained how Jesus was the fulfillment of the Temple's purpose. If that message took root in Damascus, not only the Jews in that city but Jews traveling through this important transportation hub might stop submitting to the Temple rulers. For those passionate about putting a stop to the message of Jesus, this city was the place to draw the line.

The city of Damascus was located on an oasis irrigated by the powerful and clear waters of the Amanah and the Pharpar rivers.[15] Damascus was an important commercial center located at the hub of a transportation network that sent roadways streaming in all directions to places like Arabia, Egypt, Anatolia, and Mesopotamia (Ezek. 27:18).[16] Furthermore, this city enjoyed a sizable Jewish population with multiple synagogues (Acts 9:2). That might seem surprising given the frequent tension reported between ancient Israel and Damascus.[17] But there had been quieter times when the influence of Jewish thinking and theology lived in the streets of Damascus. David established garrisons there (2 Sam. 8:6). And the Scriptures tell of at least one high-ranking resident of Damascus: Naaman, the commander of the army of Aram, who came to believe in the Lord as the one true God (2 Kings 5).

Ephesus wall painting of Paul on the Grotto of Saint Paul (sixth century AD).

Jesus encountered Saul of Tarsus on the road to Damascus for a reason. Saul was passionate about getting to Damascus in order to destroy the church, but his plan was undone when light flashed around him and the risen Lord asked a penetrating question: "Saul, Saul, why do you persecute me?" (Acts 9:4). Jesus met Saul on the

Paul's journey on the road to Damascus would have taken him past the northeast slopes of Mount Hermon.

The wall of Saint Paul's Church in Damascus is considered the location of Paul's escape from the city (Acts 9:23–25).

road to Damascus to enhance the church's growth. The Lord wanted the Kingdom of God to be proclaimed in every direction, and that could happen from a place like Damascus. Thus the Lord not only interrupted Saul's plan before he got to Damascus, but he changed Saul's perspective along the way.

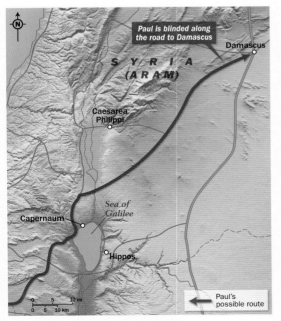

Road taken by Paul to Damascus

PETER TRAVELS TO A CENTURION'S HOME IN CAESAREA MARITIMA

ACTS 10

Paul's encounter with the risen Jesus on the road to Damascus had changed him forever. The apostle Peter also went through a remarkable change when the Lord instructed him to go to the home of Cornelius, a Roman centurion who was responsible for the soldiers stationed in the city of Caesarea Maritima.[18] Luke describes him and all his family as "devout and God-fearing" (Acts 10:2). His charitable acts and prayers were received by the Lord, so an angel was sent to Cornelius, urging him to send men to Peter in Joppa to have Peter come to his home in Caesarea Maritima for a reason (Acts 10:1–8).

As Cornelius's envoys approached the home where Peter was staying, the Lord gave Peter a vision. While on the roof of Simon the tanner's house, Peter saw a large sheet descending from heaven containing a wide variety of birds, reptiles, and four-footed animals. When he was encouraged to kill and eat, Peter hesitated because of Jewish dietary (*kashrut*) laws that forbade eating "unclean" food (Leviticus 11). The Lord immediately responded, "Do not call anything impure that God has made clean" (Acts 10:15). After this vision repeated two more times, the Lord instructed Peter to leave Joppa and go to the home of Cornelius in Caesarea.

Not keeping his feelings to himself, Peter entered Cornelius's home and announced, "It is against our law for a Jew to associate with a Gentile or visit him" (Acts 10:28). Observant Jews did not enter the home of Gentiles, particularly the home of a Roman military officer in a city like Caesarea Maritima.[19] But realizing that God does not show favoritism, Peter began to speak about Jesus. Before long, this day started to look like a reenactment of Pentecost. This time, however, the Holy Spirit came upon Gentiles while Peter was still speaking, and these Gentiles spoke in tongues and were baptized in the name of Jesus (Acts 10:30–48).

Peter's trip from Joppa to Caesarea Maritima brought the news of Jesus to those who needed to hear it and also taught Peter a powerful lesson. A big part of that lesson was shaped by his journey from Joppa to Caesarea Maritima. Joppa was the earlier seaport of Israel located on the Mediterranean Sea. Although its function as a seaport was dramatically diminished by the time of Peter, its connection to Jerusalem and Judea remained intact. By contrast, Caesarea Maritima had a decidedly Gentile orientation. Herod the Great had begun building the city in 22 BC, investing great time and energy in making this an all-weather seaport.[20]

Marble statue depicting Roman military dress.

© Dr. James C. Martin. The British Museum.

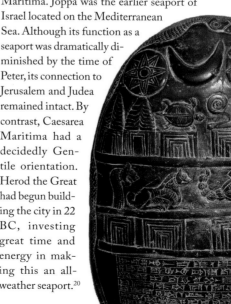

The harbor and coastline of Caesarea Maritima (view looking south).

Later Roman governors continued what Herod had begun. Caesarea became the regional capital of Rome filled with all the structures and ideology that represented the best Rome had to offer.[21] Given this Roman orientation, it is no surprise that a contingent of Roman soldiers was based there. For an observant Jew, it was those Roman soldiers who represented almost all that was wrong with the world.

The Lord summoned Peter to travel from Joppa to the home of a Roman centurion in Caesarea Maritima for a reason. It was critical for Peter to learn that "God does not show favoritism but accepts men from every nation who fear him and do what is right" (Acts 10:34–35). What better place to learn that lesson than by traveling from Joppa to the home of a Roman soldier in Caesarea Maritima. As Peter initially resisted the thought of eating food that was ritually unclean, so he initially resisted the thought of entering the home of a Gentile. But it was his trip to the home of Cornelius in Caesarea Maritima that changed all that.

Peter goes from Joppa to Caesarea Maritima

Archaeological sites of first-century AD Caesarea Maritima

◄ Dietary laws prohibited Jews from eating unclean foods such as the "creeping things" depicted on this Babylonian boundary stone. © Dr. James C. Martin. The British Museum.

Bronze statuette of a Roman soldier wearing laminated armor (*lorica segmentata*).
© Dr. James C. Martin. The British Museum.

ON THE FIRST JOURNEY PAUL DEPARTS FROM ANTIOCH OF SYRIA

ACTS 13–14

As the news of Jesus began to radiate in ever-widening circles from Jerusalem, it expanded to a growing church in Antioch of Syria. During a time of worship there, the Holy Spirit set apart Barnabas and Paul and sent them into the interior of Asia Minor armed with the gospel. This journey took them first to the island of Cyprus, then on to the coast of Asia Minor, past the coastal mountains of Pamphylia, and on to the high plateau of central Asia where they visited Pisidian Antioch,[22] Lystra, Derbe, and Iconium (Acts 13:1–14:28). This journey and the two later journeys of Paul began in Antioch. We will explore why a thriving church developed in that city and why it became the starting point for Paul's extended travels.

Antioch of Syria was a major city with half a million residents and a thriving Jewish quarter.[23] This city was filled with the best of Roman architecture, boasting magnificent public buildings, colonnaded streets, and public baths.[24] This was a city of some means, due in no small part to its unique position as a transportation hub linking eastern and western worlds. Antioch was connected to its seaport city, Seleucia Pieria, located sixteen miles to the west by the Orontes River. It was connected to the east by overland routes that connected Antioch with the major cities of Mesopotamia.[25] As merchants and travelers exchanged goods, they also openly exchanged ideas and experiences. That happened in other cities as well, but Antioch of Syria was particularly marked as a place where religious, racial, and national barriers were easily crossed.[26]

Statue of Saint Peter placed on the ledge above the altar in the Grotto of Saint Peter, which was believed to be the first church in Antioch of Syria where the early church gathered to commission Paul and Barnabas on their first journey.

All these qualities of Antioch help explain why the early church found a home there and why this city became the starting gate for the travels of Paul. As persecution filled the streets of Jerusalem and Jewish believers in Jesus scattered from that city, some traveled to Antioch. The city was also appealing because it had a large Jewish population[27] and because it was a city with an established record of tolerance to new information. Luke says that those from Jerusalem spoke only to other Jews, while some men from Cyprus and Cyrene spoke openly about Jesus to the Gentiles. The result was that

Crusader facade built in front of the Grotto of Saint Peter in Antioch of Syria (Antakya, Turkey).

many submitted to the Messiah Jesus in Antioch of Syria (Acts 11:19–26).

This city in which the Jewish and Gentile believers in Jesus were first called Christians (Acts 11:26) became the starting point for each of Paul's three journeys. The core group of the church at Antioch of Syria was composed of believers who were so passionate about their faith that they chose to flee their homes in Jerusalem rather than surrender their commitment to Jesus. Furthermore, this nucleus and those who came to the Lord around them benefited from strong leadership. Luke makes special mention of this fact: "In the church at Antioch there were prophets and teachers: Barnabas, Simeon called Niger, Lucius of Cyrene, Manaen . . . and Saul" (Acts 13:1). Barnabas and Saul, two influential teachers in the city, taught together in Antioch for one year (Acts 11:25–26).

Paul departed from Antioch of Syria on his first journey for a reason. Antioch was a huge city with a large Jewish population, a city uniquely placed as a transportation hub and a city that celebrated the open exchange of ideas and experiences. The church in Antioch was aptly suited to become the hub for outreach efforts in Asia and Europe. Consequently, the sea-lanes and roadways that radiated from Antioch of Syria became lifelines through which the Good News of Jesus traveled.

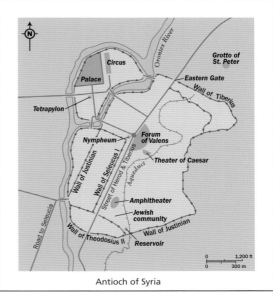

Antioch of Syria

Paul's first missionary journey

The Orontes River, running through Antioch of Syria.

Seleucia Pierea harbor.

THE FIRST CHURCH COUNCIL IS HELD IN JERUSALEM

ACTS 15:1–35

The news about the Messiah Jesus spread rapidly from Jerusalem into the neighboring Roman provinces. The response to the message was varied, and the early church was soon faced with numerous challenges. Most of the first believers in Jesus were Jews who came to recognize that Jesus was the true authority of the Temple and the fulfillment of the promises portrayed there. As Jews, they continued to worship at the Temple and circumcise their children. The expansion of the church saw many Gentiles submitting to Jesus as Lord. Throughout Jewish history, Gentiles wishing to become proselytes within Judaism had to follow the laws of Moses, including circumcision. Was this still the case now that the Messiah had come? That was the critical question raised at Antioch after Paul and Barnabas returned from teaching in cities such as Paphos, Iconium, and Pisidian Antioch—a question to be answered in the first church council, which was held in Jerusalem for a reason.

The question came to the foreground in Antioch of Syria when some men from Judea arrived at the city. In meetings with the church at Antioch they stated, "Unless you are circumcised, according to the custom taught by Moses, you cannot be saved" (Acts 15:1).[28] For Gentiles who were already putting

Wall remains of ancient Iconium.

themselves at great risk by associating themselves with a group that refused to participate in the worship of the Roman emperor, this was just another obstacle. It is no wonder that Paul and Barnabas traded sharp words in debating with these visitors (Acts 15:2).

The issue took on added significance because Antioch of Syria was a large, highly influential city[29] that was uniquely positioned as a starting point for the church's outreach to the world. If there was a place to determine if new Gentile believers in Jesus had to submit to Mosaic law, it was Antioch of Syria, for the answer given there—right or wrong—would multiply over and over again among churches throughout Asia Minor and Europe. Realizing

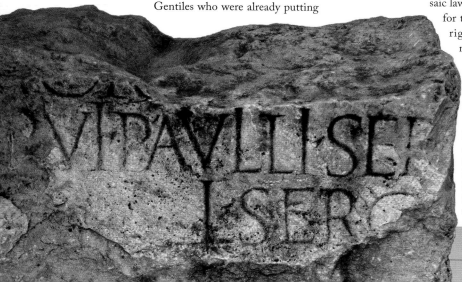

Inscription discovered at Pisidian Antioch, mentioning the Roman governor (or proconsul) Sergius Paulus, who met with Paul, Barnabas, and Mark at Paphos (Acts 13:6–12).

© Dr. James C. Martin. The Yalvac Museum.

this and aware of the risk of splitting the early church just when it needed to be united against external opposition, Paul and Barnabas urged that the matter be taken to Jerusalem (Acts 15:2).

When controversies arose in Judaism between the members of the Pharisaical party, they would often turn to Sanhedrin leaders like Gamaliel, who would provide answers (e.g., Acts 5:33–40). For the early church, however, the authority of Jesus replaced the Sanhedrin's influence. Even though Paul studied under the famous Sanhedrin Pharisee Gamaliel (Acts 22:3), Jesus was now the one to whom he submitted. So those involved in this dispute in Antioch of Syria turned to Jerusalem, not because Gamaliel was there, but because the apostles, who now represented Jesus's authority, were there.

The first church council was held in Jerusalem for a reason. While the persecution of the early church drove many from Jerusalem, the apostles remained (Acts 8:1; 15:6). These were the men who walked with Jesus and learned personally from him, as they had been given the responsibility to teach the truth on which the church was

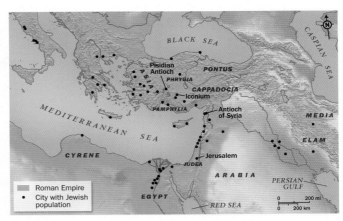

Concentrations of Jews in first-century AD Roman provinces

built (Acts 6:2). A question of this magnitude required their input. Peter in particular had struggled with this matter (see Acts 10 and Gal. 2:11–16), and it was his powerful voice that gave the compelling speech on the topic in Jerusalem: "We believe it is through the grace of our Lord Jesus that we are saved, just as they are" (Acts 15:11).[30] So the critical question that was raised in Antioch was answered in Jerusalem.

Foundation remains of the Basilica of Saint Paul at Pisidian Antioch.

ON THE SECOND JOURNEY PAUL SPEAKS TO THE AREOPAGUS IN ATHENS

ACTS 17:16–34

*P*aul's second journey covers many more miles than his first journey and has considerably more chapters in Acts devoted to it. Starting again in Antioch of Syria, Paul and his colleagues revisited churches that they had helped to establish on the prior trip: Derbe, Lystra, Iconium, and Antioch of Pisidia. After spending time in Galatia and Phrygia, the Holy Spirit used a vision delivered in Troas to direct Paul's eyes across the Aegean Sea toward Macedonia and Achaia (Acts 16:6–10). Leaving the port of Troas, Paul visited Philippi and Thessalonica, important urban centers on the Egnatian Way. When opposition in Thessalonica and later in Berea forced this team from those cities, Paul traveled south into Achaia for a short visit in Athens for a reason.

Athens was a somewhat unusual stop for Paul. As we look at the cities on the itinerary of this and his other journeys, Paul seems interested in cities with large Jewish populations and/or cities that were located at thriving transportation hubs. Neither was the case with Athens. The gleaming, golden years of the fifth century BC were long behind it—the days when Athens was the administrative center of Greece and the shining star of Greek politics, culture, and commerce.[31] By now Athens had become a quiet museum harboring the memories of the past, big on reflection but short on commerce and influence.[32] In fact, the only reason Paul seems to delay in this city is that he is awaiting the

Athenian forum and Stoa of Attalus.

arrival of Silas and Timothy, who were finishing up in Berea (Acts 17:13–15).

Athens was a city desperately searching for truth. The massive Parthenon, the temple of Athena Nike, the temple of Augustus, as well as dozens of other altars, temples, and idols combined to impress Paul with the religious quest under way in this city (Acts 17:22–23). Furthermore, Athens was the birthplace of Greek philosophy, to which the residents of Athens were especially attuned. Luke notes, "All the Athenians and the foreigners who lived there spent their time doing nothing but talking about and listening to the latest ideas" (Acts 17:21). As Paul entered the public marketplace (agora) he met such people, including the Epicurean and Stoic philosophers. Paul brought these philosophers face to face with "the good news about Jesus and the resurrection" (Acts 17:18). Their exchanges led these philosophers to invite Paul to a meeting of the Areopagus, a council whose responsibility it was to hear and evaluate new answers to old and compelling questions about the nature of good and evil, personal destiny, and the gods.[33]

Paul spoke to the Areopagus in Athens on his second journey for a reason. The troubling uncertainty that

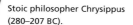
Stoic philosopher Chrysippus (280–207 BC).

© Dr. James C. Martin. Mus'ee du Louvre;
Autorisation de photographer et de filmer—LOUVRE.

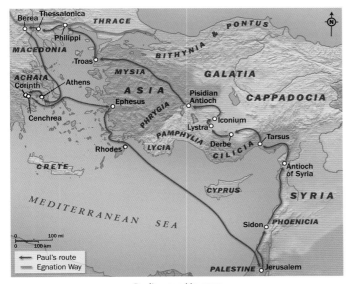

Paul's second journey

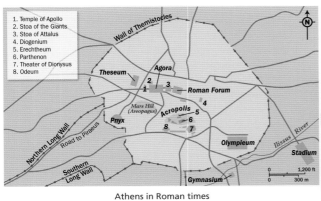

1. Temple of Apollo
2. Stoa of the Giants
3. Stoa of Attalus
4. Diogenium
5. Erechtheum
6. Parthenon
7. Theater of Dionysus
8. Odeum

Athens in Roman times

lived and breathed in this city showed the desperate need of the people to know the one and only true God. As Paul stood before the Areopagus, he was compelled to address the issue of a particular altar he had passed dedicated "TO AN UNKNOWN GOD."[34] Paul launched into an exposition on the one true God, his creation of humanity, and the need to prepare earnestly for the coming day of judgment (Acts 17:22–31). Athenians of the Areopagus greatly needed to learn what Paul was proclaiming. Paul used Athenian culture and history as the entry point for proclaiming the Good News of the Creator, God's Kingdom, and the Messiah. So Paul's stop in Athens happened for a reason.

Latin inscription dedicating this altar to an unknown God.

ON THE THIRD JOURNEY PAUL RAISES EUTYCHUS AT TROAS

ACTS 20:7–12

The combination of the outpouring of the Holy Spirit at Pentecost, the scattering of the church from Jerusalem, and two journeys of Paul resulted in the message of Jesus spreading throughout modern Turkey and Greece. Paul aspired to nurture these new communities. Following a time in Syrian Antioch, he was on the road again. We, however, will focus on Paul's weeklong stay in Troas, where he raised a young man named Eutychus—a miracle done there for a reason.

During Paul's third journey he traveled to Troas on two occasions. At that time Troas was a thriving Roman colony on the Aegean Sea that enjoyed mild weather and fertile soil.[35] The real merit of this city was its critical location and its service as a transportation hub. Overland trade routes from the east terminated here, where people and their goods could make the relatively short hop across the Aegean Sea. After crossing to Neapolis, the harbor near Philippi, they could connect with the Egnatian Way, the major highway that linked the Aegean and Adriatic seas.[36] Paul had used the port of Troas for just this reason on at least three separate occasions (Acts 16:8–10; 20:1–2, 6).

But it was his last stop there that closed with a life-giving miracle (Acts 20:7–12). The church of Troas had gathered for worship on the first day of the week,

Troas harbor basin, measuring about 400 by 200 feet.

Sunday, in commemoration of Jesus's resurrection.[37] Since Paul was leaving the next morning, eager to get to Jerusalem by Pentecost (Acts 20:16), he taught late into the night. A young man named Eutychus was sitting in the open window of the third story listening to Paul. He began to fall asleep and subsequently fell out of the window, struck the ground, and died. Paul threw himself on the body of the expired young man reminiscent of what Elijah and Elisha had done in the past (1 Kings 17:19–24; 2 Kings 4:32–37). The crowd stood in awe as life returned to Eutychus (Acts 20:10–12).

Troas could be a powerful venue to spread the gospel message. Starting from a bottleneck in the transportation system that crossed the ancient world from east to west, the message of Jesus could be told to travelers transiting Troas and have an impact thousands of miles away.

Furthermore, this miracle meant something important for Paul. After the raising of Eutychus, Paul walked from Troas to Assos instead of riding on the ship with the others (Acts 20:13). The Holy Spirit had warned Paul that he would be handed over to the Gentiles, and it seemed to Paul that his life might end shortly (Acts 21:10–14). After those experiences, perhaps that walk from Troas to Assos provided time for Paul to reflect on the recent miracle in which the Lord brought Eutychus back to life, a miracle that became an encouragement to Paul as he was warned of prison, hardships, and potential death in the days ahead.

Roman road to Assos, about nine miles south of Troas (Acts 20:13–14).

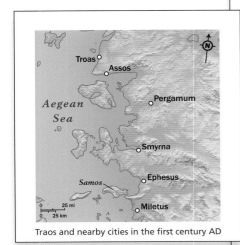

Traos and nearby cities in the first century AD

◀ Remains of the Roman bath complex at Troas.

Paul's third journey

PART 11

CITY LETTERS
AND REVELATION

Claudius I, fourth Roman emperor of the Julio-
Claudian dynasty, ruled from AD 41 to 54.

ROMANS, CORINTHIANS, GALATIANS, EPHESIANS, PHILIPPIANS, COLOSSIANS, THESSALONIANS, REVELATION

When Paul wanted to communicate with another church[1] miles from his current location, a handwritten letter was often the vehicle of choice. A quick glance at the titles of these letters reveals the name of the city or region to which it was originally written—for example Romans to Rome, Corinthians to Corinth, and Colossians to Colosse. At times the city mentioned in the title of the letter marks a city that Paul had visited on an earlier journey, and at other times Paul's letter is written to a church Paul had not yet visited. In either case, we will call these the city letters of Paul.

Each of the communities to which Paul wrote had its own unique history, geography, and culture that we can explore. A number of the cities Paul visited and honored with a letter had similar characteristics. They enjoyed a sizable Jewish population or were located at important transportation hubs.

When we look carefully at these cities, we find that they differ from one another in history, geography, and culture. By inquiring about such matters, we often obtain insights about the city or region and why he wrote a letter to them. For example, a visit to Paphos and an acquaintance with Sergius Paulus, the procurator, opened the door for Barnabas and Paul to visit Pisidian Antioch and its satellite cities in Galatia. But shortly after this visit, Paul wrote an urgent letter to the churches in Galatia because they were so quickly and unexpectedly "turning to a different gospel" (Gal. 1:6). In his letter

to Philippi, Paul describes a "citizenship" that is even more wonderful than the Roman citizenship enjoyed by the retired Roman soldiers in that city (Phil. 3:20). And he wrote two back-to-back letters to the church in Thessalonica because circumstances unfolding in the Roman Empire had required him to leave Thessalonica so quickly. In each case the letter's content had a unique link to the location.

In this final section we will focus on certain cities that received letters from Paul, surveying the qualities and circumstances of that city. We will then turn our attention to Revelation, an apocalyptic discourse that starts out as a letter written by John to seven churches in Asia Minor. It was written to these churches at the close of the first century when abuse and persecution were unsettling realities for the followers of Jesus. In response, the Lord gave John this revelation to lift their eyes to the final overthrow of evil and Satan's ultimate demise. We will explore why both the Roman government and the Lord had a purpose for John on the island of Patmos, where he received the incredible vision relayed in the book of Revelation. We will consider why this book was addressed to the seven churches in Asia Minor in general and take a closer look at the way geography motivates and shapes the message to the church in Laodicea. We will close with a look at Armageddon, the location where the kings of the nations will gather together against the Lord Almighty.

The area of Three Taverns. Believers in Jesus came to meet Paul at the Three Taverns along the Appian Way (Acts 28:15), about thirty-three miles from Rome.

Ephesus cardo (view looking west).

Laodicea cardo (view looking east).

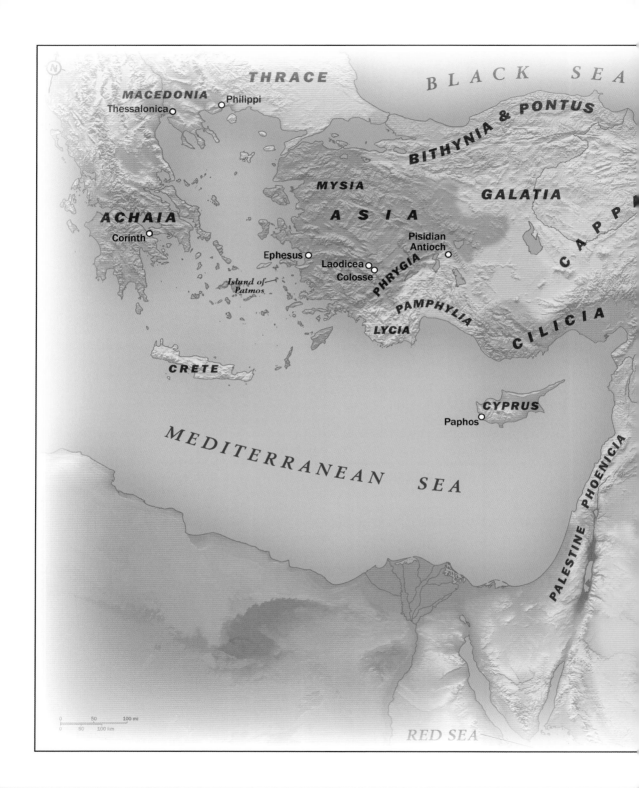

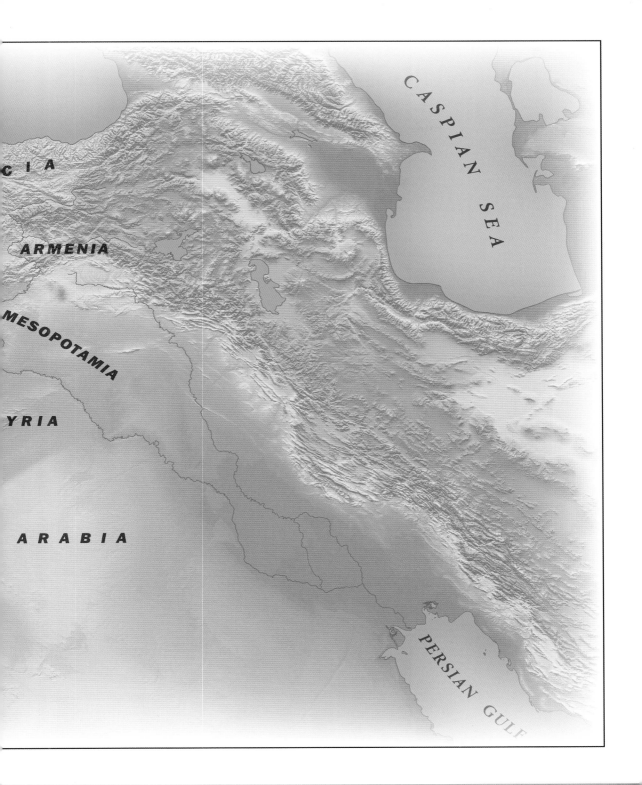

CASPIAN SEA

CIA

ARMENIA

MESOPOTAMIA

YRIA

ARABIA

PERSIAN GULF

PAUL'S URGENT CONCERN IN HIS LETTER TO THE GALATIANS

GALATIANS

We correspond with our friends, family, and associates for a variety of reasons. While some of those messages are written in a more casual and leisurely way, others brim with urgency. Paul's letter to the churches in Galatia[2] is clearly in the latter category. We will see that Paul witnessed the birth of the churches in Galatia and subsequently wrote them this urgent letter for a reason.

Paul addressed his letter "to the churches in Galatia" (Gal. 1:2). These are churches that Paul visited on all three of his journeys. Consequently, the people in cities like Pisidian Antioch, Iconium, Lystra, and Derbe had met with Paul on at least four different occasions (Acts 13:13–14:23; 15:36–16:5; 18:23). But why did he travel to this region in the first place, and why did he make repeated visits? His first visit with them may well have come at the insistence and encouragement of Sergius Paulus. He was the Roman proconsul in Paphos on the island of Cyprus. On the first journey recorded in Acts, Barnabas and Paul (along with their young assistant, John Mark) had traveled to this island and this city with the Good News about Jesus (Acts 13:4–12). While there, Sergius Paulus came to believe, "for he was amazed at the teaching about the Lord" (Acts 13:12).

The theater at Pisidian Antioch was originally built by the Greeks but later enlarged by the Romans.

Since this proconsul had family and political connections in Pisidian Antioch, he may well have encouraged Barnabas and Paul to make a stop there. He may also have provided them with a letter of safe conduct to facilitate their travels through the region.[3]

Readers of the Bible expect to find Jewish people in the Promised Land but may be surprised to find that Galatia boasted a sizable Jewish population at the time of Paul.[4] These Jewish families were familiar with the language and promises of the Scriptures. So when Barnabas and Paul entered cities like Pisidian Antioch or Iconium, they stopped first at the Jewish synagogue in order to present the news about Jesus to fellow Jews (Acts 13:14; 14:1). Given the large number of Jews and synagogues in Galatia, this region received Paul's undivided attention for days on end. And given the fact that the umbrella of protection offered by Sergius Paulus likely covered the cities connected to Pisidian Antioch by regional roadways, we find Barnabas and Paul making stops in places like Iconium, Lystra, and Derbe as well.

Caesar Augustus dedicated this temple at Pisidian Antioch to the idol Cybele (Kybele).

Aqueducts brought water into Pisidian Antioch. ▶

"Judaizers"[5] were following behind Paul and telling the new believers in the Galatian churches that no one could be brought into the fulfillment of Judaism through Jesus unless they combined that faith with the external mark of circumcision and practiced Mosaic law. In starting this letter, Paul barely gets a civil greeting out before he expresses disappointment. "I am astonished that you are so quickly deserting the one who called you by the grace of Christ and are turning to a different gospel—which is really no gospel at all" (Gal. 1:6). Then throughout the letter and in varying ways he returns again and again to the same theme: "We who are Jews by birth and not 'Gentile sinners' know that a man is not justified by observing the law, but by faith in Jesus Christ" (Gal. 2:15).

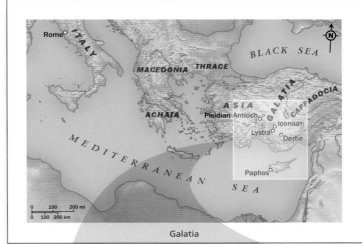

Galatia

Paul wrote his urgent letter to the Galatians for a reason. Judaizers had been going throughout Galatia demanding that the churches enforce Mosaic law. Soon after his return from the region Paul wrote this letter to the churches in Galatia to stop the teaching of the Judaizers before it became ingrained.

PAUL'S LETTER TO THE PHILIPPIANS CONCERNING CITIZENSHIP

PHILIPPIANS

During the days of Alexander the Great, the gold mined near Philippi helped support the eastward march of the Greek Empire.[6] During the days of Paul, the Kingdom of God was steadily marching in the opposite direction, delivering a message more precious than gold. When the news of Jesus crossed the Aegean Sea, it came to Philippi, a city Paul visited on both his second and third journeys (Acts 16:11–40; 20:1–5). Following both visits and while enduring imprisonment, Paul wrote a letter to the fellowship of this community—Philippians (Phil. 1:1). One of the more interesting links between Paul's visit and the letter is his use of the term *citizenship*. Paul declares himself a Roman citizen in this city for a reason.

Philippi was a Roman colony primarily filled with Gentiles who were veterans of the Roman army.[7] Citizenship was important for these former soldiers. Paul was also a Roman citizen—a unique privilege for a Jew in the first century.[8] Although Paul rarely called attention to this unique pedigree, he did so at Philippi when circumstances warranted it.

While in Philippi, Paul began to interact with a slave girl who was possessed by a spirit that enabled her to earn money for her masters as a fortune-teller. This girl began to follow Paul and his companions shouting, "These men are servants of the Most High God, who are telling you the way to be saved" (Acts 16:17). After

Section of the Via Egnatia (Egnatian Way) that crossed by the river where Paul met Lydia.

many days, Paul became annoyed, and descerning her association with the evil arts of an oracle, he commanded the spirit to come out of the girl in the name of Jesus. In doing so he stopped the flow of cash she earned. The owners were enraged and brought Paul and Silas before the magistrates emphasizing that these Jews were promoting a cause no good Roman could support. Given the recent banishment of Jews from Rome by Claudius, this was a highly incendiary charge.[9] Consequently, Paul and Silas were stripped, beaten, and jailed overnight without a trial. The next morning Paul announced that he was a Roman citizen; this panicked the magistrates so much that they attempted to make amends (Acts 16:16–40).

When Paul and Silas were publicly shamed, the message of Jesus had also been tarnished in the eyes of the Gentiles who witnessed the event. Consequently, when the magistrates wanted Paul quietly released, he demanded a public display that would counter the humiliating treatment of the previous day. (It was illegal

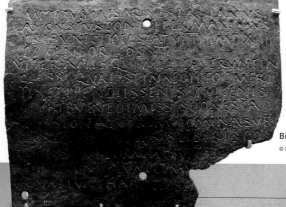

Bronze diploma granting Roman citizenship (first century AD).

for a Roman citizen to be beaten without a trial.)[10] Thus Paul announced his citizenship as leverage to restore both his reputation and the dignity of the Good News about Jesus in this Roman setting.

So it is that Paul spoke about citizenship in his letter to the Philippians for a reason. Paul's Roman citizenship certainly improved his access to the colony of retired Roman soldiers in Philippi. They had seen Paul use the power of this citizenship after he was arrested and beaten. In his letter Paul notes the fact that these retired Roman soldiers who have now submitted to Jesus share an even more important citizenship—their new King, Jesus, is more powerful than the Roman emperor, and citizenship in his Kingdom offers eternal benefits that far exceed those afforded by Rome. "But our citizenship is in heaven. And we eagerly await a Savior from there, the Lord Jesus Christ, who, by the power that enables him to bring everything under his control, will transform our lowly bodies so that they will be like his glorious body" (Phil. 3:20–21).

Remains of the forum at Philippi where Paul and Silas were taken before the Roman authorities (Acts 16:16–24).

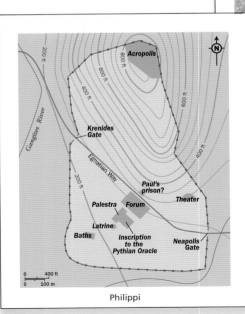
Philippi

PAUL'S RAPID DEPARTURE REQUIRES BACK-TO-BACK LETTERS TO THESSALONICA

1 AND 2 THESSALONIANS

After leaving Philippi, Paul traveled to Thessalonica where he spent three weeks at the synagogue proclaiming Jesus as the Messiah (Acts 17:2). Paul quickly left the city at night following a riot (Acts 17:5–10; 1 Thess. 2:17–20).[11] Later, when Paul arrived in Corinth, he wrote the church at Thessalonica back-to-back letters for a reason.

Thessalonica was a city that enjoyed a prime location, a diverse population, and a favorable climate for vigorous discussions and new ideas. It was located at the head of the Thermaic Gulf as the chief port of all Macedonia.[12] Here overseas shipping lanes connected with the all-important land route called the Egnatian Way[13] over which news of Jesus could expand rapidly throughout the region (as it did even in the face of persecution; 1 Thess. 1:6–8). The city had also become a cultural center and home to philosophers, poets, and teachers where a new idea would find an interested audience.[14]

Two years before Paul's arrival in Thessalonica, Claudius had issued an expulsion order in Rome. Jews had been rioting in Rome over a disagreement about *Chrestus* (from the Greek meaning "kind," i.e., "the kind ones," very possibly an allusion to Christ and his followers), which resulted in Claudius's expulsion of Jews from that city.[15] This imperial edict might well explain why there was a growing synagogue in Thessalonica. It also casts new light on the circumstances that led to Paul's departure. Jews who were jealous of Paul's message formed a mob and started a riot in the city. They dragged these followers

Excavation of the Roman forum of Thessalonica.

of Christ before the city officials and charged them with advocating a messianic king to rival the Roman emperor. They further noted that this was a problem occurring "all over the world" (Acts 17:5–8). Their choice of language is meant to create an association between these Christ followers in Thessalonica and the problems in Rome. Given the climate of the time, the charges against Paul in Thessalonica were taken very seriously and caused Paul and Silas to leave the city quickly (Acts 17:10).

Ironically, local politics soon reopened the door in Thessalonica. This city enjoyed the unique status of a free city allowed to mint its own coins and organize its own form of government. It did the latter around the *politarchs*, city officials who maintained the order and direction within the community.[16] Since the decisions of this

Milestone inscription (in Latin and Greek) of the Egnatian Way near Thessalonica.

five-man council were only valid as long as they remained in office, Paul knew a ruling that forced him from the city would expire with the term of the current *politarchs*.[17]

The time would come when he might safely return to this city. In the meantime he furthered the encouragement of the church in Thessalonica by sending Timothy (1 Thess. 3:2) and two back-to-back letters that answered questions and concerns that had not been addressed due to his rapid departure. The unique politics of the time and of the city itself help us understand why Paul left and why he wrote two back-to-back letters to the church in Thessalonica, filling the void until he could personally return to the city on his third journey.

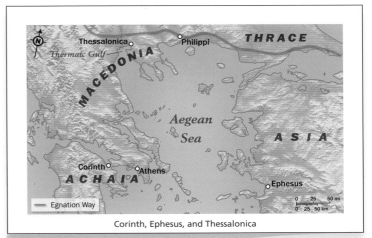

Corinth, Ephesus, and Thessalonica

The harbor of Thessalonica.

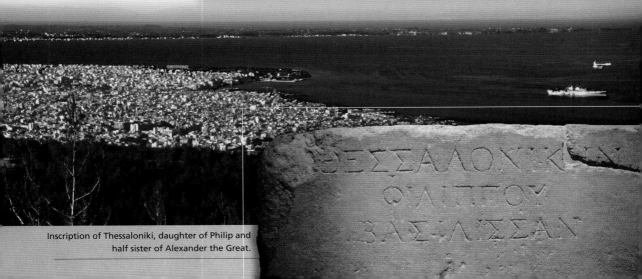

Inscription of Thessaloniki, daughter of Philip and half sister of Alexander the Great.

PAUL'S WARNING TO THE CHURCH AT CORINTH ABOUT ASSIMILATION

1 AND 2 CORINTHIANS

Paul had a deep and abiding interest in Corinth, a city he visited during his second and third journeys (Acts 18:1–17; 20:1–3) and to which he wrote two letters (1 and 2 Corinthians). Paul labored in this city, feeling the press of danger and frustration with their response to his message. So the Lord spoke to him in a vision urging him to continue speaking "because I have many people in this city" (Acts 18:10). Paul continued his work there for a year and a half. But despite this investment of time and energy, some in the church at Corinth were prone to identify with the idolatrous culture of the city. As we learn more about Corinth, we will come to appreciate why it was a city of both promise and frustration for Paul. We will also see that he wrote two letters to the church in Corinth for a reason.

When Emperor Claudius expelled the Jews from Rome, many refugees like Aquila and Priscilla came to Corinth (Acts 18:1–2). Even before Paul's arrival, both the city and the Jewish synagogue were filling with an increasing number of Jews.[18] Consequently, it is no surprise that Paul went to the synagogue every Sabbath to speak about Jesus (Acts 18:4). Despite the fact that the synagogue ruler himself and his entire household believed in the Messiah Jesus, certain men from the synagogue became abusive, raising charges against Paul with the proconsul, Gallio. Nevertheless, as a result of Paul's efforts, "many

Corinth (bottom right) was strategically located near the Corinthian Gulf.

of the Corinthians who heard him believed and were baptized" (Acts 18:8).

Corinth was fast becoming a large and important commercial center in Greece, a city attractive to both Gallio and Paul.[19] Gallio was the proconsul of Achaia, and although his name may not be familiar to us, he was famous in his time. He was the brother of Seneca and a man identified as the "friend of Claudius," the Roman emperor.[20] Someone with this reputation gave prominence to the city by his mere presence.

Since no city in Greece was better situated as a commercial center, it became both the chief city of Achaia and a lucrative trade center. Corinth and its two sea ports, Lechaeum and Cenchrea, formed a triangle that linked the mainland of Greece with the Aegean world (Asia) as well as the Adriatic world (Italy).[21] Since travel around the southern coast of the Peloponnese was treacherous, a stone-paved roadway called the *di-olkos* linked the two harbor cities allowing cargo and passengers to travel overland between the Aegean and

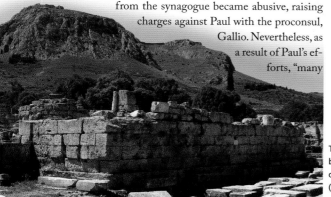

The judgment platform and hill of the Acrocorinth in the background. Paul was brought before Gallio, the proconsul of Achaia, at the judgment platform known as the Bema (Acts 18:12–17).

Adriatic Seas. This meant that a regular flow of merchants, sailors, and military delayed for the crossing had the opportunity to hear Paul speak.[22] No wonder Paul spent so much time there. This was a city where the Good News of Jesus might touch hundreds of people on any one day and on the next day travel with them to the far-flung corners of the Roman Empire.

But those who delayed in Corinth were not always attracted to such wholesome pursuits. The city also had a reputation for violence and coarse immorality.[23] Its streets held temples and shrines dedicated to the likes of Apollo or the baths of Asclepius. But it was the worship of Aphrodite that most shaped Corinth's reputation as an immoral city. Aphrodite promised to share fertility with all those who worshiped her by joining themselves to the temple prostitutes who worked throughout the streets of the city.[24]

After Paul left, the young church began to rejoin the old vices of Corinthian culture. Paul's first letter calls them out on this very topic: "Brothers, I could not address you as spiritual but as worldly—mere infants in Christ" (1 Cor. 3:1). This and the second letter from Paul address distortions in lifestyle and worship that had tainted the church. Corinth was a city of promise and frustration for Paul. That is why he spent time there and why he wrote two letters to guide this church that lived among numerous and easily accessible vices.

Road leading to the harbor at Cenchrea. According to Romans 16:1, there was a church meeting at the home of Phoebe at Cenchrea.

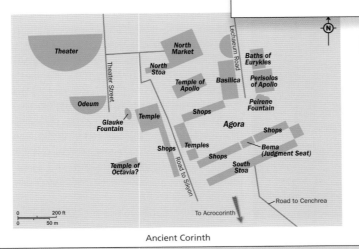

Ancient Corinth

PAUL WRITES TO UNIFY THE JEWISH AND GENTILE BELIEVERS AT ROME

ROMANS

Throughout the first century, Rome was the city that controlled the world. So it is only fitting that this city with its finger on the pulse of an empire might also find itself touched by the Kingdom of God. A church consisting of Gentiles and Jews came to life in Rome, and that community received a letter from the apostle Paul for a reason.

The introduction of Paul's letter to Rome indicates that it was not addressed to the church in Rome but "to all who are in Rome" (Rom. 1:7). That and other clues throughout the letter suggest that there was significant fragmentation in the city. The early church at Rome initially developed under the influence of three powerful factors: the outpouring of the Holy Spirit at Pentecost, Gentile believers in Jesus moving to Rome, and Paul's imprisonment at Rome. By the middle of the first century, the city of Rome had a Jewish population of around twenty thousand.[25] Luke tells us that at least some of these Jews had been in Jerusalem and were filled with the Holy Spirit at Pentecost (Acts 2:10). Once

Palatine Hill contained the palatial residences of Roman emperors, including Augustus, Tiberius, and Domitian.

they returned to their homes, they surely would have shared their experiences in Jerusalem with other Jewish families in Rome. Thus the earliest evidence we have for the church in Rome is linked to this event.

Rome was also touched by Gentiles who had become disciples of Jesus and traveled to this city from the eastern Mediterranean. That is because Rome was a transportation hub that connected to its empire through sea-lanes and roadways. A brief glance at a map suggests that the Italian Peninsula is ideally suited to sea traffic, with the Tyrrhenian, Ionian, and Adriatic seas marking three of its four borders. But it is particularly in Rome where land travel meets sea travel. Here seaborne travelers could move up the navigable waters of the Tiber River from Ostia and connect to the famous Roman road system that radiated to all the major cities of the ancient world.[26] Among those travelers and merchants were Gentiles who had come to know Jesus through their encounter with the churches of the eastern Mediterranean.[27]

It was this church, comprised of both Jewish and Gentile believers in Jesus, that Paul visited when he was imprisoned in Rome. While he awaited trial, he lived

Carcere Mamertino (Mamertine Prison) was believed to be the place where Paul and Peter were imprisoned while in Rome.

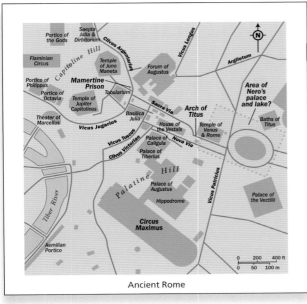

Ancient Rome

under some form of arrest while still having access to those who wished to visit him (Acts 28:11–31). But before Paul arrived there physically (see Rom. 1:10–15), he sent a letter, known to us as the book of Romans, to this community. Paul wrote this letter from Corinth during his third journey and addressed it "to all in Rome who are beloved by God and called to be saints" (Rom. 1:7). These followers of Jesus not only needed to hear the basics of God's teaching from an apostle but also needed to unite themselves in the face of growing opposition. Prior to Paul's arrival we know of no apostle who had personally traveled to Rome. Consequently, this church required a briefing on the basics of the faith, and that is what they get in Paul's letter to the Romans (e.g., Rom. 3:9–31).

Paul wrote to unify the Jewish and Gentile believers at Rome for a reason. Division between Jew and Gentile may have roots in Claudius's expulsion of the Jews from Rome due to rioting over *Chrestus*. It is assumed that this reflects a heated debate within the Jewish and Gentile church in Rome, and it is possible that bad feelings may have continued.[28] But a new age was dawning, that of Nero,[29] who as emperor of Rome persecuted Jewish and Gentile followers of Jesus like never before. Thus Paul's letter to the church at Rome was written as an urgent call for the disciples of Jesus to unite for mutual support in the face of upcoming persecution by Nero.

Nero Claudius Caesar Augustus Germanicus (AD 37–68), the fifth and final Roman emperor of the Julio-Claudian dynasty.

PAUL ENCOURAGES EPHESIAN BELIEVERS TO RETAIN UNITY DESPITE PERSECUTION

EPHESIANS

In the letter written "to the saints at Ephesus" (Eph. 1:1), Paul celebrates the blessings the Lord showers on his church and holds up a picture of what it means to be one in Christ. The church at Ephesus was on its way. Through three years of Paul's labor (Acts 20:31), the Holy Spirit had established a church in Ephesus that remained influential for centuries.[30] But during the first century Paul wrote a letter to the Ephesian fellowship encouraging them to retain unity despite the political, social, and financial persecution under way. We will see that this church, in this city, needed to hear that message for a reason.

The city of Ephesus enjoyed a significant Jewish population.[31] When Paul arrived in this city, he spent the first three months boldly and persuasively teaching about Jesus in the synagogue (Acts 19:8). When many there refused to listen and even began to publicly malign the followers of Jesus, Paul moved to the lecture hall of Tyrannus, where he continued to work for another two years (Acts 19:9–10).

The location of Ephesus on the Aegean coast made it an important commercial center.[32] And the emperor thought it important to establish a college of messengers here.[33] It is no surprise, therefore, that Paul chose to preach so long at this hub of human movement. When he did, "all the Jews and Greeks who lived in the province of Asia heard the word of the Lord" (Acts 19:10).

Years later, during the time of Paul's imprisonment, he wrote the church in Ephesus a letter (Ephesians).[34] In particular he encouraged these disciples to remain focused on Christ and to remain united in the face of coming persecution. Paul's call to remember the key message of Christ (Eph. 2:1–10) was critical to people living in Ephesus, who were surrounded by other religious attractions. In Acts we hear about two of those attractions. Luke reported that "a number who had practiced sorcery brought their scrolls together and burned them publicly" (Acts 19:19). These may well have been the famous "Ephesian Writings," scrolls that contained magical practices and incantations designed to manipulate life.[35] The second and even larger attraction unique to Ephesus was the great temple of Artemis (also known as Diana). Artemis was an idol of nature who promised to provide fertility to those who came to worship at the massive, marble temple built in her honor.[36] People would flood into Ephesus from throughout the region in order to honor this image. When they did, they boosted the local economy by purchasing votive offerings from the local artisans. As the church took root in Ephesus, the local artists began to suffer financially since there was less demand for these images. At one point, things became so tense that a riot developed, and a public demonstration was held in the theater at Ephesus (Acts 19:23–41). Eventually the city clerk dismissed the assembly, but the temple and its attraction continued. Thus Paul urged the Ephesian church to remain focused on Christ in the face of these destructive alternatives.

Paul encouraged Ephesian believers to retain unity despite persecution. Rejection of Artemis, witchcraft, divination, and emperor worship had already brought persecution to the church at Ephesus. Upcoming events would continue to

Idol of Artemis (Diana) of Ephesus (first century AD).
© Dr. James C. Martin. The Ephesus Museum.

The harbor road, theater, and cardo of Ephesus (aerial view looking east).

The Ephesus theater, with a seating capacity of seventeen to twenty-five thousand, was originally built by the Greeks and later renovated under the Roman rulers Claudius, Nero, and Domitian.

bring untold hardship their direction (Eph. 2:11–22; 4:1–16). Nero was the emperor of Rome at the time,[37] and he soon began to blame the followers of Jesus for problems that he himself had caused. As scapegoats, Gentile believers in the Messiah Jesus were considered traitors who were disloyal to the Roman emperor, and they were subject to various forms of persecution, torture, and execution. In the face of that hardship, Paul urged the church at Ephesus to recognize the true enemy, to remain united, and to put on the full armor of God while standing firm against the devil's schemes (Eph. 6:10–18).

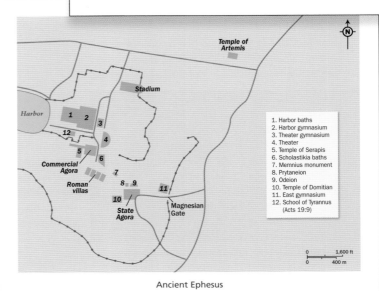

1. Harbor baths
2. Harbor gymnasium
3. Theater gymnasium
4. Theater
5. Temple of Serapis
6. Scholastikia baths
7. Memnius monument
8. Prytaneion
9. Odeion
10. Temple of Domitian
11. East gymnasium
12. School of Tyrannus (Acts 19:9)

Ancient Ephesus

PAUL RESPONDS TO HERESY IN A LETTER TO THE COLOSSIANS

COLOSSIANS

The church at Colosse is not mentioned by name in the book of Acts, and it is an ancient site virtually untouched by archaeological investigation.[38] But when we read Colossians, the letter sent by Paul to the churches in this region, one thing does become clear: they were struggling with various heresies, a struggle that would come to a conclusion when they joined Paul in asserting the adequacy of Christ.

If Paul did visit Colosse, it was most likely during the third journey when he traveled from Syrian Antioch to Ephesus. During the early stages of that trip Paul's goal was to strengthen the disciples throughout Galatia and Phrygia while traveling to Ephesus (Acts 18:23). Presuming that Paul took the main road through Asia Minor, he would have traveled within a few miles of Colosse. But there is no evidence that even a few hours of his time were spent in this city. With Acts and archaeology silent on the subject, the start of the church in Colosse and neighboring churches in Laodicea and Hierapolis (Col. 4:13–16) remains a mystery.

Although Paul had not visited the fellowships personally (Col. 2:1), he had received reports about their circumstances (Col. 1:9). The reports appear to have come from two individuals, Epaphras and Onesimus, both of whom were with Paul during the time of his imprisonment in Rome when he wrote Colossians (Col. 1:7–8; 4:9). We know that when Paul was in Ephesus on his second journey the Good News of Jesus spread throughout the Roman province of Asia (Acts 19:10). It is very possible that Epaphras was among those who traveled from Ephesus, during Paul's stay there, and visited cities like Colosse. By contrast, Onesimus was a slave from Colosse who had joined Paul after running away from his master.[39] Thus what Paul lacked in personal contact with the churches in these cities he gained via the eyewitness reports he received from these two men.

The news that Epaphras and Onesimus offered Paul was not good. The church at Colosse was deeply embattled in heresy.[40] Paul discussed or alluded to at least three separate issues that had arisen in this church. First he mentioned the intrusion and competition of

This Greek inscription (third century AD) discovered in Miletus reveals five (of seven) prayers to unnamed archangels.

Classical Greek philosopher Socrates (ca. 470–399 BC).

human philosophy—deceptive philosophy that leans on the "basic principles of this world rather than on Christ" (Col. 2:8). He further spoke about certain Jewish practices that had been fulfilled in Jesus and therefore were no longer required to be adopted into God's family. He mentioned the better circumcision they have received from Christ (v. 11) and urged the believers of Colosse not to allow themselves to be judged for not observing dietary rituals, religious festivals, New Moon celebrations, or Sabbath days (v. 16). Finally, Paul touched briefly on the topic of angel worship that threatened "to disqualify them for the prize" (v. 18).

Paul responded to heresy in a letter to the Colossians for a reason. The common denominator linking all these mistaken beliefs was a failure to see Christ as the full and adequate answer to the meaning of life.[41] Consequently, Paul encouraged the church at Colosse to remain faithful to the teachings they first received about Jesus. Since they had apparently lost touch with those basics, he presented an extended discourse reviewing the nature and role of the Messiah in their lives (Col. 1:15–23; 2:13–23). So far as we know, Paul may never have made a personal stop in Colosse, and many details of this city's heritage continue to elude us. But we do know that Paul wrote a letter to this church to confront false teachings and bring their focus back to the church and to the full and total adequacy of Christ.

The acropolis of Colosse (aerial view looking south).

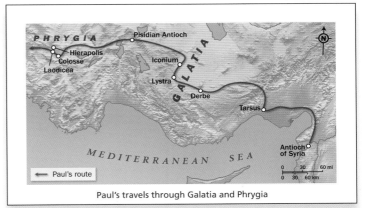

Paul's travels through Galatia and Phrygia

Cities of Phrygia: Hierapolis, Laodicea, Colosse

JOHN RECEIVES A REVELATION ON THE ISLAND OF PATMOS

REVELATION 1

Patmos is an island in the Aegean Sea lying off the west coast of modern Turkey, approximately thirty-five miles from the ancient harbor at Miletus. Eight miles long and six miles wide, the island boasts but a small amount of living space. Since it was off the major shipping lanes and had a limited supply of fresh water, it was destined to have a small population. But what impresses us even more than its small size and poor natural resources is the isolation of this rocky island.[42] The Romans sent John to this island for a reason, and God used this setting to reverse the intended outcome of the Roman government.

Following Jesus's ascension into heaven in the early years of the first century, John and the other apostles had remained in or near Jerusalem. By the close of the first century, tradition indicates John was at work in Ephesus.[43] During those intervening years the church had witnessed explosive growth at the same time it had endured painful persecution. Rome was governed by the Flavian dynasty, which used the imperial cult of emperor worship as a way of uniting the empire. By the time of the revelation to John, the emperor Domitian was the head of the Roman Empire. He was not well educated, had no record as a war hero, lacked social graces, and was generally cruel. In a desperate attempt to lift his credibility, he commanded that he be addressed as *dominus et deus noster,* "our lord and god."[44] The emperor sought to exterminate those who

Cave of the Apocalypse on the island of Patmos.

refused to acknowledge him as deity or follow this national religion.

The Romans recognized that John was encouraging and advancing efforts that opposed the imperial cult. They sought to silence him by isolating him on the island of Patmos, which doubled as a Roman detention center.[45] The Lord used the quiet isolation of Patmos to pull back the curtain of eternity and to reveal a vision that John preserved in the book of Revelation.

Statue of the Roman emperor Domitian.

Emperor Nero (AD 37–68). The numeric equivalent in Hebrew script for Caesar Nero (qsr nrwn) is 100 + 60 + 200 + 50 + 200 + 6 + 50, which totals 666—the number given to the Antichrist in Revelation 13:18.

The island of Patmos with the monastery of AD 1088 at the top and the Cave of the Apocalypse in the center.

As John began the book of Revelation, he described himself as "your brother and companion in the suffering and kingdom and patient endurance that are ours in Jesus" (Rev. 1:9). John had felt the pain of persecution, but he had also received a revelation from God. By sharing this vision with the church, John assured the churches of Asia Minor that the Lord who loved them was still in control of the world. Using symbolic language, John described a revelation that confused those who wished to harm and yet brought comfort to those in harm's way.

John received a revelation on the island of Patmos for a reason. Persecution can shorten rather than lengthen one's view of life. Real healing and help for those living under persecution comes in getting the big picture presented in Revelation. As John's gaze turned away from the landscape of his island prison, his eyes were freed to see future events and know that the final destruction of Satan was coming—a showdown in which the ultimate victory of Jesus over the adversary was assured. The Romans had sent John to Patmos to prevent him from offering encouragement to the church. In turn, God used the island of Patmos as the setting in which to reveal the vision destined to help and sustain the church during times of persecution.

The island of Patmos

WATER AND WEALTH ARE RELATED TO THE CHURCH AT LAODICEA

REVELATION 3:14–21

The book of Revelation addresses disciples of Jesus living throughout time who might be facing marginalization, persecution, or even a martyr's death.[46] When the Holy Spirit filled John with the words of this book, some of its first readers were living in seven cities of ancient Asia Minor. The churches in these cities were either started or enjoyed significant growth during Paul's second journey when he remained in Ephesus for around three years (Acts 20:31). During his stay there and under his influence, "all the Jews and Greeks who lived in the province of Asia heard the word of the Lord" (Acts 19:10). While the bulk of material in Revelation was addressed to all seven churches, each of them received a special note from the Lord unique to their local situation (Revelations 2–3). Here we will explore the last of those seven special notes—the one addressed to the church at Laodicea. To whom and how it was written was for a reason (Rev. 3:14–22).

Ironically the last church addressed with a special note[47] comes in for some of the harshest criticism, which was directed at its apathy and dependence on

The forum of Laodicea (view looking northeast).

wealth. The local geography of Laodicea is used either to illustrate or explain the Lord's concerns, beginning with the city's apathy. Every expectation is that those who come to know Jesus as their Lord will naturally be excited to live lives that distinguish them as his disciples (John 15:1–17). When the Lord looked at the church of Laodicea, he saw apathy rather than fruit of faith. Note how these verses call attention to the apathy in Laodicea using *water* language: "I know your deeds, that you are neither cold nor hot. I wish you were either one or the other! So, because you are lukewarm—neither hot nor cold—I am about to spit you out of my mouth" (Rev. 3:15–16). The metaphor relies on our knowledge of the hot and cold water sources in the region. Hot water came from the famous hot springs of Hierapolis (modern Pamukkale, Turkey), approximately eight miles north of Laodicea, and the cold water (snow melt) came from Colosse (modern Honaz), a little over four miles east along the Lycus Valley. The reputation of these two cities as hot and cold water sources was well-known in the area. Laodicea had no local water supply; it had to be piped in from over four miles away.

The waters near Laodicea have beneficial distinctions: hot healing springs and fresh drinking water.

Ancient stone water pipes brought water into the city of Laodicea.

Laodicea had neither a hot nor a cold water reputation. Therefore the note to the church in Laodicea describes its reputation as lukewarm and thus not beneficial.

The second concern the Lord had with the church at Laodicea was related to money. We know they were very wealthy. When a devastating earthquake ruined the city in AD 60, the residents were able to decline the rebuilding assistance offered by the Roman Senate because they had sufficient wealth to undertake the rebuilding on their own.[48] Laodicea became a strong commercial and banking center fostered by its prime location on the east/west roadway that bisected Asia Minor. The region was also well known for its glossy black wool and its eye salve made from Phrygian stone.[49]

Water and wealth are related to the church at Laodicea for a reason. Laodicea was situated between two cities famous for their water qualities—qualities that Laodicea lacked. The city did, however, have abundant wealth. To some the blessing of this wealth had become a distraction, harming their relationship with the Lord. In that light, the Lord used local color when offering a solution to their situation: "I counsel you to buy from me gold refined in the fire, so you can become rich; and white clothes to wear, so you can cover your shameful nakedness; and salve to put on your eyes, so you can see" (Rev. 3:18).

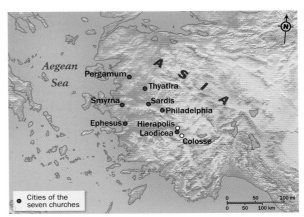

Cities of the seven churches

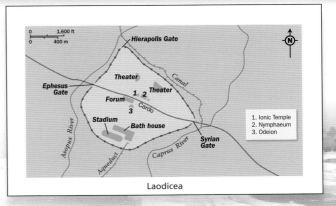

Laodicea

The hot springs of Hierapolis (known as Pamukkale, or "cotton castle," near Denizli, Turkey) lie on the north side of the Lycus Valley, across from Laodicea.

THE FINAL BATTLE AT ARMAGEDDON NEAR MOUNT CARMEL

REVELATION 16

T he book of Revelation has brought comfort and encouragement to embattled disciples of Jesus since it was written. It is addressed to men, women, and children wearied by attacks from Satan's schemes and discouraged by conflicts with an enemy committed to their ruin. Although the fight seems interminable, the inspired words of Revelation offer a different reality. The arrival of Jesus set in motion a series of events that will bring history to a climactic end when the Lord will destroy the adversary and his minions once and for all—forever. The Revelation to John reveals that this final battle will occur at Armageddon (Rev. 16:16). This vision reminds us of two earlier battles that took place in this same area. We will see that this final battle takes place in Armageddon near Mount Carmel for a reason.

Armageddon is a Hebrew place name best decoded as "Mount of Megiddo." Although this particular phrase is not used elsewhere in the Bible, we do know the location of Megiddo, which rests on the southwest side of the Jezreel Valley and is clearly one of the most strategic locations in the Promised Land.[50] In particular we note that it was where Josiah was killed in a battle against Egypt in his attempt to keep Israel safe (2 Chron. 35:20–24). Thus when "the kings of the whole world"

Painting of "Jesus on Throne" at the Russian Orthodox Church of the Ascension (Jerusalem).

are gathered "for the battle on the great day of God Almighty" (Rev. 16:14), we can rest assured this will be a significant battle. This battle will bring an end to the adversary (Rev. 16:17), and "Babylon the Great" will finally fall (Rev. 16:19).[51]

Another implication of the battle setting is often overlooked. This battle will occur in association with the "mountain" of Megiddo, most likely the ridge of Mount Carmel that rises above Megiddo. Let's consider what the mention of Mount Carmel has to do with the description of this conflict. The book of Revelation often invites its readers to recall images and events from Scripture. For example, Revelation invites us to think about another battle that started on Mount Carmel and ended in the Jezreel Valley. During the days of Elijah the prophet, King Ahab and Queen Jezebel had encouraged and sponsored Baal worship in Israel. This led Elijah to call for a contest to determine who deserved the title of God (1 Kings 18:21). Both Elijah and the four hundred prophets of Baal made altars for their sacrifices. Whichever sacrifice was divinely ignited would prove

Megiddo (view looking northeast). Many believe we get the word *Megiddo* from the name Har Mageddon (or Armageddon), "mountain of Megiddo."

The Jezreel Valley, the battleground of history (view looking west).

to represent the true God. Following the total failure of Baal and the awe-inspiring ignition provided by the Lord, Elijah commanded that the prophets of Baal be seized and executed at the base of the mountain in the Jezreel Valley not far from Megiddo (1 Kings 18:40). It is this unquestionable victory of the Lord that casts the hope and promise over the coming battle at Armageddon. Just as Baal and his prophets met their end at the base of Mount Carmel near Megiddo, so Satan and his forces will meet their end at the Mountain of Megiddo.

Mutiny against the King of the Universe will come to a close. The adversary who seduced humanity into thinking that a fulfilled life was found in his lies rather than God's Word will be dealt with once and for all (Rev. 20:10). We have hoped for a Rescuer since humanity's first mutiny against God, starting in the Garden of Eden. Now we can look to the Promised Land and to the Nazareth Ridge, where Jesus lived. Throughout much of his time in Galilee, Jesus walked by or gazed down on "Armageddon," the battleground of history. We now join him

in looking to this same place in certainty of the day when he will return to destroy evil once and for all—a victory that will occur where it does for a reason.

Maranatha. Come, Lord Jesus!

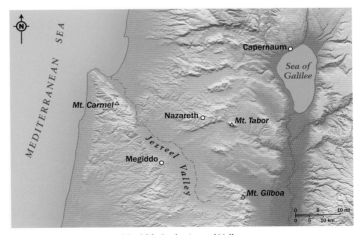

Megiddo in the Jezreel Valley

NOTES

Part 1 The Need for Rescue and the Promised Land

1. Biblical references also include 2 Kings 19:12; Isaiah 37:12 (Eden in Tel Assar); 51:3; Ezekiel 28:13; 31:9, 16, 18; 36:35; Joel 2:3 (Garden of); Amos 1:5 (Beth Eden).

2. For a more detailed discussion of the location, see Barry J. Beitzel, *The Moody Atlas of Bible Lands* (Chicago: Moody, 1985), 74–75.

3. I. Cornelius, "*Gan*," in *NIDOTTE*, ed. Willem A. Van Gemeren (Grand Rapids: Zondervan, 1997), 1703.

4. While the Greek term *paradeisos* used by the Septuagint provides us with our English word *paradise*, it is a Persian loan word used to describe a royal, parklike enclosure. Joachim Jeremias, "*Paradeisos*," in *TDNT*, vol. 5, ed. Gerhad Kittel and Gerhard Friedrich (Grand Rapids: Eerdmans, 1967), 765–66.

5. Priit J. Vesilink, "Water, The Middle East's Critical Resource," *National Geographic* (May 1993): 48.

6. Yohanan Aharoni, *The Land of the Bible: A Historical Geography* (Philadelphia: Westminster, 1979), 3.

7. John Sailhamer, *The Pentateuch as Narrative*, Library of Biblical Interpretation (Grand Rapids: Zondervan, 1992), 134.

8. David A. Dorsey, *The Roads and Highways of Ancient Israel*, The ASOR Library of Biblical and Near Eastern Archaeology (Baltimore: Johns Hopkins University Press, 1991), 57.

9. Carl G. Rasmussen, *Zondervan NIV Atlas of the Bible* (Grand Rapids: Zondervan, 1989), 57.

10. The archaeological evidence from this period indicates that residents of the Levant frequently responded to climatic misfortune by marching directly for the abundant natural resources available in Egypt. James K. Hoffmeier, *Israel in Egypt: The Evidence for the Authenticity of the Exodus Tradition* (New York: Oxford University Press, 1996), 68.

11. For a helpful summary of the options, see Eugene H. Merrill, *Kingdom of Priests: A History of Old Testament Israel* (Grand Rapids: Baker, 1987), 35–36.

12. Sailhamer, *Pentateuch as Narrative*, 134.

13. A single tomb was used for multiple burials. Alfred J. Hoerth, *Archaeology and the Old Testament* (Grand Rapids: Baker Books, 1998), 105.

14. Standing stones were erected for various purposes, including the commemoration of an important event. Carl F. Graesser, "Standing Stones in Ancient Palestine," *The Biblical Archaeologist* 35 (1972): 37.

15. Aharoni, *The Land of the Bible*, 57.

16. Dorsey, *Roads and Highways of Ancient Israel*, 119.

17. Ibid., 196.

18. The location of the Egyptian capital city depends on the dating of Joseph's arrival in Egypt. It is our position that the date of his arrival coincided with the Egyptian Middle Kingdom (1991–1782 BC), specifically, the Twelfth Dynasty (1991–62 BC). During the Twelfth Dynasty the capital was located at Itj-Tawy on the west bank of the Nile between Memphis and the Faiyum. For a summary of this and other possible dates, consult John J. Davis, *Paradise to Prison: Studies in Genesis* (Salem, WI: Sheffield, 1998), 266–67. For a discussion of the dating issues, see Hoerth, *Archaeology and the Old Testament*, 57–59.

19. "From Dan to Beersheba" became a formula frequently used to mark the northern and southern boundaries of the Promised Land (Judg. 20:1; 1 Sam. 3:20; 2 Sam. 3:10, passim).

20. Amihai Mazar, *Archaeology of the Land of the Bible, 10,000–586 B.C.E.*, The Anchor Bible Reference Library (New York: Doubleday, 1992), 197.

21. Dorsey, *Roads and Highways of Ancient Israel*, 121, 180.

Part 2 The Journey from Egypt to the Promised Land

1. Denis Baly, *The Geography of the Bible: A Study in Historical Geography* (London: Lutterworth Press, 1957), 12–13.

2. Some scholars believe the "new king" (Exod. 1:8) was a Hyksos ruler. For a discussion see Hoerth, *Archaeology and the Old Testament*, 157.

3. The archaeologist of Tell ed-Dab'a, Alfred Bietek, has suggested that Tell ed-Dab'a had two names: in the Eighteenth Dynasty, *Peru-nefer*, and in the Nineteenth Dynasty, *Rameses*. For a discussion of this site in English, see Bryant G. Wood, "The Royal Precinct at Rameses," *Bible and Spade* 17 (2004): 45–51. Archaeological discoveries in Egypt include papyrus baskets used as coffins.

4. Anson F. Rainey and R. Steven Notley, *The Sacred Bridge: Carta's Atlas of the Biblical World* (Jerusalem: Carta, 2006), 68.

5. This association with Tell ed-Dab'a is broadly accepted even by those who date the Exodus to different periods (fifteenth versus thirteenth century). Beitzel, *Moody Atlas of Bible Lands*, 86; K. A. Kitchen, *On the Reliability of the Old Testament* (Grand Rapids: Eerdmans, 2003), 255–56; Rasmussen, *NIV Atlas of the Bible*, 88.

6. For a discussion on the possible location of these sites, see Kitchen, *Reliability of the Old Testament*, 259–61.

7. E.g., Lake Ballah, Lake Timsah, Great Bitter Lake, and Little Bitter Lake.

8. Hoffmeier, *Israel in Egypt*, 179–80.

9. Beitzel, *Moody Atlas of Bible Lands*, 92.

10. These men are never called *mraglim*, military spies, as those who are sent out at other times (Gen. 42:9; Josh. 2:1).

11. For an overview of those Egyptian records, see Rainey and Notley, *The Sacred Bridge*, 65–76.

12. Ibid., 76.

13. Aharoni, *The Land of the Bible*, 174–75.

14. Mazar, *Archaeology of the Land of the Bible*, 243.

15. Aharoni, *The Land of the Bible*, 31.

16. A skill still used by Bedouin in the region. Arie Issar, *Water Shall Flow from the Rock: Hydrology and Climate in the Land of the Bible* (New York: Springer, 1990), 121.

17. The "rock" to which Moses was to speak is translated from the Hebrew word sela‘. This is not the generic word for *rock* but an infrequently used word for the softer porous rock found in the Wilderness of Zin. For a further discussion, see John A. Beck, "Why Did Moses Strike Out? The Narrative-Geographical Shaping of Moses's Disqualification, Numbers 20:1–13," *Westminster Theological Journal* 65 (2003): 135–41.

18. Rephidim is located in the southern Sinai where the predominant rock is granite. Since this rock absorbs no water, there would be no natural expectation that striking the rock would produce water.

19. Efraim Orni and Elisha Efrat, *Geography of Israel*, 3rd ed. (Philadelphia: Jewish Publication Society, 1971), 108.

20. Wadi Fidan or Wadi Musa would be the most likely passages in view for the Israelites. Rasmussen, *NIV Atlas of the Bible*, 56.

21. Pisgah and Nebo are two separate but associated heights that lie nine miles east of the northern rim of the Dead Sea. Yohanan Aharoni, Michael Avi-Yonah, Anson F. Rainey, and Ze'ev Safrai, *The Macmillan Bible Atlas*, 3rd ed. (New York: Macmillan, 1993), 49.

22. A circa ninth to seventh century BC ink inscription has been discovered at Tell Deir Alla near the mouth of the Jabbok River. The subject of this inscription is "Balaam, son of Beor." Kitchen, *Reliability of the Old Testament*, 412–13.

Part 3 Conquest and Settlement of Canaan

1. Carl Ritter, *The Comparative Geography of Palestine and the Sinaitic Peninsula*, vol. 4 (New York: Greenwood, 1968), 51, 53.

2. William F. Lynch, *Narrative of the United States' Expedition to the Jordan River and the Dead Sea* (Philadelphia: Lea and Blanchard, 1849), 255.

3. Some have questioned the reliability of the biblical account of Jericho's fall since they claim that no archaeological evidence of a late Bronze Age city exists on this site. But that evidence does exist. For an accessible summary of the debate and evidence, see Walter C. Kaiser Jr., *A History of Israel from the Bronze Age through the Jewish Wars* (Nashville: Broadman and Holman, 1998), 151–54.

4. A. Zertal has proposed that a one-acre cultic site contains remains of the altar built by Joshua. For a discussion, see Mazar, *Archaeology of the Land of the Bible*, 348–50.

5. Gibeon was part of a four-city coalition of Hivites (Gibeon, Kephirah, Beeroth, Kiriath Jearim), which controlled the road that went from the coastal plains to the hill country. Gibeon was an important city, "it was larger than Ai, and all its men were good fighters" (Josh. 10:2).

6. This region was later assigned to the tribe of Benjamin.

7. For a study of the specific language used, see David M. Howard Jr., *Joshua*, vol. 5, *The New American Commentary* (Nashville: Broadman and Holman, 1998), 300–307.

8. In at least one case, the tribes contested the allotment based on this criterion. See Joshua 17:14–18.

9. Howard, *Joshua*, 321.

10. John A. Beck, *The Land of Milk and Honey* (St. Louis: Concordia, 2006), 33–34.

11. Baly, *The Geography of the Bible*, 41–66.

12. Karel Van Der Torn, "Theology, Priests, and Worship in Canaan and Ancient Israel," in *Civilizations of the Ancient Near East*, vol. 3, ed. Jack M. Sasson (Peabody, MA: Hendrickson, 1995), 2043–45.

13. Hoerth, *Archaeology and the Old Testament*, 221.

14. Kaiser, *A History of Israel*, 184.

15. The borders of Naphtali, Zebulun, and Issachar meet there (Josh. 19:10–23, 32–39).

16. Judges 5:8. The Israelite soldiers lacked not only state-of-the-art weapons but basic tools for war itself.

17. At the time of Joshua, Manasseh and Ephraim had complained that their assigned territory included the Jezreel Valley, where chariots consistently held the day (Josh. 17:16). This problem is also cited in Judges 1:19.

18. On summer nights in the interior plains of the Promised Land, one could expect this cooling to produce dew on at least half the nights. From June through August the Geva area in the Harod Valley receives dew about seventeen nights per month. Jacob Katnelson, s.v. "Dew," *Encyclopedia Judaica*, vol. 5, 1602.

19. Michael Zohary, *Plants of the Bible* (Cambridge: Cambridge University Press, 1982), 26.

20. Mark Stratton Smith, "Myth and Mythmaking in Canaan and Ancient Israel," in *Civilizations of the Ancient Near East*, vol. 3, ed. Jack M. Sasson (Peabody, MA: Hendrickson, 1995), 2033.

21. Cheryl A. Brown, "Judges," in *Joshua, Judges, Ruth*, vol. 5 of *New International Biblical Commentary: Old Testament* (Peabody, MA: Hendrickson, 2000), 192.

22. The Egyptians called these former residents of the Aegean world and their invading partners the "Sea Peoples." Mazar, *Archaeology of the Land of the Bible*, 300–307.

23. Rainey and Notley, *The Sacred Bridge*, 110.

24. David M. Howard Jr., "Philistines," in *Peoples of the Old Testament World*, ed. Alfred Hoerth, Gerald L. Mattingly, and Edwin M. Yamauchi (Grand Rapids: Baker, 1994), 241–43.

25. Lucian Turkowski, "Peasant Agriculture in the Judean Hills," in *Palestine Exploration Quarterly* 101 (1969): 23.

26. Orni and Efrat, *Geography of Israel*, 111.

Part 4 The United Monarchy of Israel

1. Aharoni, Avi-Yonah, Rainey, and Safrai, *The Macmillan Bible Atlas*, 68.

2. The Lord had directed Joshua to bring the Ark of the Covenant into battle at Jericho (Josh. 6:1–20), so this deployment enjoyed divine sanction.

3. A concubine was viewed as a wife without inheritance rights.

4. The location of this site is disputed, but all alternatives place it near Gibeah of Benjamin. Aharoni, *The Land of the Bible*, 286.

5. Dorsey, *Roads and Highways of Ancient Israel*, 117, 138, 183.

6. The sycamore provided figs and the raw materials for roof rafters. Additionally, the terebinth produced a resin used for caulking, for shellacking wall paintings,

and in the mummification process in Egypt. Zohary, *Plants of the Bible*, 68. Aharon Kempinski and Ronny Reich, *The Architecture of Ancient Israel* (Jerusalem: Israel Exploration Society, 1992), 7. Philip J. King and Lawrence E. Stager, *Life in Biblical Israel*, Library of Ancient Israel (Louisville: Westminster John Knox, 2001), 109.

7. George A. Smith, *The Historical Geography of the Holy Land* (New York: Armstrong and Son, 1907), 209. Anson F. Rainey, "The Biblical Shephelah of Judah," *Bulletin of the American Schools of Oriental Research* 251 (1983): 3.

8. Moisture-laden air masses are driven up the western side of the central mountains. This rising air cools and disgorges its moisture west of the watershed line. As the air mass crests the central ridge and descends, it slowly warms, withholding rain from the eastern slopes. This area lies beneath a rainfall shadow.

9. Orni and Efrat, *Geography of Israel*, 62.

10. While the Hebrew of Judges 7:1 leaves some question on the relationship of the Midianite camp to Mount Moreh, Psalm 83:9–10 locates it on the north side of the mountain near Endor. Ironically, Endor is where Saul approached a medium and learned of his coming fate. See Rainey and Notley, *The Sacred Bridge*, 139.

11. Jezreel is Hebrew for "may God sow."

12. Orni and Efrat, *Geography of Israel*, 96.

13. This risk became reality as the Israelites abandoned their towns in these valleys (1 Sam. 31:7).

14. Explorers sent out by Joshua to retrieve evidence of the Promised Land's fertility brought back a massive cluster of grapes from this region—powerful evidence of the land's productivity (Num. 13:23–24).

15. George A. Turner, *Historical Geography of the Holy Land* (Grand Rapids: Baker, 1973), 279.

16. A high place was either a naturally occurring hill or a constructed platform. The fact that such locations could be orthodox worship sites is supported by Samuel's use of a high place (1 Sam. 9:12). Since such locations were also associated with pagan worship, Israelites who used such locations to blend Canaanite worship with worship of the Lord were roundly condemned. Roland De Vaux, *Ancient Israel: Its Life and Institutions*, Biblical Resource Series (Grand Rapids: Eerdmans, 1997), 288.

17. The Lord forbade the worship of any images, expressing his presence through visual absence. Hoerth, *Archaeology and the Old Testament*, 174.

18. We are not given any information as to the time or the circumstances of Saul's massacre of the Gibeonites, but it was a grave breach of the covenant entered into by Joshua in the name of the Lord (Josh. 9:15–27). Therefore when Saul, as head of the Israelite nation, committed an atrocity against the innocent Gibeonites, God saw to it that this did not go unjudged.

19. De Vaux, *Ancient Israel*, 320.

20. Hazor, Megiddo, and Gezer all have city gates dated to this period. The similar floor plan of those gates has been associated with Solomon's fortification efforts. Aharoni, Avi-Yonah, Rainey, and Safrai, *The Macmillan Bible Atlas*, 85.

21. Kitchen, *Reliability of the Old Testament*, 108–10.

22. Although Gezer had been defeated by Joshua (Josh. 12:1, 12), assigned to Ephraim, and made a Levitical city (Josh. 21:21), it remained a Canaanite stronghold into the time of the Judges (Judg. 1:29).

23. This includes the Israeli army that used this route in its bid to reclaim Jerusalem in 1967. Turner, *Historical Geography of the Holy Land*, 186.

Part 5 The Divided Kingdom and Assyrian Invasion

1. Solomon employed two different branches of public labor for his building projects. Non-Israelites were conscripted to do forced labor particularly in Lebanon. Israelites were also required to provide unpaid service to Solomon, but this work occurred within Israel and was considered more honorable than the work imposed on non-Israelites (1 Kings 5:13–17). Rehoboam threatened to make life more difficult for the northern tribes by requiring the same humiliating and difficult work his father had pressed upon the non-Israelites. Rainey, *The Sacred Bridge*, 167–68.

2. This east/west roadway leaves the International Highway at Socoh (Sharon Plain), following gentle slopes toward Shechem. East of Shechem this road links to the Wadi Faria and goes to the Jordan Valley, connecting to a route that leads into the Transjordan. Dorsey, *Roads and Highways of Ancient Israel*, 174–75.

3. Consider the way in which the northern tribes came to David at Hebron in order to ask him to be their king (2 Sam. 5:1–2).

4. It is unclear if Jeroboam intended for the bull to represent the throne of the Lord or Baal, but royal subjects of various persuasions would have found something meaningful to worship. De Vaux, *Ancient Israel*, 334.

5. This shrine was easily accessible by using major roadways emanating from Megiddo and Beth Shan. Beitzel, *Moody Atlas of Bible Lands*, 67–68.

6. Rainey and Notley, *The Sacred Bridge*, 169.

7. The biblical authors use the name Samaria in two different ways. It may designate the city or the region (Northern Kingdom) associated with that capital city.

8. Twice by Aram (1 Kings 20:1–12; 2 Kings 6:24) and once for three years by Assyria (2 Kings 17:5–6).

9. Aharoni, *The Land of the Bible*, 334.

10. Rainey and Notley, *The Sacred Bridge*, 199.

11. Merrill, *Kingdom of Priests*, 345.

12. For a more detailed discussion of this story in its location, see John A. Beck, "Geography as Irony: The Narrative-Geographical Shaping of Elijah's Duel with the Prophets of Baal," *Scandinavian Journal of the Old Testament* 17 (2003): 291–302.

13. Aharoni, *The Land of the Bible*, 111.

14. Mount Carmel enjoys a heavy dewfall 250 nights per year. Beitzel, *Moody Atlas of Bible Lands*, 52.

15. Yohanan Aharoni, "Mount Carmel as Border," in *Archäologie und Altes Testament* (Tübingen, Germany: JCB Mohr, 1970), 2.

16. Subsequent Roman inscriptions also identify Mount Carmel with Baal worship. Ephraim Orni and Michael Avi-Yonah, s.v. "Carmel, Mount," *Encyclopedia Judaica*, vol. 5, 186. Note that an altar to the Lord once stood on this location as well (1 Kings 18:30).

17. Note particularly 2 Kings 17 and the prophecy of Amos.

18. Beitzel, *Moody Atlas of Bible Lands*, 126.

19. Joseph Blenkinsopp, "Ahab of Israel and Jehoshaphat of Judah: The Syro-Palestinian Corridor in the Ninth Century," in *Civilizations of the Ancient Near East*, vol. 2, ed. Jack M. Sasson (Peabody, MA: Hendrickson, 2000), 1312.

20. This renaissance in Israel would come to a close as Tiglath-Pileser reanimated Assyrian imperialism in 745 BC, leading to the destruction of Samaria in 722 BC.

21. The same Hebrew verb (*hfk*) is used repeatedly in Genesis 19 to describe the overthrow of Sodom and Gomorrah.

22. It would have been possible for Jonah to board one of the trading ships that regularly traveled from Joppa to Ugarit. From Ugarit, Jonah could have joined the overland routes to Nineveh. But his plan was to leave for Tarshish, not Ugarit (Jonah 1:3).

23. The location of Tarshish is uncertain, though many place it on the southwestern shore of Spain. For a discussion see, Beitzel, *Moody Atlas of Bible Lands*, 122–23.

24. Jonah further reveals this attitude in his interaction with the sailors on the ship (Jonah 1:8–16) and in his reaction to the remarkable repentance in Nineveh (Jonah 4:1–3).

25. Victor H. Matthews and Don C. Benjamin, *Social World of Ancient Israel, 1250–587 BCE* (Peabody, MA: Hendrickson, 1993), 47–48.

26. The *soreq* is a dark red grape considered the choicest of the land. King and Stager, *Life in Biblical Israel*, 98.

27. Victor H. Matthews, "Treading the Winepress: Actual and Metaphorical Viticulture in the Ancient Near East" in *Food and Drink in the Biblical Worlds*, Semeia 86 (Atlanta: Society of Biblical Literature, 1999), 26.

28. One route past Lachish provided access to the Ridge Route near Hebron and the second travels north northeast past Azekah and Beth Shemesh. Dorsey, *Roads and Highways of Ancient Israel*, 154, 195.

29. Hezekiah's revolt took place during the transition that saw Sennacherib replace Sargon II as ruler of Assyria (705 BC).

30. Hezekiah expanded and strengthened the walls of Jerusalem while constructing a tunnel that could bring fresh water into the capital city in the face of an Assyrian siege (2 Chron. 32:2–5, 30).

31. Sennacherib's own account of this foray speaks of forty-six Judean cities he placed under siege. Rainey and Notley, *The Sacred Bridge*, 243. Isaiah 36:1 makes the same observation, and Micah 1:10–16 provides a partial listing of those cities.

Part 6 The Babylonian Invasion, Exile, and Return to the Promised Land

1. Josiah eliminated false idols, temples, and priests from the land, including the persistent worship of the golden calf at Bethel. He rebuilt and reanimated the Temple at Jerusalem. And when the book of the Law was discovered in the process, he led Judah in a covenant renewal (see 2 Kings 22–23; 2 Chron. 34–35).

2. Beitzel, *Moody Atlas of Bible Lands*, 34.

3. Baly, *The Geography of the Bible*, 152.

4. Mazar provides a summary of this campaign that is preserved in the archaeological record. Widespread destruction both within Jerusalem and throughout the region shows the breadth and ferocity of this campaign. Mazar, *Archaeology of the Bible*, 458–60.

5. The new era in view has been understood in a variety of ways. Some have interpreted this change in the Dead Sea as symbolic of the New Testament church. Others interpret this chapter as a literal change in this body of water during the

millennial period. And still others see it as a mix of the two. For a discussion, see Gleason L. Archer Jr., *A Survey of Old Testament Introduction* (Chicago: Moody, 1974), 373–76.

6. Orni and Efrat, *Geography of Israel*, 102.

7. The spring of Eglaim may reside on the east shore of the Dead Sea opposite En Gedi at Mazra, or it may lie north of En Gedi at En Feshka. Rasmussen, *NIV Atlas of the Bible*, 233.

8. Tahpanhes has been identified with Tell Defenneh.

9. Isaiah indicates that Jewish refugees had begun to flow into these areas as early as the time of the Assyrian invasion of the land (Isa. 11:11). While in Egypt, Jeremiah directed words of warning to God's people living throughout these regions (Jer. 44:1). For more on Yeb, see Beitzel, *Moody Atlas of Bible Lands*, 146–47.

10. Rainey and Notley, *The Sacred Bridge*, 270.

11. While some associated the judgment of Obadiah with Edom's rebellion during the reign of Jehoram (2 Kings 8:16–20), we believe that the Babylonian invasion of the land provides the more convincing backdrop.

12. For a more detailed treatment, see Kenneth G. Hoglund, "Edomites," in *Peoples of the Old Testament World*, ed. Hoerth, Mattingly, and Yamauchi, 335–47.

13. Aharoni, *The Land of the Bible*, 40.

14. Rasmussen, *NIV Atlas of the Bible*, 56.

15. This policy is recorded not just in the Bible but also in the Cyrus Cylinder, a barrel-shaped clay artifact from this period. This cylinder preserves a decree of Cyrus that directs Mesopotamian deportees to return to their homeland and restore their religious shrines. This is exactly the same public policy we see expressed in the royal edict preserved within the book of Ezra (1:2–4).

16. Hoerth, *Archaeology and the Old Testament*, 389.

17. Yehud encompassed much of the former kingdom of Judah.

18. Merrill, *Kingdom of Priests*, 481.

19. Edwin M. Yamauchi, "Persians," in *Peoples of the Old Testament World*, ed. Hoerth, Mattingly, and Yamauchi, 120–21.

20. John Bright, *A History of Israel*, 3rd ed. (Philadelphia: Westminster Press, 1981), 374.

21. Josephus, *Jewish Antiquities*, 11.1.2.

22. Ben Witherington III, *New Testament History: A Narrative Account* (Grand Rapids: Baker Academic, 2001), 30–35.

23. Ibid., 36.

24. Josephus, *Jewish Antiquities*, 12.3.3–4.

25. 2 Macc. 4:7–17.

26. 1 Macc. 16–23; 2 Macc. 5:15–21.

27. 1 Macc. 1:62; 2 Macc. 6:1–11. Josephus, *Jewish Antiquities*, 12.5.1–4.

28. 1 Macc. 1:47; 2 Macc. 6:2.

Part 7 The Birth and Early Years of Jesus

1. Because there was more than one "Bethlehem" in the Promised Land, the Lord provided additional identification. This Bethlehem was located in the tribal territory of Judah. Ephrathah was either an alternate name for the village or the name of its district. Rasmussen, *NIV Atlas of the Bible*, 234.

2. The Greek word *kataluma*, often translated as "inn," refers to the guest room within a typical family home. Luke is aware of the Greek word for a traveler's inn (*pandocheion*) and uses it in Luke 10:34. See Witherington, *New Testament History*, 66.

3. Early Christian writers from the second through the fifth century like Justin Martyr, Origen, and Jerome all provide witness of a specific cave in Bethlehem associated with Jesus's birth. John McRay, *Archaeology and the New Testament* (Grand Rapids: Baker, 1991), 156.

4. Emperor Hadrian (AD 135) attempted to eliminate the memory of Jesus's birth at this location by building a pagan worship site there dedicated to Adonis (Venus). But his efforts to eliminate the memory only served to mark the birth cave of Jesus, waiting for the day of Emperor Constantine when a Byzantine church was built there (AD 339). A Christian church has continuously marked this cave from the fourth century to the present. Jerome Murphy-O'Connor, *The Holy Land: An Oxford Archaeological Guide from the Earliest Times to 1700*, 4th ed. (Oxford: Oxford University Press, 1998), 200–201.

5. During the time of Jesus, the hill country of Judah became the Roman province of Judea.

6. The wheat was ground and became the famous bread of Bethlehem. Bethlehem means "house of bread" in Hebrew.

7. Mishnah, *Qiddushin* 4:14.

8. Mishnah, *Baba Qama* 10:9.

9. Jacob camped beyond Migdal Eder south of Bethlehem (Gen. 35:21). The Mishnah says that animals raised between Jerusalem and Migdal Eder are fit for

use in the Temple rituals (*Sheqalim* 7:4). Since Bethlehem lies between Jerusalem and Migdal Eder, these may well have been animals designated for Temple sacrifice.

10. The Magi were not astrologers but high officials in the Parthian government, perhaps holding positions similar to that of Daniel. For a defense of their identity as such, see James Martin, *Exploring Bible Times: The Gospels in Context* (Amarillo, TX: Bible World Seminars, 2005), 46–47.

11. The Persian identification of the Magi is supported by second-century Christian art found in the catacombs of Rome depicting these visitors in Persian garments. And the reason the invading Persians spared the Church of the Nativity in Bethlehem (AD 614) was that they saw a mosaic depicting the Magi, who were wearing Persian headdress. Paul L. Maier, *In the Fullness of Time* (San Francisco: Harper Collins, 1991), 48. We further note that they must have been traveling for some time since the star that led the Magi had appeared up to two years prior to their arrival (Matt. 2:7, 16).

12. For a helpful summary of this history, see Witherington, *New Testament History*, 51–61.

13. See ibid., 53–57.

14. Aharoni, Avi-Yonah, Rainey, and Safrai, *Macmillan Bible Atlas*, 179. Alexandria alone hosted a significant Jewish quarter. That city, with a million residents, had a Jewish population approaching 300,000.

15. Martin, *Exploring Bible Times*, 50.

16. In the culture of first-century Judaism, many parents taught their children the Scripture at age five, oral law at age ten, and religious duties at age thirteen. Mishnah, *Abot* 5:21.

17. While some insist that pious Jews would have avoided Samaria and traveled on roads east of the Jordan River, such a journey would have taken them into the idolatry of the Decapolis. Both the Gospel accounts (Luke 9:51–56 and John 4:4) as well as Josephus (e.g., *Jewish Antiquities,* 20:118) indicate that it was customary for Galilean Jews to travel to Jerusalem via Samaria.

18. According to Deuteronomy 6:7, parents were instructed to teach their children during times of travel. Alfred Edersheim, *The Life and Times of Jesus the Messiah* (New York: Longmans, Green, and Co., 1904), 247.

19. Martin, *Exploring Bible Times*, 53.

20. For a further discussion, see ibid., 60–63.

21. Based on John 3:23, some scholars locate this event near Aenon south southeast of Beth Shan. See Beitzel, *Moody Atlas of Bible Lands*, 169.

22. This Bethany is on the east side of the Jordan River and is, therefore, different from the Bethany near Jerusalem that is on the west side of the Jordan River.

23. The Bordeaux Pilgrim (AD 333), Theodosius (AD 530), and Anonymous Piacenza (AD 570) all direct us to this location for Jesus's baptism. Jack Finegan, *The Archaeology of the New Testament*, 2nd ed. (Princeton: Princeton University Press, 1992), 13.

24. The Greek name "Jesus" is the equivalent of the Hebrew name "Joshua" (i.e., *Yeshua*).

25. Finegan, *The Archaeology of the New Testament*, 13.

26. Ibid., 203–4.

27. Sepphoris was the capital of Galilee with a population of 50,000 people. First-century Nazareth had a population of 1,500 to 2,000 residents. Rasmussen, *NIV Atlas of the Bible*, 166.

28. Rainey and Notley, *The Sacred Bridge*, 349.

29. The widespread influence of Hellenism would have been an affront to conservative Jewish families like Mary and Joseph's. They may very well have chosen Nazareth as their hometown because it offered some level of insulation from these pagan influences. For a discussion, see Martin, *Exploring Bible Times*, 31–32.

Part 8 Jesus's Messianic Mission in Samaria, Galilee, and Phoenicia

1. Large water jars carved from stone were expensive, but the Mishnah indicates such containers, when properly covered, prevented the transfer of ritual impurity. Mishnah, *Kelim* 10:1.

2. G. S. P. Freeman-Grenville, Rupert L. Chapman III, and Joan E. Taylor, eds., *The Onomasticon of Eusebius of Caesarea* (Jerusalem: Carta, 2003), 65.

3. Finegan, *Archeology of the New Testament*, 63–64.

4. In the later days of his ministry in Galilee, public perception of Jesus appears to have escaped these reservations.

5. The light mentioned in Isaiah 9:1–2 is clearly linked to the Messiah. See also Isaiah 42:6; 49:6.

6. The basaltic soils and stones around the Sea of Galilee come in various shades of black and dark gray.

7. Josephus, *Jewish War*, 1.16.4.

8. For a fuller discussion, see Beitzel, *Moody Atlas of Bible Lands*, 170–71.

9. Beitzel, *Moody Atlas of Bible Lands*, 100.

10. New Testament Sychar may either be the same as Old Testament Shechem or Askar, located just northeast of ancient Shechem. Rasmussen, *NIV Atlas of the Bible*, 252.

11. For a discussion on the different theological perspectives of Jews and Samaritans, see Richard L. Niswonger, *New Testament History* (Grand Rapids: Zondervan, 1988), 61–63.

12. The Gospel writers each recorded that this miracle occurred within a region associated with a city. There are various similar-sounding yet different Greek names for that city: Gerasa, Gadara, Gergesa. See Rainey and Notley, *The Sacred Bridge*, 359; Finegan, *Archaeology of the New Testament*, 115–16; McRay, *Archaeology and the New Testament*, 166–67.

13. Rasmussen, *NIV Atlas of the Bible*, 171.

14. Mendel Nun, *The Sea of Galilee and Its Fishermen in the New Testament* (Kibbutz Ein Gev: Kennereth Sailing Co., 1989), 54.

15. For example, Peter, who was careful to keep all Jewish dietary laws and had never entered the home of a Gentile until after the resurrection, came from this area (Acts 10:9–48). For further discussion, see Martin, *Exploring Bible Times*, 70.

16. Bethsaida is Aramaic for "house of the fisherman." This and other indicators direct our attention to the north shore of the Sea of Galilee. Bethsaida, mentioned as the home of Philip, Andrew, and Peter, is in Galilee (John 1:44; see also 12:21). El-Araj is a ruin that lies closer to the lakeshore and in the first century may have been west of the Jordan inlet in the territory of Galilee. For further discussion, see Rainey and Notley, *The Sacred Bridge*, 356–59; McRay, *Archaeology and the New Testament*, 168–70.

17. Martin, *Exploring Bible Times*, 66.

18. That is, Solem. Rasmussen, *NIV Atlas of the Bible*, 252.

19. That is, Nein. Ibid., 246.

20. Today this miracle is commemorated by the Church of the Multiplication of Loaves and Fishes at Tabgha. Here a contemporary church stands over a fourth-century church foundation. Murphy-O'Connor, *The Holy Land*, 278–79.

21. For a discussion of the issues involved in identifying and locating the Bethsaida of the Gospels, see Rainey and Notley, *The Sacred Bridge*, 356–59; McRay, *Archaeology and the New Testament*, 168–70.

22. This miraculous provision of food also recalls a similar event from the life of Elisha (2 Kings 4:42–44).

23. For a summary of the history, cultural achievements, and expertise of the Phoenicians, see William A. Ward, "Phoenicians," in *Peoples of the Old Testament World*, ed. Hoerth, Mattingly, and Yamauchi, 183–206. LaMoine F. DeVries, "Tyre: Citadel on the Sea," in *Cities of the Biblical World* (Peabody, MA: Hendrickson, 1997), 78–82.

24. The Phoenicians referred to their land as Canaan and to themselves as Sidonians. Perhaps Matthew calls her a Canaanite in order to recall the harm the Canaanites had frequently done to God's people in the past. Charles F. Pfeiffer and Howard F. Vos, *The Wycliffe Historical Geography of Bible Lands* (Chicago: Moody Press, 1967), 197.

25. In a similar way, a widow at Zarephath, a town near Tyre and Sidon, came to believe in the Lord through the ministry of Elijah (1 Kings 17:24).

26. See David G. Hansen, *In Their Sandals: How His Followers Saw Jesus* (Longwood, FL: Xulon Press, 2007), 33–40.

27. For a discussion of the Decapolis, see Rainey and Notley, *The Sacred Bridge*, 362.

28. Martin, *Exploring Bible Times*, 70–71.

29. Ibid., 86–87.

30. This is in contrast to Caesarea Maritima, the port city built by Herod the Great on the Mediterranean Sea.

31. Pan is the Greek idol associated with fields, forests, flocks, and shepherds. In the Greek period, Caesarea Philippi was named Panias after this idol. When Caesar Augustus provided Herod the Great with extended landholdings, Herod dedicated a marble temple to the worship of Augustus for use in this place. McRay, *Archaeology and the New Testament*, 171–73.

32. Martin, *Exploring Bible Times*, 93–94.

33. It is likely that Herod Philip built up Caesarea Philippi and made it his capital city in order to exploit its critical location. DeVries, "Caesarea Philippi," in *Cities of the Biblical World*, 267.

34. F. F. Bruce, *New Testament History* (New York: Doubleday, 1969), 186.

35. To transfigure is to change one's outward appearance or form.

36. Murphy-O'Connor, *The Holy Land*, 366.

37. Rasmussen, *NIV Atlas of the Bible*, 171.

38. These details appear in each of the Synoptic Gospel accounts (Matt. 17:1–13; Mark 9:2–12; Luke 9:28–36).

39. Jesus notes the incongruity of this fact (Luke 17:17–18), for Jews generally had a much lower opinion of Samaritans and much lower expectations of them (John 4:9). See Witherington, *New Testament History*, 189–91.

40. Hansen, *In Their Sandals*, 55–59.

41. This is where we find him shortly after the account of Naaman's healing (2 Kings 6:13). The servant girl's suggestion that the prophet lived in Samaria (2 Kings 5:3) can easily be explained by the fact that Elisha would have frequently traveled to Samaria in order to discuss matters of state with the king. Dothan itself lies approximately eleven miles northwest of Samaria.

42. While Luke provides no more detail than that, medieval tradition indicates this miracle occurred at Ginae (Jenin), a village that lies just four miles north of Dothan. Turner, *Historical Geography of the Holy Land*, 121. This may, in part, be associated with Josephus's observation that Ginea (Ginae) is located on the border between Samaria and Galilee (Josephus, *Jewish Antiquities*, 20.6.1).

Part 9 Jesus's Last Days in and around Jerusalem

1. The Mishnah directs survivors to bury their dead on the day of their loved one's passing (Mishnah, *Sanhedrin* 6:5). From the time of the fourth century and continuing to this day, a cave in Bethany has been marked and visited as Lazarus's tomb. See Murphy-O'Connor, *The Holy Land*, 133–35.

2. See Martha's concern expressed in John 11:39. Edersheim, *Life and Times of Jesus the Messiah*, vol. 2, 324–25.

3. See John 11:36 and 11:45. When John uses the term *Jews*, he is most often referring to religious leaders among the Jews.

4. Babylonian Talmud, *Sanhedrin* 43a : "And it is tradition: On the eve of Pesach they hung Jeshu [the Nazarene]. And the crier went forth before him forty days (saying) '[Jeshu the Nazarene] goeth forth to be stoned, because he has practiced magic and deceived and led astray Israel. Anyone who knoweth aught in his favour, let him come and declare concerning him.' And they found naught in his favour. And they hung him on the eve of Pesach. Ulla says, 'Would it be supposed that [Jeshu the Nazarene] a revolutionary, had aught in his favour?'"

5. This was an entry so noteworthy that each of the four Gospel writers take note of it. See Matthew 21:1–11; Mark 11:1–10; Luke 19:28–40; John 12:12–19.

6. The palm branches mentioned in John 12:13 have been associated with Jewish liberation and independence (1 Macc. 13:51; 2 Macc. 10:7). In AD 71 following Jerusalem's fall to Rome, the Romans minted a special group of coins. One version of this *Judea Capta* coin mocks the defeated Jews by displaying a woman kneeling beneath the gaze of a Roman solider. She is kneeling beneath a palm tree, the symbol of Jewish freedom.

7. Jesus indicates that Psalm 118 is messianic in nature (Matt. 21:42).

8. Bread prepared for use in the Temple was considered to have been made in the city of Jerusalem if it was made in Bethphage. Mishnah, *Menahot* 11:2.

9. While the Gospel writers do not detail the route from Bethphage, we may confidently trace its route to his entry point into the Temple complex via the southern steps. The main entryway into the Temple lay at the top of those steps where the money changers were at work. Martin, *Exploring Bible Times*, 121.

10. Faith from the biblical perspective is: "Acting in accordance to God's truth, even though every fiber in one's being may not want to and the desired result is not immediately realized." Martin, *Exploring Bible Times*, 122.

11. Zohary, *Plants of the Bible*, 58–59.

12. Within Jewish tradition, this structure became a symbol of political power. Babylon Talmud: *Seder Nezikin, Baba Bathra* 3b.

13. McRay, *Archaeology and the New Testament*, 129–33.

14. Mishnah, *Abodah Zarah* 3:3, 9.

15. Christianity has traditionally associated this meal with Thursday of Passion Week. For a discussion of the problems and solutions associated with assigning a particular day, see Martin, *Exploring Bible Times*, 129–30; Witherington, *New Testament History*, 141–43. A special thanks to Dr. James Fleming of Biblical Resources in LaGrange, Georgia. In 1980 Dr. Fleming brought to my attention the cultural context of the Bible, including meals related to the Passover and the Last Supper.

16. The first-century Church of the Apostles that lies beneath the Crusader Church of Saint Mary appears to have been a Jewish-Christian synagogue used by Jewish believers in Jesus. Finegan, *Archeology of the New Testament*, 232–35.

17. Edersheim, *Life and Times of Jesus the Messiah*, vol. 2, 494.

18. Tombs near the Church of All Nations would have been avoided by Jews wishing to remain ceremonially clean. So the location of Jesus's struggle is likely farther north on the Mount of Olives than church tradition suggests.

19. Murphy-O'Connor, *The Holy Land*, 128–29.

20. William D. Edwards, Wesley J. Gabel, and Floyd E. Hosmer, "On the Physical Death of Jesus Christ," *Journal of the American Medical Association* 255 (March 21, 1986): 1456.

21. Martin, *Exploring Bible Times*, 133.

22. Josephus, *Jewish War*, 2.411.

23. Josephus, *Jewish Antiquities*, 13.298; Babylonian Talmud: *Pesahim* 57a.

24. The Great Sanhedrin itself was divided into three smaller courts that met in various locations throughout the Temple complex: the Chamber of Hewn Stone, the gate of the Temple Mount, and the gate of the courtyard. Mishnah, *Sanhedrin* 11:2.

25. Caiaphas had not inherited the position according to the Lord's instructions, but he was assigned the post since he had impressed Pilate with his ability to obtain taxes from the people. Witherington, *New Testament History*, 148–50. This corruption in office finds its roots deeply set in the intertestamental world (2 Macc. 4:7, 23–24).

26. Mishnah, *Sanhedrin* 4:1.

27. Bruce, *New Testament History*, 197.

28. For a mortal to claim he was divine merited the death penalty (John 19:7).

29. Note that when Paul was condemned by the Sanhedrin, he was taken to the Roman governor in Caesarea Maritima for his trial (Acts 23:33; 24:1).

30. The Stone Pavement mentioned in the Gospels may have been located at either Herod's palace or the Antonia Fortress (although those stones are now in secondary use).

31. For a description of Roman trial proceedings, see Witherington, *New Testament History*, 152.

32. Pilate had killed Galileans worshiping at the Temple (Luke 13:1–2), taken money from the Temple to underwrite an aqueduct, accepted bribes, and caused riots. See Martin, *Exploring Bible Times*, 139–41.

33. Philo, *On the Embassy to Gaius*, 299–303.

34. Edwards, Gabel, and Hosmer, "On the Physical Death of Jesus Christ," 1457.

35. Seneca, *De Ira III*, 17.4–19.2.

36. The location of the crucifixion is also called Calvary from the Latin, *calva*, which means "skull."

37. Liturgical worship services were held on the site of the Church of the Holy Sepulcher until AD 66. In a bid to discourage worship there and destroy the memories associated with the place, Hadrian (AD 135) filled in the quarry in order to make a platform for a pagan temple and shrine. But his efforts served only to secure the memory of the location in advance of the Christian emperors, who passionately sought restoration of such sites. Early in the fourth century, Emperor Constantine constructed the first of what became a series of churches enlisted to honor this sacred ground. Murphy-O'Connor, *The Holy Land*, 45–48. In 1883 General Charles Gordon pointed to a hill, associated with a garden and a tomb, which he believed was a better fit for Calvary than the Church of the Holy Sepulcher. Based on his reading of Matt. 27:33, and presuming that Calvary was a hill that resembled a skull, Gordon popularized a location now known as Gordon's Calvary. McRay, *Archaeology and the New Testament*, 206–16.

38. For a discussion of the various forms of crucifixion, see Martin, *Exploring Bible Times*, 146–47.

39. Origen, *Contra Celsum*, 6.10. Note that the Romans used this form of execution on all ethnic groups including Romans. Martin Hengel, *Crucifixion in the Ancient World and the Folly of the Message of the Cross* (Philadelphia: Fortress Press, 1982), 22–23.

40. Martin, *Exploring Bible Times*, 152.

41. Two locations in Jerusalem claim to be the location of Jesus burial: the Garden Tomb (associated with Gordon's Calvary) and the Church of the Holy Sepulcher. See McRay, *Archaeology and the New Testament*, 206–17.

42. See Mishnah, *Sanhedrin* 6:6; 10:1; *Sotah* 9:15.

43. Niswonger, *New Testament History*, 175.

44. Psalm 16:10.

45. On one occasion Jesus appeared to five hundred of his followers at one time (1 Cor. 15:6).

46. Since the fourth century, Christian tradition has remembered this event at churches erected on the northwest shore of the Sea of Galilee at Heptapegon (the seven springs). Today the Chapel of the Primacy of St. Peter marks the spot. Finegan, *Archeology of the New Testament*, 92–94.

47. Such a meal was part of an ancient Jewish custom known as a "meal covenant." It is represented in Psalm 23:5 as a meal that signals forgiveness and acceptance. Martin, *Exploring Bible Times*, 154.

Part 10 The Good News Travels from Jerusalem to the World

1. The word *church* used here and in the coming pages is not used to describe a building but a gathering of Jesus's followers who have come together and submit

to his authority. They may meet in a synagogue, a home, or even along a river. But in each case, they are individually and collectively part of the "body of Christ," Jesus's church.

2. The fire in particular is a phenomenon closely associated with a manifestation of God's presence (see, e.g., Exod. 3:2; 19:18; 40:38).

3. These steps provided an area large enough to accommodate the growing crowds in a place where the apostles' voices could be heard. Furthermore, people were used to coming there for instruction because the rabbis frequently used these steps to teach. And finally, a large ritual bath complex (*miqva'ot*) associated with these steps provided the water that might be used for the thousands seeking baptism. See Rainey and Notley, *The Sacred Bridge*, 370.

4. Bruce, *New Testament History*, 208.

5. Estimates range from 125,000 to 500,000. Witherington, *New Testament History*, 180.

6. Colonnaded porches surround the courts of the Temple complex. Solomon's Colonnade was the one on the east side, rising above the Court of the Gentiles. Finegan, *Archeology of the New Testament*, 194.

7. McRay, *Archaeology and the New Testament*, 110.

8. The word *Samaria* may refer both to the biblical city of Samaria (also called Sebaste during the period of the book of Acts) and to the region that lay between Galilee and Judea. See Rasmussen, *NIV Atlas of the Bible*, 174; Rainey and Notley, *The Sacred Bridge*, 370.

9. Note that this is not Philip the apostle, who is unmentioned by name in the book of Acts.

10. On the Samaritans, see Witherington, *New Testament History*, 189–91.

11. Christian tradition traces Philip's journey south on the Ridge Route toward Hebron with the baptism occurring in the springs at Beth Zur. Both the Bordeaux Pilgrim and the Medeba map link the baptism to this site. Rainey and Notley, *The Sacred Bridge*, 371. It is possible that the Ethiopian treasurer would have taken his chariot down the paved Roman road that led through the Elah Valley and on to the International Highway en route to Gaza. Rasmussen, *NIV Atlas of the Bible*, 174.

12. This would have been particularly compelling for a man who had just come from Jerusalem, where a eunuch was forbidden the right to worship at the Temple.

13. The Ethiopia from which the royal treasurer hailed is located where Nubia and southern Sudan are today. In the Old Testament, this region is called Cush. J. Alexander Thompson, s.v. "Ethiopia," *Zondervan Pictorial Encyclopedia of the Bible*, vol. 2, 411–12.

14. Jesus says that his gospel must be preached in Jerusalem, in all Judea and Samaria, and to the ends of the earth (Acts 1:8). In this regard, it is striking to note that Ethiopia lay outside the bounds of the Roman Empire. Witherington, *New Testament History*, 193.

15. Aharoni, Avi-Yonah, Rainey, and Safrai, *The Macmillan Bible Atlas*, 182.

16. McRay, *Archaeology and the New Testament*, 233.

17. Damascus is the capital of Aram.

18. This is a different city than Caesarea Philippi located at the base of Mount Hermon.

19. Gentile homes were associated with cemeteries and so were deemed unclean. For a discussion, see Martin, *Exploring Bible Times*, 136–37.

20. Finegan, *Archeology of the New Testament*, 131–32.

21. DeVries, "Caesarea Maritima, Seaport Gateway to Herod's Kingdom," in *Cities of the Biblical World*, 255–63.

22. Although Pisidian Antioch lies within the province of Phrygia, it became known as Pisidian Antioch because it was located near the border with Pisidia.

23. Seleuchus I founded Antioch of Syria about 300 BC. This general of Alexander the Great and heir to a portion of his empire was committed to rewarding those who assisted him in achieving his political and military objectives. In doing so, he did not discriminate. Greek, Macedonian, and Jewish soldiers alike were given full citizenship and land in Antioch. Beitzel, *Moody Atlas of Bible Lands*, 178; Witherington, *New Testament History*, 224–25.

24. For an overview of the city at the time of Paul, see McRay, *Archaeology and the New Testament*, 227–32.

25. Rasmussen, *NIV Atlas of the Bible*, 180.

26. McRay, *Archaeology and the New Testament*, 232.

27. Josephus describes the city as having more Jews than any other in Syria. Josephus, *Jewish War*, 7.3.3.

28. Traditional Jewish teaching indicates that the need to circumcise Gentile converts was debated in Judaism between those with different feelings on the topic. See Bruce, *New Testament History*, 282–84.

29. See the previous chapter for more details on Syrian Antioch; also see McRay, *Archaeology and the New Testament*, 227–32.

30. This decision was coupled with the demand that Gentile believers separate themselves from food and practices associated with pagan temples, which is the

point made by James in his address (Acts 15:19–21). See Witherington, *New Testament History*, 246–48.

31. DeVries, "Athens, City of Gods, Goddesses, Monumental Building, and Temples," in *Cities of the Biblical World*, 351–58.

32. McRay, *Archaeology and the New Testament*, 299–300.

33. For more on these philosophies of life and the Areopagus, see Witherington, *New Testament History*, 289–91.

34. A number of ancient authors (Pausanias, Apollonius of Tyana, Diogenes Laertius, and Oecumenius) mention such an altar in their writings. While no such altar to an unknown god has been discovered in Athens, one was found in Pergamum during a 1909 excavation. McRay, *Archaeology and the New Testament*, 304.

35. Pfeiffer and Vos, *Wycliffe Historical Geography of Bible Lands*, 315.

36. Rasmussen, *NIV Atlas of the Bible*, 183.

37. Comparing Acts 20:7 and Luke 24:1, we find Luke using parallel language in association with the resurrection of Jesus on the first day of the week (i.e., Sunday).

Part 11 City Letters and Revelation

1. As mentioned before, the word *church* is used here and in the coming pages not to describe a building but a community of Jesus's followers. They may be meeting in a synagogue, a home, or even along a river. But in each case, they are part of the body of Christ, the church.

2. A debate continues as to whether Paul's use of *Galatia* in this letter refers to ethnic Galatians who lived in the northern part of this province or to the churches established in the southern part of the province during Paul's first missionary journey. We find ourselves persuaded by the evidence that supports the latter view. For a summary of both views and the evidence associated with each, see D. A. Carson, Douglas J. Moo, and Leon Morris, *An Introduction to the New Testament* (Grand Rapids: Zondervan, 1992), 290–93.

3. Witherington, *New Testament History*, 232–33.

4. This is due in part to a decree of Antiochus (ca. 200 BC) that called for two thousand Jewish families to be settled here as "guardians" against sedition in the region that later became the Roman province of Galatia. Josephus, *Jewish Antiquities*, 12.3.4.

5. Perhaps Ebionites, from the Hebrew meaning "the poor ones." Justin Martyr refers to this group in his *Dialogue with Trypho* as those who differ from other Jewish believers in Jesus in that they mandated the practice of the laws of Moses.

6. Pfeiffer and Vos, *Wycliffe Historical Geography of Bible Lands*, 451, 454.

7. Octavian and Anthony settled their veterans here in 42 BC after their defeat of Brutus and Cassius. Bruce, *New Testament History*, 307.

8. Witherington, *New Testament History*, 261.

9. In AD 49, shortly before Paul's visit to Philippi, Claudius expelled Jews from Rome due to rioting over *Chrestus*. It is generally assumed that this may reflect a heated debate between Jewish and Christian communities in Rome. Carson, Moo, and Morris, *Introduction to the New Testament*, 243.

10. The Lex Portia required that a Roman citizen was entitled to a trial before being scourged or executed. Those who failed to provide this trial were subject to banishment.

11. Carson, Moo, and Morris, *Introduction to the New Testament*, 352.

12. Rasmussen, *NIV Atlas of the Bible*, 183.

13. The Egnatian Way connected the Aegean Sea with the Adriatic Sea. McRay, *Archaeology and the New Testament*, 282–83.

14. Ibid., 293.

15. Suetonius, *Lives of the Twelve Caesars*, 25. See Bruce, *New Testament History*, 297–98, 308.

16. In 1867 an arch was discovered that spanned the Egnatian Way on the west side of Thessalonica. The inscription on that arch includes a reference to the "time of the Politarchs." McRay, *Archaeology and the New Testament*, 295.

17. Witherington, *New Testament History*, 263.

18. A partially preserved inscription discovered in Corinth mentions a "synagogue of the Hebrews." Although it dates to the centuries after Paul's visit, it may well mark the location of the earlier synagogue Paul visited. See McRay, *Archaeology and the New Testament*, 319.

19. Pfeiffer and Vos, *Wycliffe Historical Geography of Bible Lands*, 480.

20. An inscription from Delphi refers to Gallio in just these terms. McRay, *Archaeology and the New Testament*, 226–27.

21. Ibid., 313–15.

22. Paul may have joined Aquila in making tents for those delayed in Corinth (Acts 18:1–3).

23. "Not for every man is a trip to Corinth." Strabo, *Geography*, 8.6.20.

24. McRay, *Archaeology and the New Testament*, 315–17.

25. Harry J. Leon, *The Jews of Ancient Rome* (Philadelphia: Jewish Publication Society, 1960), 4–9.

26. The *Milliarium Aureum*, the Golden Milestone, was located at the west end of the Roman forum. It listed all the major cities of the empire and the distance to them along the road system. McRay, *Archaeology and the New Testament*, 344.

27. See Romans 11:11–24. Bruce, *New Testament History*, 393.

28. Witherington, *New Testament History*, 330.

29. Ibid., 333–40.

30. Bruce, *New Testament History*, 326.

31. Josephus mentions this community in *Jewish Antiquities*, 14.10.12; 14.10.25.

32. Although located several miles from the sea itself, the harbor at Ephesus was linked to the Aegean by the Cayster River. Pfeiffer and Vos, *Wycliffe Historical Geography of Bible Lands*, 359–60.

33. Witherington, *New Testament History*, 280.

34. For a discussion of the captivity letters see ibid., 326–29.

35. See Bruce, *New Testament History*, 328.

36. When it was rebuilt in the sixth century BC it measured 377 feet by 197 feet—the largest building in the Greek world. McRay, *Archaeology and the New Testament*, 256.

37. Witherington, *New Testament History*, 333–40.

38. McRay, *Archaeology and the New Testament*, 249.

39. The book of Philemon tells us more about him. This book is also a letter likely written and delivered at the same time as Colossians. In the letter of Philemon Paul urges Philemon, Onesimus's owner, to forgive his slave for running away and to receive him as a Christian brother.

40. Paul directs that this letter also be read in Laodicea (Col. 4:16). It may well be that the same problems were beginning to take hold in this community as well.

41. Carson, Moo, and Morris, *Introduction to the New Testament*, 335–36.

42. Pfeiffer and Vos, *Wycliffe Historical Geography of Bible Lands*, 402–3.

43. McRay, *Archaeology and the New Testament*, 257.

44. Witherington, *New Testament History*, 390–94.

45. Ibid., 274.

46. Witherington, *New Testament History*, 403.

47. If we place the seven churches of Ephesus, Smyrna, Pergamum, Thyatira, Sardis, Philadelphia, and Laodicea on a map and overlay the ancient road system, we will find that all the cities mentioned are located along key transportation arteries. And we will further find that if we start at Ephesus and follow the cities listed in the order they are presented in Revelation, we will trace a geographical semicircle just as a courier would in moving from one city to the next on the ancient roads. McRay, *Archaeology and the New Testament*, 243.

48. Ibid.

49. Pfeiffer and Vos, *Wycliffe Historical Geography of Bible Lands*, 377–78.

50. Beitzel, *Moody Atlas of Bible Lands*, 34.

51. Whether one views this battle as literally occurring within the Jezreel Valley or sees the Jezreel Valley as symbolic of the battle location, these insights apply.

SCRIPTURE INDEX

Dr. James Martin founded Bible World Seminars in 1989 and has taught more than two hundred biblical study programs on location in Israel, Egypt, Jordan, Turkey, and Greece. Ordained in the Evangelical Presbyterian Church, he served in the pastorate in Amarillo, Texas, from 1978 to 1982. In 1980 and 1982 he worked on postgraduate studies in Jerusalem with Israeli scholars, focusing on the historical, cultural, and geographical context of the Bible. From 1983 to 1989 he was program director and instructor at the Jerusalem Center for Biblical Studies, where he taught biblical studies on location. He finished a doctor of ministry in biblical studies from Fuller Seminary in 1991, with a focus on the cultural context of the Gospels and development of the Bible World Seminars Israel study syllabus titled "Exploring Bible Times: The Gospels in Context."

Over the past twenty-five years, Dr. Martin and his wife, Stacey, have also been involved in photography and video filming throughout the Middle East and Europe, concentrating on the historical, geographical, cultural, and archaeological aspects of the Bible. Their photos appear in works such as the *Tyndale Illumina Bible*, the *NIV Archaeological Study Bible*, the *Zondervan Pictorial Encyclopedia of the Bible*, *Zondervan's Pictorial Bible Dictionary*, *Halley's Bible Handbook*, *The Bible in Ninety Days*, and numerous magazines and resources related to the world of the Bible.

Dr. John Beck earned his PhD in theology (Hebrew and Old Testament) from Trinity International University in 1997. For sixteen years, he taught courses in Hebrew and Old Testament at various colleges and universities. During the last ten years, he has worked closely with Dr. James Martin both as a teacher in Israel and as a consultant for various publications.

Dr. Beck has studied the role of geography in biblical communication and has published articles in *JETS*, *SJOT*, *WTJ*, and *BibSac*. He also authored the article on geography for Baker's *Dictionary for Theological Interpretation of the Bible*. He recently published *The Land of Milk and Honey: An Introduction to the Geography of Israel* and *God as Storyteller: Seeking Meaning in Biblical Narrative*.

Colonel David G. Hansen, PhD, served in the US Army for thirty-five years. He taught at the US Army War College for nine years as chairman of the Department of National Security and Strategy and as a tenured professor who held the General Maxwell D. Taylor chair. He left active military service with academic degrees in geography (BA, University of Nebraska at Omaha) and international relations (MA, University of Texas). He then taught regional geography at Penn State for eight years while finishing his PhD in biblical studies at Trinity Theological Seminary.

Hansen's on-site research in the Middle East includes extensive travel and participation in archaeological excavations. At the request of both the Israel Defense Forces and the Royal Jordanian Army, he was an academic consultant for the higher education of their professional military officers. He has published articles in several journals about the impact of geography on military affairs and on the Bible, and has authored one book and contributed chapters to other books.

Hansen currently travels, writes, and teaches with Bible World Seminars and Youth With A Mission. He is an associate professor in the College of Archaeology and Biblical History at Trinity Southwest University, and is a member of the special faculty (Geography and Archaeology) for Trinity College of the Bible and Trinity Theological Seminary.